REGULATORY WAVES

All governments, in various ways, regulate and control nonprofit organizations. Nongovernmental organizations (NGOs), while hopeful of supportive regulatory environments, are simultaneously seeking greater autonomy both to provide services and to advocate for policy change. In part to counter increasing statutory regulation, there is a global nonprofit sector movement toward greater grassroots regulation – what the authors call self-regulation – through codes of conduct and self-accreditation processes. This book drills down to the country level to examine both sides of this equation, examining how state regulation and nonprofit self-regulation affect each other and investigating the causal nature of this interaction. Exploring these issues from historical, cultural, political, and environmental perspectives, and in sixteen jurisdictions (Australia, Brazil, China, Ecuador, England and Wales, Ethiopia, Ireland, Israel, Kenya, Malawi, Mexico, Scotland, Tanzania, Uganda, United States, and Vietnam) the authors analyze the interplay between state control and nonprofit self-regulation to better understand broader emerging trends.

Oonagh B. Breen is a senior lecturer at the Sutherland School of Law, University College Dublin where she teaches NGO law. Her research focuses on comparative charity law regulation and governance and the development of more structured legal relationships between the state and the nonprofit sector. She has been a Research Fellow at Harvard's Hauser Center for Nonprofit Organizations (2009) and an Ian Potter Foundation Fellow at the Australian Centre for Philanthropy and Nonprofit Studies (2016) and serves on the boards of both the International Society for Third-Sector Research and the International Center for Not-for-Profit Law.

Alison Dunn is an independent researcher, having recently retired from the position of Senior Lecturer at Newcastle Law School, Newcastle University. Her research interests are in charity law and the law relating to nonprofits, particularly governance and the regulation of political activities of charities and nonprofit organizations, on which she has published widely. She is editor of *The Voluntary Sector, the State and the Law* (2000).

Mark Sidel is Doyle-Bascom Professor of Law and Public Affairs at the University of Wisconsin-Madison. In 2016 he is also serving as the Charles Stewart Mott Foundation Visiting Chair in Community Foundations at the Lilly Family School of Philanthropy at Indiana University. Sidel has served as president of the International Society for Third-Sector Research and as visiting professor of law at Harvard, Melbourne, Institut d'Etudes Politiques de Paris (Sciences Po), and other institutions.

Regulatory Waves

COMPARATIVE PERSPECTIVES ON STATE REGULATION AND SELF-REGULATION POLICIES IN THE NONPROFIT SECTOR

Edited by

OONAGH B. BREEN
University College Dublin

ALISON DUNN

MARK SIDEL
University of Wisconsin

CAMBRIDGE
UNIVERSITY PRESS

CAMBRIDGE
UNIVERSITY PRESS

University Printing House, Cambridge CB2 8BS, United Kingdom

One Liberty Plaza, 20th Floor, New York, NY 10006, USA

477 Williamstown Road, Port Melbourne, VIC 3207, Australia

314-321, 3rd Floor, Plot 3, Splendor Forum, Jasola District Centre, New Delhi - 110025, India

79 Anson Road, #06-04/06, Singapore 079906

Cambridge University Press is part of the University of Cambridge.

It furthers the University's mission by disseminating knowledge in the pursuit of education, learning and research at the highest international levels of excellence.

www.cambridge.org
Information on this title: www.cambridge.org/9781316617755

First published 2017
First paperback edition 2018

A catalogue record for this publication is available from the British Library

Library of Congress Cataloging in Publication data
Names: Breen, Oonagh, editor. | Dunn, Alison, 1969– editor. | Sidel, Mark, editor.
Title: Regulatory waves : comparative perspectives on state regulation and self-regulation policies in the nonprofit sector / edited by Oonagh B. Breen, University College Dubin; Alison Dunn; Mark Sidel, University of Wisconsin ; foreword by Marion Fremont-Smith.
Description: Cambridge [UK] : Cambridge University Press, 2016. | Includes index.
Identifiers: LCCN 2016027430| ISBN 9781107166851 (Hardback) | ISBN 9781316617755 (Paperback)
Subjects: LCSH: Nonprofit organizations–Law and legislation. | Nonprofit organizations–Political aspects. | Nonprofit organizations–History.
Classification: LCC K656 .R43 2016 | DDC 346/.064–dc23 LC record available at https://lccn.loc .gov/2016027430

ISBN 978-1-107-16685-1 Hardback
ISBN 978-1-316-61775-5 Paperback

Contents

v

Notes on Contributors

Susan Appe is Assistant Professor of Public Administration at Binghamton University, New York. Her research focuses on government/nonprofit relations and the dimensions and evolution of the nonprofit sector in both developed and developing countries. She examines how government policy influences and shapes civil society and nonprofit organizations and their work in social development, and how and why nonprofit organizations form civil society networks and the implications of doing so. In addition, she researches the challenges and opportunities in nonprofit management education, particularly in the context of Latin America, and studies the development of international service learning in public affairs education. She has published articles related to government/nonprofit relations and collaborative governance and has taught several courses in arts management, public administration, and public policy. She has been awarded several research fellowships that include a Fulbright in Colombia (2006), a Fellowship at the University of Texas at Austin's RGK Center on Philanthropy and Community Service (2010), and a Rotary International Ambassadorial Scholarship in Ecuador (2010). She received her PhD in Public Administration and Policy from the Nelson A. Rockefeller College of Public Affairs and Policy at the University at Albany, State University of New York.

Putnam Barber is Senior Advisor at the Nancy Bell Evans Center on Nonprofits and Philanthropy at the University of Washington Evans School of Public Affairs, Seattle, and is the Book Review Editor for *Nonprofit and Voluntary Sector Quarterly*. He has taught on nonprofits in the MPA program at the University of Washington and Seattle University. He is an advisor to the American Law Institute's project to develop a volume presenting "A Restatement of the Law of Charitable Nonprofit Organizations." In addition to his work with the Nancy Bell Evans Center, Putnam has worked for many years to build strong nonprofits and communities in his home state of Washington through service with the Evergreen State Society, Executive Alliance, and Institute of Public Service at Seattle University. He was a founding member of the board of Washington Nonprofits, an association that connects nonprofits throughout the state.

Oonagh B. Breen is a senior lecturer at the Sutherland School of Law, University College Dublin where she teaches NGO law. A Yale Law School graduate and a qualified barrister, her research focuses on comparative charity law regulation and governance and the development of more structured legal relationships between the state and the nonprofit sector. A former Fulbright Scholar and Government of Ireland Research Fellow, Oonagh holds an ARNOVA Emerging Scholar Award (2006) and an International Center for Not-for-Profit Law (ICNL)/Cordaid Distinguished Research Award (2008). She has been a Research Fellow at Harvard's Hauser Center for Nonprofit Organizations (2009) and an Ian Potter Foundation Fellow at the Australian Centre for Philanthropy and Nonprofit Studies (2016) and currently serves on the boards of both International Society for Third-Sector Research and ICNL. Oonagh has published extensively in the field of charity regulation both nationally and internationally and has participated actively in policy processes leading to the reform of charity law in Ireland.

Noy Brindt is a PhD student in the law faculty of Haifa University, Israel. His doctoral work is focused on institutional analysis of nonprofit organizations' legal frameworks. His research interests include organization law, nonprofit theories, nonprofit economic analysis, and organizations' institutionalism. Noy is an attorney at law (LLB, LLM) and an economist (BA). He works as a researcher at Van Leer Forum for Civil Society Organizations and at the Van Leer Jerusalem Institute and serves as legal advisor for nonprofit organizations.

Alison Dunn is an independent researcher, having recently retired from the position of Senior Lecturer at Newcastle Law School, Newcastle University. She received her PhD from Leicester University. Her research interests are in charity law and the law relating to nonprofits, particularly governance and the regulation of political activities of charities and nonprofit organizations. She has undertaken appointment panel work for the Judicial Appointments Commission in the Ministry of Justice for the first judicial appointees to the charity law tribunal for England and Wales, as well as commissioned socioeconomic research on trustee exemption clauses for the English Law Commission. She is editor of *The Voluntary Sector, the State and the Law* (2000).

Megan M. Farwell is a doctoral student at the University of Pennsylvannia's School of Social Policy and Practice. She has collaborated on several research projects examining the third sector and has direct experience in program administration at the community, city, and county level. She holds an MPA degree and a Master of Social Work degree from the University of Washington; her thesis examined changes to nonprofit operations and service provision during the Great Recession.

Marion R. Fremont-Smith is a senior research fellow at the Hauser Institute for Civil Society of the Center for Public Leadership at the Harvard Kennedy School. She joined the Hauser Center for Nonprofit Organizations at Harvard, the predecessor to the institute, in 1988 and since then has conducted research on governance and accountability of nonprofit organizations. She is the author of *Governing Nonprofit Organizations: Federal and State Law and Regulation* (2004). Marion is also currently serving as Co-Reporter of the Restatement of the Law of Nonprofit Charitable Organizations of the American Law Institute. She has published two other books and numerous papers on government regulation of nonprofit organizations. Fremont-Smith's interest in nonprofit organizations began in the 1960s when she served as assistant attorney general and director of the Division of Public Charities in Massachusetts. In 1964 she joined the Boston law firm of Choate, Hall and Stewart where she specialized in tax and nonprofit law. She was elected partner in 1971, retiring in 2004. Fremont-Smith received a BA from Wellesley College in 1948 and a JD from Boston University School of Law in 1951.

Mary Kay Gugerty serves as the Nancy Bell Evans Professor in Nonprofit Management at the University of Washington Evans School of Public Affairs, Seattle. Her scholarship seeks to increase our understanding of how individuals and organizations engage in collective action and build institutions of collaborative governance. She currently directs research projects funded by the National Science Foundation to examine the design of nonprofit voluntary regulation programs, by the United States Agency for International Development (USAID) to investigate how community-based organizations can improve outcomes for female farmers in Tanzania, by Google to explore how nonprofits can collect decision-driven data to support program improvement, and by the International Development Research Centre (IDRC) to study the strategies and influence of think tanks in developing countries. Mary Kay is the lead editor of *Voluntary Regulation of Nonprofit and Nongovernmental Organizations: An Accountability Club Framework* (Cambridge University Press, 2010), along with numerous journal articles. She holds a PhD in political economy and government from Harvard University, an MPA from the John F. Kennedy School of Government at Harvard, and a BA in political science and economics from Georgetown University.

Michael D. Layton is one of the foremost experts on philanthropy and the nonprofit sector in Mexico. He is currently an independent consultant and researcher. Prior to this, Michael was a Professor of International Relations at the Autonomous Technological Institute of Mexico, where his achievements include creating the Project on Philanthropy and Civil Society, developing Mexico's first national survey on giving and volunteering (ENAFI), and participating in the creation of fondosalavista.mx, Mexico's premier transparency website for foundations and nonprofits. Michael is the author and editor of numerous books and articles on the nonprofit sector in Mexico and Latin America and was a Visiting Scholar in the Center on Philanthropy and Public Policy, Sol Price School of Public Policy, University of Southern California. He earned a master's degree and a doctorate in political science from Duke University (1993, 1997), and he graduated with a bachelor's degree in philosophy from Haverford College (1982).

Nissan Limor, PhD, is a senior research fellow at the Institute for Law and Philanthropy, Buchmann Faculty of Law, Tel-Aviv University; a faculty member of the College for Academic Studies, Or Yehuda; and Chair of the Center of Civic Responsibility in this college. His academic work covers a variety of areas, including civil society, third-sector organizations, higher education, and economy of education. He taught previously at the Hebrew University of Jerusalem, the Paul Baerwald School of Social Work and Social Welfare, MA Program for Management of Nonprofit and Community Organizations, and at Ben-Gurion University of the Negev, Guilford Glazer School of Business and Management, MA Program for Management of Nonprofits. Nissan has written and edited six books (on nonprofit management, regulation, and auditing) and numerous articles and policy and position papers. He has also served as a Senior Research Fellow and the Head of the Van Leer Forum for Civil Society Organizations, at the Van Leer Jerusalem Institute. He is a former Director General of the Office of the President of Israel, and a former Director General of the Israeli Council for Higher Education.

Marcelo Marchesini da Costa is a PhD student in Public Administration and Policy at the Nelson A. Rockefeller College of Public Affairs and Policy, University at Albany, State University of New York. His research is focused on nonprofit/government relations and governance in Brazil and other Latin American countries. He has been awarded scholarships from the Latin

American Council of Social Sciences (CLACSO) and from the Brazilian research agencies CNPq and Capes. His professional experience includes several years working in Brazilian agencies in the areas of health, culture, and social development.

Myles McGregor-Lowndes, OAM, is Professor and Founding Director of the Australian Centre of Philanthropy and Nonprofit Studies (ACPNS). ACPNS has a multidisciplinary research focus located in the Queensland University of Technology (QUT) Business School and is known for its research in nonprofit law, governance, fundraising, and philanthropy. Myles has written extensively about nonprofit tax and regulation, nonprofit legal entities, government grants, and standard charts of accounts as a means of reducing the compliance burden. He was a member of the 2010 Productivity Commission Report on the Nonprofit Sector for the Australian Government, which made extensive recommendations for the reform of the sector. He is a founding member of the Australian Tax Office Charities Consultative Committee and the Australian Charities and Not-for-profits Commission Advisory Board and served as Chair of the Australian Council for International Development Code of Conduct Committee. In June 2003, Myles was awarded a Medal of the Order of Australia (OAM) "For service to the community by providing education and support in legal, financial and administrative matters to nonprofit organizations."

Mark Sidel is Doyle-Bascom Professor of Law and Public Affairs at the University of Wisconsin, Madison, and consultant for Asia at the International Center for Not-for-Profit Law (ICNL). He has served as president of the International Society for Third-Sector Research, the international academic association working to strengthen research on civil society, philanthropy, and the nonprofit sector; on the US Council on Foundations Community Foundations National Standards Board; as consultant to the Ford, Gates, and Asia foundations, Norwegian government, ICNL, US Department of Justice, US Department of State, UK Serious Organised Crime Agency, and other groups; and visiting professor at Harvard, Melbourne, Institut d'Etudes Politiques de Paris (Sciences Po), and other institutions. Earlier Sidel served with the Ford Foundation in Beijing, Hanoi, Bangkok, and New Delhi. His books include *Central-Local Relations in Asian Constitutional Systems* (forthcoming, co-edited), *Regulation of the Voluntary Sector: Freedom and Security in an Age of Uncertainty* (2010), and *Law and Society in Vietnam* (Cambridge University Press, 2008).

Foreword

This volume meets the hopes of every author: it is authoritative, timely, and groundbreaking. Since the latter half of the twentieth century, members of the charitable sector, regulators, and scholars have been increasingly interested in the operations of the sector, its marked growth worldwide, questioning the purpose of regulation, and attempting to devise optimum systems of regulation that are geared to the needs of a specific country. In some instances, that perceived need may be to gain or keep control of the sector; in others, it may be to provide greater freedom to the sector to permit it to better meet the needs of society. To date there has been no attempt to study the interplay of state and voluntary regulation in one country, let alone the sixteen that this volume provides. Furthermore, no study has succeeded in analyzing the relationship of the size and extent of government regulation with the size and extent of self-regulation, nor considered the relationship of these two components of the regulatory framework as their respective power and influence fluctuate over time. Finally, no study has attempted to look at the extent of regulation vis-à-vis self-regulation as a series of waves that ebb and flow over time within specific jurisdictions as well as among others, some geographically adjacent, others aligned by the nature of their governing structure. In short, there is enough material in Chapter 1 to provide scholars with subjects for many years of research and analysis.

Among the country- and region-specific studies of regulation and self-regulation in sixteen jurisdictions, Chapter 2, on the waves of regulatory power in Britain, provides a vivid picture of the shifting powers of the chief regulators, the Charity Commissioners, over centuries – historically, the waves of regulation. The chapter contains a description of what is categorized as fairly sudden changes in the powers of the Commissioners during the last twenty years, with self-regulation expanding while the power of the Commissioners was declining and, within the last ten years, the emergence of what is described as "co-regulation." This is a new form of cooperation between state regulators and organizations created to provide self-regulation. The change in roles has led to a division of powers, permitting the Charity Commission to conserve resources and focus on enforcement, rather than providing advice on compliance, matters which the self-regulators will in turn provide.

Co-regulation also appears to be developing in China where the government is supporting nonstate actors to coordinate data gathering. It appears that the Israeli government may also be considering using nonprofit self-regulators for state purposes. Co-regulation is one of the subjects delineated in this study that warrants greater attention in all countries, not just those noted in the study in which government regulation has been notably strong and co-regulation appeared to be the only choice when the political will was aimed at reducing the scope of central government regulation.

"We do not yet know whether this will be a receding wave or what might be designated a tidal wave." One of the unique contributions of the studies in this volume is the manner in which the authors address the overriding question posed in its title. And one should approach the volume with this in mind. If, in fact, the case studies do not help one to predict the answer to the question of what kind of a wave is about to reach the shore, they do indicate that one of the most important factors may be the political one. And if the political situation in a particular jurisdiction is the overriding factor determining the nature and scope of government regulation, charitable nonprofits may not be able to control outcomes. Nonetheless, the final sets of recommendations are ones that will prepare the nonprofit sector for what is to come, strengthening its responses to attempts to preempt its autonomy and thereby preventing it from carrying out its essential role in meeting the needs of society.

The authors and editors are to be commended for these groundbreaking studies. Readers will be rewarded by the insights on regulation, self-regulation, and co-regulation. In addition, the descriptions of the shifting waves of power between regulators and nonprofit organizations regarding the degree of state control of the sector within individual countries and among common geographical areas are invaluable. The concluding chapter contains suggestions for improving self-regulation. They reflect a distillation of the information gathered in the individual case studies. Even for one who might disagree with the conclusion that self-regulation is the answer to the future of all-encompassing regulation, this book is a milestone in research on the nonprofit sector, one that warrants attention and, one hopes, inspires broader and more in-depth studies of its kind.

Marion R. Fremont-Smith
Hauser Institute for Civil Society
Harvard University

Acknowledgments

This project was conceived and began life in the midsummer heat of Siena, Italy, in July 2012. During a coffee break between sessions at the biennial conference of the International Society for Third-Sector Research (ISTR), the conversation of the co-editors of this book turned to the notion of regulatory cycles in the nonprofit arena. As we shared updates from each other's jurisdictions, our curiosity grew as we began to ponder whether the transitions and links we were witnessing between state regulation and self-regulation in our home countries were being replicated in other parts of the world and, if so, how these changes between regulatory forms could be explained or perhaps even predicted. The ebb and flow of what was to become the *Regulatory Waves* project that started at ISTR was to continue over the following four years as we invited nonprofit scholars in eleven other jurisdictions to come on this journey of discovery with us.

We are indebted to ISTR for providing us with the reflective space to start this conversation in Siena and then in allowing us to present two sessions of workshop papers at the 2014 conference in Muenster, Germany, and a progress update on the work at the ISTR Latin American Regional Conference in Puerto Rico in 2015. We are equally grateful to the Association for Research on Nonprofit Organizations and Voluntary Action (ARNOVA) for facilitating conference sessions on the *Regulatory Waves* project at its annual conferences in Hartford, Connecticut, in 2013 and Denver, Colorado, in 2014. The value of international collaborative forums such as ISTR and ARNOVA should not be underestimated in their bringing together nonprofit lawyers and academics from many disciplines and allowing a natural sharing of learning to occur. For us, these academic gatherings provided an opportunity to convene our team of collaborators, allowing us to keep the momentum going. They also introduced us to new scholars who, intrigued by our research question, came to our workshops, joined our ranks, and subsequently became valued members of our team as this project took shape.

We are extremely grateful not only to the contributors to this volume but to our many unnamed but much appreciated colleagues in both ISTR and ARNOVA who attended our sessions, plied us with constructive and critical questions, and continued to support us in the completion of this project long after the conference banners had been taken down and the circus had left town for another year.

We also gratefully acknowledge support from our universities and other institutions. In this regard, Oonagh Breen's attendance at ISTR and ARNOVA meetings was made possible by the generous support of both University College Dublin (UCD) Seed Funding and UCD Sutherland School of Law research awards. Alison Dunn's attendance at ISTR and ARNOVA meetings was made possible by generous funding support from Newcastle Law School, Newcastle University, and the funding attached to her Vice Chancellor's Distinguished Teaching Award (2013). Mark Sidel's participation at the ISTR and ARNOVA meetings and research in China and Vietnam was made possible by generous support from the University of Wisconsin-Madison, University of Wisconsin Law School, International Center for Not-for-Profit Law (ICNL), United Nations Development Programme (UNDP), and the Luce Foundation (via a grant to Indiana University).

We are honored that one of the founding figures in nonprofit law, Marion Fremont-Smith, graciously agreed to write the Foreword to this volume. Marion's long career focusing on the regulation and governance of nonprofit organizations and her expertise not just in US regulation but also her abiding interest in Asian and Anglo/Irish nonprofit regulatory regimes made her a perfect choice. We thank her sincerely for her kind comments.

We are grateful for the interest in this project and the strong support provided by Matt Gallaway, Finola O'Sullivan, and the exceptional law team at Cambridge University Press. We offer our sincere thanks, too, to the peer referees who reviewed our book proposal and made excellent constructive suggestions.

We hope that this work will provide a solid foundation from which to continue the important task of theorizing the regulation of the nonprofit sphere. We believe that the insights into the interactions between state regulation and self-regulation of nonprofit organizations in this work provide a useful basis for reexamining the nature and longer-term policy implications of such regulatory waves not just in the area of nonprofit law but in the broader area of regulatory governance more generally. We look forward to continuing this conversation with policymakers, academics, and stakeholder organizations in both the nonprofit sphere and beyond.

Oonagh B. Breen
Alison Dunn
Mark Sidel

1

Regulatory Waves

An Introduction

OONAGH B. BREEN, ALISON DUNN, AND MARK SIDEL

1.1 INTRODUCTION

The same water – a different wave.
What matters is that it is a wave.
What matters is that the wave will return.
What matters is that it will always return different.
What matters most of all: however different the returning wave,
it will always return as a wave of the sea.[1]

Regulatory intervention in the nonprofit sphere tends to come in waves. Such intervention often takes the form of statutory regulation and, in recent decades, frequently includes self-regulatory initiatives as well. In more recent years, combinations of self-regulation and statutory regulation – sometimes referred to as "hybrid" or "co-regulation" – have also begun to emerge. Academic scholarship has tended to focus on these forms of regulation as distinct entities, examining their strengths and weaknesses in the context of individual models of regulatory governance.[2] To date, however, there has been no scholarly attempt to undertake an examination of both kinds of nonprofit regulatory frameworks with a view to discerning the contributing factors that might cause a state to switch between one form of regulatory regime (for example, statutory regulation) and another (for instance, self-regulation or co-regulation), or to combine them. Neither has there been a comparative analysis of the possible environmental factors that inform or perhaps influence the frequency, timing, or degree of switching between nonprofit regulatory regime types, nor how they influence each other in practice.

---

[1] Marina Tsvetaeva, "Poets with History and Poets without History," (1934), first published as "Pesnici sa istorijom i pesnici bez istorije," *Ruski Arhiv* 26–27 (1934): 104–142.
[2] Mary Kay Gugerty and Aseem Prakash eds., *Voluntary Regulation of NGOs and Nonprofits: An Accountability Club Framework* (Cambridge: Cambridge University Press, 2010).

A short word on terminology, as used in this book, is perhaps merited here. Statutory regulation is concerned with a government-driven process resulting in either primary or secondary legislation giving effect to the regulatory goals. The regulation, developed with or without nonprofit sector input, applies universally to those entities covered by the legislation. In the case of nonstatutory regulation, the sector rather than the state takes up the role of developer and enforcer of the regulatory regime. The democratic nature of nonstatutory regimes depends on the sector's composition and its commitment to collective action. Once initiated, unlike statutory regulation, nonstatutory regimes are normally dependent on voluntary adherence and compliance. Enforcement and sanction imposition generally lack state imprimatur and may be dependent on a contractual enforcement basis. Between the polar ideals of pure statutory and nonstatutory regulatory regimes lies the emerging sphere of co-regulation or hybrid regulation. This regulatory form tends to be developed by or on behalf of the sector (like self-regulation) but with the active funding or participation of the state (like statutory regulation). While compliance and enforcement in the first instance lie with the sector, co-regulation is often viewed as complementary or supplementary to statutory regulation such that ineffective enforcement of co-regulation may result in the triggering of the state's default power to regulate statutorily.

This book explores whether there is an underlying relationship between statutory and nonstatutory regulation models in the context of nonprofit regulatory frameworks and sets out to investigate the extent to which the nature of the regulatory conversations occurring in sixteen jurisdictions inform the resulting regulatory models, influences, and regulatory relationships. By delving into the regulatory narrative and analyzing the factors that inform the interaction between statutory and nonstatutory regimes, we seek to glean a better understanding of the catalysts for regulatory change. Exploration of the country narratives at hand allows us to highlight the common trends emerging in these country case studies. Drawing on these shared experiences, we can begin to articulate policy principles that may assist decision makers to choose the best options for effective facilitation and management of the third sector from among the array of regulatory tools on offer.

This work posits that there is an ongoing causal relationship existing between statutory and nonstatutory regulation of the nonprofit sector. As with the ebb and flow of the tide, so with the ebb and flow of statutory and nonstatutory regulation; in some cases, one form growing in strength as the other lessens its hold over the sector, or the two co-existing in some uneasy or easy form. An initial hypothesis might be to view the relationship between regulatory forms as a zero sum game. When statutory regulation is in the ascendancy, one might think, there is less room (or need) for nonstatutory (self-regulatory) intervention; whereas when statutory regulation fails to deliver, space is created for more innovative self-regulation or co-regulatory options to come to the fore. An alternative explanation might posit the view that while statutory regulation remains solely within the domain of the state, the state and the nonprofit sector compete over self-regulation, making it a contested space for either the extension of state control or the extension of nonprofit autonomy from the state. Other plausible explanations for the seeming ebb and flow between the statutory and nonstatutory regulatory cycles of the nonprofit sector exist. For example, this may be a long game: in some jurisdictions, the nonprofit sector may recognize the ascendancy and dominance of state regulation, and set about building self-regulation and semi-autonomous nonprofit sector bodies over a long period (twenty to thirty years, for example), as a way of moving toward some more autonomy for the sector, even as the state highly and restrictively regulates. Additionally there are also broader environmental, political, and historical factors that influence and drive how the relationship between statutory and nonstatutory cycles of regulation is balanced. It remains the case, however, that the nature and mechanisms of this relationship and the rationale for the use of one form of regulation over another at a particular time has not been the subject of systematic study or comprehensive discussion.

1.2 THE WHAT, WHY, WHEN, AND HOW OF REGULATION

I Keep six honest serving-men
(They taught me all I knew);
Their names are What and Why and When
And How and Where and Who.
I send them over land and sea,
I send them east and west;
But after they have worked for me,
I give them all a rest.[3]

Many rationales exist for the regulation of the nonprofit sector. These rationales range from the state's concern to protect public trust and confidence in the integrity of the nonprofit sector, thereby encouraging greater giving, to safeguarding public funds devoted to charitable ends from fraudulent abuse. The government may also have an altogether less noble vested interest either in controlling

---

[3] Rudyard Kipling, "The Elephant's Child," in Rudyard Kipling, *Just So Stories* (New York: Country Life Press, 1902).

altruism and philanthropy, so as to minimize nonprofit challenge or dissent, or in ensuring alignment of sector activities with the state's objectives, and preventing the nonprofit sector (or elements of it) from joining forces with those who would challenge government. On a more neutral note, a government may wish to regulate to prevent unfair competition arising vis-à-vis charities and other sectors, to better protect vulnerable beneficiaries or to incentivize public giving toward certain causes, whether through fiscal policy or otherwise.

Achievement of these broad aims may be brought about through regulation that takes either an enabling form (thereby creating a supportive framework for the encouragement of a flourishing sector) or one that is more prescriptive in nature (limiting access to the benefits typically associated with public benefit or charitable status, or restricting the rights of such qualifying entities to engage in certain activities). Within this context, the common regulatory themes that emerge tend to focus on the need to promote better accountability and transparency among nonprofit organizations, the requirement to introduce or strengthen public benefit requirements, the push toward better nonprofit governance, the importance of enhanced fiscal regulation ensuring both transparency of funding sources and ultimate destination of donated funds, the creation of restrictions on and procedures for formation and registration of organizations, discretionary powers accorded to government, restrictions on activities, and other matters of regulation.

Common approaches to the meeting of these aims include the development of comprehensive statutory frameworks for nonprofits, the creation of new or the improvement of existing national registers and the strengthening of state agency supervisory and oversight powers, and detailed regulatory provisions for certain types of nonprofit organizations, such as foundations or advocacy groups. Yet regulation in these areas does not fall solely within the domain of the state; increasingly, the nonprofit sector has entered this sphere of oversight in its own right, seeking to create and impose its own self-regulatory norms or to work in conjunction with the state in the achievement of a co-supervisory regime. The "how" of regulation thus ranges widely from statutory legislation, both primary and secondary, overseen by an appointed regulator(s) or courts, to sector codes of conduct or certification and accreditation schemes, aimed at preempting or supplementing statutory regulation, to the encouragement of certain types of nonprofit conduct, the enforcement of which is not left entirely to the sector but depends rather on the cooperation of the state and nonprofit sector working together and without either of which the regime is simply unenforceable.

Important questions remain to be explored: How do regulation and self-regulation interact? How does that shifting mix between regulatory forms impact the nonprofit sector, and particular parts of it, such as advocacy organizations, community-based groups, foundations, and others? Is there an ideal mix of statutory and nonstatutory regulation for the best governance of nonprofit organizations, and, if so, what is it? How suitable are these different forms of regulation for the specific requirements of the nonprofit sector and its regulatory goals? What burdens does each regime option impose on the nonprofit sector and on government?

The questions posed here may be seen as broad regulatory governance questions common to both regulatory governance and multilevel governance models. Regulatory governance theorists are concerned with understanding the forms that regulation takes and the processes of delegation to independent regulatory institutions. Multilevel governance theorists, on the other hand, focus on arrangements "for making binding decisions that engage a multiplicity of politically independent but otherwise interdependent actors – private and public – at different levels of territorial aggregation in more or less continuous negotiation/deliberation/implementation, and that [do] not assign exclusive policy competence or assert a stable hierarchy of political authority to any of these levels."[4] The interplay of both delegation of statutory control and the renegotiation of policy competences between state and nonstate actors has a particular resonance within the nonprofit sphere, particularly in light of new public management, making the sector an ideal forum in which to explore modern and emerging regulatory perspectives on government and nongovernment regulation.

In recent years, similarities between emerging nonprofit regulation regimes have led us to question whether regulatory patterns spread between countries, and, if so, what the underlying conditions are that encourage this regulatory domino effect. The first decade of this century saw a strong preference for the creation or enhancement of charity regulatory frameworks based on overarching regulator-based supervisory control, evidenced in New Zealand (2005), Scotland (2005), England and Wales (2006), Northern Ireland (2008), Ecuador (2008), and Ireland (2009). And this has been the long-term trend in other countries we discuss in this volume, including China, Vietnam, and parts of Latin America and Africa. The mid-2000s also saw the parallel emergence of greater community-based self-regulation or co-regulation in the different jurisdictions of the United Kingdom (2007), Ireland (2008), and Uganda (2006). Both patterns have been at work in China and Israel, first strong state regulation to the virtual exclusion of

---

4   Philippe Schmitter, "Neo-Functionalism," in *European Integration Theory*, ed. Antje Wiener and Thomas Diez (Oxford: Oxford University Press, 2004), 49.

self-regulation, and now some development of the self-regulatory side, though state regulation certainly remains dominant.

The second decade of the millennium continues to witness ongoing regulatory change. As some countries press ahead with new central regulators (Australia, Ireland, Scotland), others are retrenching by either dismantling independent regulators in favor of direct state control (New Zealand) or moving more toward the empowerment of the nonprofit sector to oversee itself through a variety of mechanisms framed as co-regulation partnerships (England and Wales). There continue to be longstanding patterns of dual and more control mechanisms over nonprofits, both regulatory and self-regulatory (as is prevalent in the United States, Brazil, and Ecuador), while there is also evidence of the emergence of nascent self-regulatory, transparency, and accountability frameworks (though not independent regulators) in state-dominated frameworks (the "long game" in China and Vietnam) and the emergence of competing self-regulatory initiatives in state-centered federal frameworks (India and Mexico). While government macro policies may recognize the vital role played by civil society organizations in advancing government policy, the realpolitik of state acceptance of broadened civil organization activities as well as their accrued public power can lead to increased tension between the state and the nonprofit sector (Israel, Ecuador).

The regulatory environment in a given jurisdiction is often shaped by the broader relationship that exists between the state and nonprofit sector. Thus, to understand the former, we may need to first categorize or classify the context in which nonprofits engage with the state. In terms of engagement, a number of options exist ranging from collaboration at one end of the spectrum to cooption and challenge at the other.

1.2.1 *Collaborative Relationships*

The types of problems that form the subject of government/nonprofit sector collaboration are often noncontractible and seemingly intractable. These problems, to which there are no easy answers, require policy solutions to issues concerning social exclusion, long-term unemployment, environmental concerns, and development aid assistance, to name a few. In some instances, it is difficult to formulate exactly what the policy question should be. Unlike commercial collaborative ventures in which the parties will agree on the intended product and decide clear performance indicators to guide their collaboration, the areas giving rise to nonprofit sector/government collaboration are often cases in which a government does not have a clear image of the specifics of the policy or project that it wants to produce. Government knows, however, that it cannot find the answer on its own. This type of collaboration, in the words of Linden, requires "lateral and systemic thinking. It requires more partnerships, fewer rigid boundaries. It supports knowledge sharing, not knowledge hoarding ... [and] leaders who connect their work to a higher purpose."[5] To this extent, partnership represents the new language of public governance.[6]

The reasons for government and nonprofit sector collaboration are as varied as they are complex. There are, for instance, moral motivations on both sides. Claims of democratic deficit – that is, the worrying trend of citizen detachment from involvement in and responsibility for government – confront governments in many societies.[7] In an effort to address this trend, governments see collaboration with nonprofit organizations as a way to bridge the perceived gap between bureaucracy and citizens.[8] By engaging with nonprofit organizations and utilizing their expertise on the ground, government reaches out to citizens active at local level, offering citizens a chance to be part of a policy solution and thereby reaffirming and encouraging active citizenship.[9] The nonprofit sector's moral motivation lies in the desire to make policy outcomes more responsive to nonmajoritarian concerns regarding, for example, social exclusion, by representing voices that may not be otherwise adequately heard in the policy process.

There are also pragmatic motivations driving state/sector collaboration. Governments have a financial incentive to achieve greater efficiency. Modern welfare states face difficulties in satisfying the heterogeneous needs of citizens by themselves and have sought out nonprofit organizations, among others, to meet the demand. Two different rationales exist for this growing interdependence between state and sector.

---

[5] Russell M. Linden, *Working across Boundaries: Making Collaboration Work in Government and Nonprofit Organizations* (San Francisco, CA: Jossey-Bass, 2002), 238.

[6] Helen Sullivan and Chris Skelcher, *Working across Boundaries: Collaboration in Public Services* (Basingstoke: Palgrave Macmillan, 2002).

[7] See, for example, Robert Putnam, *Making Democracy Work: Civic Traditions in Modern Italy* (Princeton, NJ: Princeton University Press, 1994); Robert Putnam, *Bowling Alone: The Collapse and Revival of American Community* (New York: Simon & Schuster, 2000); Francis Fukuyama, *Trust: The Social Virtues and the Creation of Prosperity* (New York: Simon & Schuster, 1995).

[8] Putnam, *Bowling Alone*, n. 7, 49.

[9] David Hulme and Michael Edwards, "NGOs, States and Donors: An Overview," in *NGOs, States and Donors: Too Close for Comfort*, ed. David Hulme and Michael Edwards (Basingstoke: Palgrave Macmillan, 1997), 6 (noting that "under the New Policy Agenda NGOs ... are seen as vehicles for 'democratisation' and essential components of a thriving 'civil society', which in turn are seen as essential to the success of the Agenda's economic dimension").

On the one hand, the contraction of the welfare state and the increased emphasis on value for money leads government to contract out more public service provision to the most competitive tender, which in many (though not all) cases results in a nonprofit partner providing the service.[10] Collaboration thus starts out as a cost-effective strategy that along the way is transformed into an ideology. Lowering expectations regarding new state funding, while encouraging greater cost-effectiveness and productivity (for the state, but not always for the collaborative partner delivering the service), the state encourages an ideology of "doing more with less." Nonprofit organizations' familiarity with this ideology makes them ideal partners when the question turns from delivery to the design of such services.[11] Examples abound in Australia, England and Wales, Brazil, and Israel.

On the other hand, those who view the welfare state as expanding rather than contracting argue that the state needs to make strategic alliances with the nonprofit sector in order to meet the expanded commitments of the welfare state. In other words, collaboration is necessary because of the state's lack of capacity to meet sufficiently the individualistic and growing needs of citizens.[12] Given the finite level of resources, nonprofit sector incentives for collaboration lie in the possibility of influencing the future direction of public funding and being on the inside of policy delivery.

Strategically, the opportunity to contract around local elected representatives, although unlikely to be expressed as an explicit motivation for collaboration by either side, may appeal implicitly to both the nonprofit sector and central government when local government is seen as part of the policy problem. Working with nonprofit organizations allows a state to decentralize

---

[10] Lester M. Salamon, *Partners in Public Service: Government-Nonprofit Relations in the Modern Welfare State* (Baltimore, MD: Johns Hopkins University Press, 1995), 198 (observing that in America, "[g]overnment-nonprofit cooperation took shape not as a matter of conscious policy but as an adaptation to powerful political realities – the political strength of the voluntary sector, the widespread public hostility to governmental bureaucracy, and the general tepidness of public support for welfare services"). See also Steven Rathgeb Smith and Michael Lipsky, *Nonprofits for Hire: The Welfare State in the Age of Contracting* (Cambridge, MA: Harvard University Press, 1993).

[11] See Arthur T. Himmelman, "On the Theory and Practice of Transformational Collaboration: From Social Service to Social Justice," in *Creating Collaborative Advantage*, ed. Chris Huxham (London: Sage, 1996), 19–44.

[12] Claire F. Ullman, *The Welfare State's Other Crisis: Explaining the New Partnership between Nonprofit Organizations and the State in France* (Bloomington: Indiana University Press, 1998).

programs even in areas where historically local government is weak, thereby empowering local communities.[13]

In the search for policy solutions, a further motivation for government to collaborate with the nonprofit sector stems from the knowledge that many policy problems are perennial and intractable. Involving the nonprofit sector in the policy process enables the government to share the burden of policy failure with the sector, even when the policy issue itself relates to the very regulation of the sector. The inability of a nonprofit organization to distance itself sufficiently from results it helped to broker can effectively silence stakeholder criticism,[14] a result often incorrectly classified as government cooption. As the state and sector begin to explore the contours of policy collaboration in many areas including nonprofit regulation, questions arise as to the efficacy of such hybrid regulation; the ground rules for its effective operation, including who creates them; and the relative challenges in ensuring collaborative regulation does not blur into cooption.

In some states, there is another dimension to this collaborative process. Here the state understands the substantive value of working with the nonprofit sector, but also understands that in working with and delegating provision of services to nonprofits, nonprofits are also guided (through fiscal and contractual mechanisms) toward provision of social services and away from advocacy. Thus "cooption" as a government strategy fits well with the other, and perhaps more public, rationales for state/nonprofit collaboration.

1.2.2 *Relationships of Cooption*

At the opposite end of the spectrum to collaboration, state cooption of the nonprofit sector is often driven by funding or political dependencies on government. Often the underdeveloped state of the sector, particularly in, but not limited to, post-transitional democracies means that the sector is both fragmented and fragile, lacking in autonomy and heavily dependent on the

---

[13] See Kathleen McLaughlin and Stephen Osborne, "A One-Way Street or Two-Way Traffic? Can Public-Private Partnerships Impact on the Policy-Making Process?," in *Public-Private Partnerships: Theory and Practice in an International Perspective*, ed. Stephen Osborne (London: Routledge, 2000), 326.

[14] This outcome is particularly evident in nonprofit involvement in social partnership in Ireland: Oonagh B. Breen, *Crossing Borders: Comparative Perspectives on the Legal Regulation of Charities and the Role of State-Nonprofit Partnership in Public Policy Development* (New Haven, CT: Yale Law School, 2006), arguing that social partnership was used to implicate community/voluntary players who might otherwise have dissented. See also Martha S. Feldman and Anne M. Khademian, "Managing for Inclusion: Balancing Control and Participation," *International Public Management Journal* 3(2) (2000): 149–167.

state, or sometimes international donors, for funding support whether by way of grant aid or contract. This, in turn, affects the nature of the relationship between state and sector and the form of regulation imposed. In the same way that one may question whether collaboration between state and nonprofit sector inevitably leads to cooption in all but the most robust regimes, one might equally ask whether in developing economies cooption of the nonprofit sector should always be viewed negatively as undermining the sector, or whether it might be viewed as an intermediate step in the development of the nonprofit sector and an incremental step toward future state/sector collaboration. The chapters on East Africa and Latin America (most notably the case studies of Ecuador and Brazil) provide excellent case studies and insights into these questions. Equally, the chapters considering Ireland, Israel, China, and Malawi point to the difficulties that a weak nonprofit sector infrastructure will face when it engages in self-regulation or co-regulation with government. Chronic lack of resources, leading to the sector's overreliance on the state for funding support not just for programmatic purposes but also for engagement in self-regulatory regimes, can seriously undermine the efficacy of the latter regimes at worst or, at best, skew the focus of the regulatory purpose. And yet the case studies of Ireland and Israel hold out some hope that from (repeated) lessons of failure can spring potential for renewed future engagement that seeks to succeed more on the collaborative than the cooption end of the scale. The case studies from China and Vietnam also indicate that, when viewed as a long process of strengthening the role of transparency and quality within the nonprofit sector, even the most nascent, episodic self-regulatory chapters can play a role in building the nonprofit sector over decades.

1.2.3 *Challenging Relationships*

Not all state/sector relationships fall into the mutual (collaborative) or forced (coopted) cooperation category. There are times when both sides view the other with distrust and as a threat to its authority (in the case of government) or its existence (in the case of nonprofits). The distrust may have historical roots (as in the case of Mexican government's distrust of the Church transferring in more modern times to distrust of secular nonprofit organizations engaged in the same poverty relief area as previous religious institutions) or it may be more cultural (as in Ecuador where public mistrust of government extends to public mistrust of nonprofit organizations as corrupt extensions of government). Or it may be directly political, in states that have known strong government, such as China and Vietnam, and where the government seeks to channel and mold nongovernmental entities toward nonchallenging social service provision and away from what is often perceived to be antigovernment advocacy.

Challenging the state – an increasingly common role for nonprofits migrating from the sphere of service delivery to that of advocacy for fundamental freedoms and rights – changes the dynamic between the parties. In regulatory terms, the hostility engendered can lead a state to impose a more prescriptive registration and oversight regime based on a command and control model than ostensibly is warranted by nonprofit activities. In those countries in which civil society space itself is contested, one might expect to find little room and indeed little appetite for nonprofit self-regulation. The Mexican experience in navigating this territory allows us to interrogate this hypothesis and the related issue of whether self-regulation is more prevalent or successful in those states where collaborative or even cooption relationships exist.

Gaining a better understanding of these relationship stages – collaboration, cooption, and challenge – their proximity to each other on the cycle of regulation and overlap, the climate conditions that precede each stage, and the triggers for the metamorphosis of one stage into the other (or not) helps to inform our understanding of the world of nonprofit regulation.

1.3 EMERGING TRENDS IN THE INTERACTION OF STATE REGULATORY AND NONSTATUTORY REGULATORY INITIATIVES

Turning then to the manner in which state regulatory and self-regulatory initiatives have affected or impacted on each other, we can discern a number of common trends across the case studies. The threat of government action is a key driver for self-regulation efforts. Self-regulatory regimes are often a preemptive response to a feared statutory regulatory regime. Evidenced instances of this behavior abound in Africa, with the clearest examples of self-regulation being triggered by government moves to regulate emerging in those cases in which the risk of centralized regulation was perceived as imminent, the state's initial reform efforts were characterized as hostile and nonconsultative, and the proposed reforms were viewed by international donors as undermining the democratic transition or development of the country (namely, Ethiopia, Uganda, and Kenya). Self-regulation as a long-term partial coping mechanism toward strong state regulation is also an important feature in states with restrictive nonprofit regulatory regimes such as China and Vietnam.

Developed countries, however, also respond to the stimulus of threatened government reform, with the threat of statutory regulation of fundraising prompting nationwide self-regulatory regimes in both Ireland and Great

Britain. The United States and Australia provide an interesting federal cross comparison on this issue. In the United States, the Senate Finance Committee encouraged the formation of a Panel on the Nonprofit Sector, drawn from the nonprofit sector to examine and make recommendations for improving nonprofit governance as a way of preempting the Finance Committee's own sweeping proposals regarding nonprofit governance, donor-advised funds, deductibility of appreciated property, and supporting organizations' periodic substantiation of eligibility for tax exemption. The panel's final recommendations in June 2005 recommended both legislative action and nonstatutory recommendations, providing the sector with an opportunity to propose what it considered were proportionate and reasonable measures.[15]

In contrast, the 2014 attempts of the Australian government to abolish its newly established federal regulator, the Australian Charities and Not-for-profits Commission, and to replace it with an undefined form of charity self-reporting drew the ire of the sector, with the majority of respondents to the public consultation process indicating their satisfaction with the new central regulator and warning against a return to purely tax oversight (which was viewed as not fit for purpose in the broader nonprofit regulatory sense) or some form of self-reporting self-regulation.

As well as the threat of government action, a complementary driver for self-regulation efforts is under-regulation often brought about by a lack of government action to regulate. This regulatory gap is evident particularly in Scotland where, in the face of an inadequate regulatory framework and lack of action by government, the nonprofit sector initiated self-regulation in order to stem falling trust and confidence as a result of various sector governance scandals. This in turn led the nonprofit sector to lobby government to provide a workable sector-specific state regulatory regime, demonstrating how one regulatory initiative pushes for the next regulatory wave.

Another catalyst in the move toward self-regulation, particularly in the developing country context, has been the role of donor influence. Donor support has played a crucial role in underwriting collective action and creating a protective space for associational activity. International donors, spurred on by fears that democratic reforms might be threatened, tend to be the most likely to act. In Kenya and Uganda, the causal nature of this relation reveals that when governments adopt a more hostile approach toward regulatory

---

[15] Panel on the Nonprofit Sector, *Strengthening Transparency, Accountability and Governance of Charitable Organizations: A Final Report to Congress and the Nonprofit Sector* (Washington, DC: Independent Sector, June 2005).

reform, donors are more likely to intervene, whereas a less hostile state attitude results in lower donor involvement.

Greater donor involvement correlates to strong nonprofit cohesion, thus creating a fertile environment for self-regulation to occur. In contrast, lower donor involvement was causally connected with the weakening of the sector through the fracturing of nongovernmental organization (NGO) associations. Thus, in Tanzania where multiple associations competed for support, as well as in Malawi where a single association failed to mobilize sufficient support from the sector, weaker donor involvement in the reform process adversely affected the ultimate reform outcomes. Similar patterns emerge in Brazil, where the disengagement of international funders in the mid-1990s led to increased nonprofit dependency on state government for funding. The effect of this disengagement changed the nature of the regulatory relationship between the state and the sector by crowding out the space for self-regulatory efforts in an environment that encouraged greater reliance on government and less nonprofit autonomy. But the influence of donor engagement is variable and idiosyncratic. In two states with similar forms of one-party government and roughly similar policies toward the nonprofit sector, donor engagement has played relatively little role in the development of a self-regulatory impulse in China, while it has, at the most nascent stages, been very important in Vietnam.

A third trend of note that the case studies identify is the positive correlation between the existence of a state mandate for self-regulation and the likely success of such self-regulation. A good example in this regard is the development of the fundraising self-regulation regime in Great Britain. Motivated primarily as an alternative to statutory intervention, government supported the establishment of a self-regulatory regime when it recognized and experienced firsthand the past shortfalls of statutory regulation in the control of charitable fundraising. The nonstatutory scheme received state funding in its formative years, and its success rates were measured against achievement benchmarks developed by government. Following a five-year statutory review, the state granted the nonstatutory regime a further five-year stay on the introduction of statutory regulation to allow additional time to bed the nonprofit regime down (although recent fundraising scandals have raised questions as to whether that reprieve will be honored).

The British state-mandated experiment can be contrasted with the Irish fundraising nonstatutory regulatory experience, which, initially borne of nonprofit sector initiative and supported by the state, became latterly coopted by government. The Irish state, in paying the piper here also called the tune, resulting ultimately in the staying of further development of the regime, at the state's specific request, at a critical time in the nonstatutory regime's infancy, causing the experiment to flounder, largely as a consequence.[16]

In the absence of a state mandate, the development of self-regulation institutions among nonprofits appears to require some form of selective incentive underwritten by external patrons or broad sectoral agreement on the need for some self-regulatory or semi-autonomous action to strengthen quality, transparency, and accountability in the nonprofit sector. In the case of Ethiopia, the sponsoring nonprofit offers members quite concrete benefits based on external donor support and relatively strong administrative capacity. In the case of Uganda, the sponsors of the quality assurance mechanism hold out the prospect that accredited nonprofits will be better candidates for donor funding, thereby providing the necessary carrot to engagement. In contrast, the Australian experience illustrates how successful a sophisticated self-regulatory regime can be when it evolves to meet nonprofit stakeholders' accountability needs while simultaneously proving useful to government as a means of co-regulation.

1.3.1 *The Impact of Wider Political Agendas*

The relationship between the state and the nonprofit sector in each country and the extent to which there is a wider political and/or nonprofit sector agenda to the development, or lack of development, of state regulation and self-regulation in each country also influences the emerging regulatory pattern. Nowhere is this more evident than in Australia where strong political catalysts have been the driving force behind nonprofit regulatory reform. One of the more reflective nations when it comes to conceptualizing optimum regulatory options, Australia's commitment to new public management theory with its contracting out of government services has seen Australia enter a new regulatory space in which the rules for regulating the type of state/sector collaboration now commonly occurring have yet to be worked out.

As the Australian study reveals, the favored form of regulation changes with the government and its political ideology; moves toward statutory regulation and the creation of a central charity regulator tend to occur when the government is Liberal Democratic, whereas pushes for smaller government

---

[16] One of the earliest examples of the relationship between state mandates (or at least facilitation) of self-regulation and the growth of self-regulatory regimes was in the Philippines, the site of the first formal nonprofit self-regulatory scheme in Asia. There, a government mandate that recognized certification through the self-regulation process (the Philippine Council for Nonprofit Certification [PCNC]) for charitable tax purposes was a key driver in the acceptance of the PCNC certification process in the 1990s.

and more self-regulation come when the Conservatives hold power. Interestingly, the main impetus and support for greater central regulation has come from the nonprofit sector (a trend we see replicated in both Ireland and Scotland), leaving space when a willing government partner is in power to explore further the possibility for co-regulation.

A similar pattern driven by a combination of political ideology and public finances may be found in England and Wales where again the need for a more robust regulatory framework flowed very much from a new public management model that needed to be able to contract out to reliable and functioning nonprofits. Legislative reform of charity regulation came with the Labour government in the late 1990s and the turn of the century. Yet again, as in Australia, a shift in power to the Conservatives in England has brought about a change in regulatory policy with the launch of a "Big Society" model, focused on moving from "state action to local action." The goals of Big Society with their small state imperative, coupled with the ensuing economic recession and the need to put in place extensive fiscal austerity measures, have seen a vast reduction in the budget of the charity regulator, the Charity Commission for England and Wales, and a push toward new co-regulation and greater self-regulation.

The case study of Scotland reveals the impact of a different type of political agenda brought about as a result of constitutional change. Devolution of power from the UK government to Scotland in 1999 opened up a previously nonexistent space in which policy and regulation specific for Scotland could be created. Charity law was part of the powers devolved to the newly formed Scottish Executive (latterly Scottish Government), and this enabled the call for a workable Scottish charity law statutory framework to come to fruition. The political agenda was toward nation building and making devolution work. The opening up of a new policy environment had a threefold effect on the nonprofit sector in terms of generating a political need to harness nonprofit organizations' expertise, providing greater opportunities for state/sector partnerships and creating a new forum in which nonprofit organizations could lobby for legal and policy change.

One further interesting example of the impact of wider political agendas can be seen in Brazil wherein the extent of statutory regulation has, to a large extent, crowded out nonprofit self-regulation initiatives aside from those focusing on better nonprofit coordination and information sharing. Engagement by the nonprofit sector with government has predominantly focused on the improvement of state regulation of nonprofits rather than any independent agenda to promote self-regulation (which was also the position in Scotland). Failures by the state to deliver on its regulatory promises, however, has led both to the growth of Abong (the influential nonprofit platform) and to greater public revolt against government, unrelated to the nonprofit sector. The unexpected reaction of this broader section of civil society pressured the Brazilian government to bring forth its new regulatory framework for civil society organizations in 2015, focused on securing better partnerships between nonprofits and the state, falling perhaps more within the domain of cooption than collaboration at the present moment in time. There are similarities to these developments in China and Vietnam, where self-regulation is so nascent as to be sometimes invisible, in part because the nonprofit sector has focused significantly on seeking amelioration to some of the strictest forms of government regulation and on institutions of soft autonomy (a foundation coordinating center, for example) rather than on the development of institutions of self-regulatory autonomy.

1.3.2 *The Interplay between State Regulatory and Self-Regulatory Initiatives*

In state/nonprofit relationships characterized by mistrust on both sides and giving rise to a hostile regulatory environment, it is not unusual to find command and control type legislation in place that focuses ostensibly on making nonprofits more accountable and subjecting them to stricter oversight, particularly in relation to matters of registration and taxation. Elements along these lines define relationships in Mexico, in East Africa, in Ecuador over the past twenty years, and in China and Vietnam. This often harsh regulatory environment often resulted at worst in the outright repression of nonprofits or, at best, in their cooptation by the state. In the presence of weak political institutions, the state's ability or willingness to deliver on its promised statutory regime is greatly limited, and a policy window opens for nonstatutory intervention. In the presence of strong state institutions (such as in China, Vietnam, or England and Wales), the state delivers on its promised statutory regime (or overdelivers, in the view of many nonprofits), and the development of self-regulation is a long game to be developed over several decades, often beginning with softer coordinating, quality strengthening, transparency, and informational initiatives and groups rather than formal self-regulation itself.

Thus, in Mexico, the government's lack of effective implementation of its regulatory framework has provided the necessary space for nonprofit self-regulation to emerge. Interestingly, the purpose of such regulation is not to ensure greater nonprofit accountability but rather to rule out state manipulation and corruption of nonprofit funds. Similarly, with the spread of political liberalization in Africa and the simultaneous proliferation of NGOs, the authoritarian control frameworks for supervising NGOs proved unworkable.

At a time of often fundamental political transition and transformation, African states find themselves struggling to manage relationships with NGOs, opening a new space for greater input from the nonprofit sector in the regulation of this space, the success or otherwise of which is often related to the level of associational collective action exercised, as can be seen in a comparison of the Kenyan and Malawi experiences. From failure, however, comes the potential for learning and future success – a trend evident in both Ireland and Israel when it comes to self-regulatory efforts.

Ecuador, too, provides an interesting example of seizing the policy window. The recent emergence of a new nonstatutory "regulator" in the form of the Ecuadorian Confederation of Civil Society Organizations grew out of a nonprofit collective assembled initially to respond to government consultation on statutory regulation proposals. The government's abandonment of its regulatory plans left the collective free to continue their coordination, leading the group toward the development of a self-regulatory framework instead and the consolidation of the collective as a confederation. Whether this Ecuadorian cycle of nonstatutory regulation will be short lived remains to be seen. Despite a great start with the confederation's reports on collective accountability in 2010 and 2011, new fears exist that the state's new decree on the role of civil society organizations in policy formation is seeking to foreclose the regulatory space and exclude nonprofit self-regulation as a regulatory tool.

An interesting outcome of judicial intervention in the United States has been the extent to which US case law has influenced the direction and form of permissible statutory regulation. As the courts limited the power of the legislature to restrict charitable solicitation across the states, statutory officials (in the form of the National Association of State Charities Officials)[17] turned from statutory regulation to nonstatutory collective regulation in the form of the Charleston Principles. Notwithstanding the judicial pushback, no fewer than forty-eight of the fifty states have focused on the introduction of statutory regulation of fundraising in preference to nonstatutory models, an outcome at odds with the Australian experience where nonstatutory fundraising codes have, in some instances, moved from being temporary political fixes to being viewed as more permanent federally endorsed solutions.

Finally, the Irish study reveals that the interplay between statutory and nonstatutory regulation itself may be informed by the manifold interactions of the state and nonprofit sector in separate but related policy spheres. The

---

[17] An interesting departure in itself when one recalls that the body in question, the National Association of State Charity Officials, has no authority over members' actions or authority to publish binding regulations.

Irish case study highlights how even failed attempts at state/sector collaborative policymaking on substantive matters can in turn influence the next wave of nonprofit regulation. The experiences gleaned by nonstate actors from such state/sector interactions, whether vested processes or not, can be transformative. Exposure to the politics of decision making forges new nonprofit leaders who have potential to deliver innovative nonstatutory regulatory solutions when statutory regulation promises more than it can deliver or fails to deliver at all. Further examples of "learning from the feet of failure" can be found in the Mexican and Ecuadorian chapters, albeit in all three instances, the threat of state cooption still visibly hangs in a Damoclesian fashion over these efforts.

1.4 THE COUNTRY CASE STUDIES

This book uses a series of country case studies to analyze if, and how, statutory regulation, self-regulation and co-regulation interrelate in practice in the nonprofit sphere. These case studies do so by examining the waves and types of nonprofit regulation against their historical, economic, political, and policy context and alongside any wider environmental factors that may have informed or influenced them. The country case studies cover sixteen jurisdictions that span Asia, Australia, North and Latin America, Europe, and sub-Saharan Africa. While not representative of regions – and not intended to be – the case studies, nonetheless, have been chosen specifically to provide a range of global comparative examples. In so doing, these case studies are intended to present a broad spectrum of environmental and policy contexts in order to tease out the factors that might – or equally might not – drive the use of different regulatory tools in nonprofit regulation. The case studies cover both civil law and common law jurisdictions so that analysis is not limited, and comparisons between legal regimes might also be made.

The country case studies begin in Chapter 2 where Alison Dunn provides a comparative analysis of the two jurisdictions of Great Britain. We shall see that in England and Wales, where strong state regulation is in place, there is government encouragement for nonprofits to take greater responsibility via self-regulatory and co-regulatory practices, whereas in Scotland, where the state framework was neglected, self-regulation has been sidelined in the push for a comprehensive and cohesive statutory regime. In both British jurisdictions nonprofit regulatory reform occurred at propitious moments when the nonprofit sector's push for reform aligned with a new government seeking to harness the sector in its own vision of governance.

In Chapter 3 Oonagh B. Breen investigates the waves of nonprofit regulation in Ireland. This fifty-year retrospective demonstrates how the development – or not – of regulatory policy is closely woven into, and shaped by, the relationship between the nonprofit sector and the state. In examining the processes of dialogue and collaboration between the sector and the state, the chapter illustrates how nonprofit regulatory policy can develop over time on an episodic basis, and how the many false starts and failed initiatives can nonetheless provide valuable learning experiences for all parties.

A comparative analysis of five jurisdictions in sub-Saharan Africa is the subject of Chapter 4. Here Mary Kay Gugerty analyzes the development of nonprofit regulatory tools in Kenya, Malawi, Tanzania, Uganda, and Ethiopia. Within each of these countries, a set of regulatory waves emerges as governments and NGOs propose and respond to regulatory initiatives. Distinct phases of contestation, nongovernmental professionalization, and the development of more sophisticated and professional systems of self-regulation can be traced through these regulatory waves, but we shall see differing results across the countries, including, in some cases, a severe crackdown on nonprofit activity.

The influence of state-dominated regimes is also a theme in Chapter 5, in which Mark Sidel undertakes a comparative investigation of the emergence of self-regulation in the Chinese and Vietnamese nonprofit and philanthropic sectors. The analysis in this chapter demonstrates that, in different ways, the attempts at self-regulation in both countries are attempts to begin a long-term process of establishing some autonomy from the state for semi-independent transparency and accountability mechanisms. But in both countries, the state remains dominant, including in the nascent self-regulatory sphere.

Tension between the state and the nonprofit sector is also evident in Israel, a country examined by Nissan Limor and Noy Brindt in Chapter 6. Although there have been self-regulatory initiatives in Israel, there is little division of labor between the state and the sector in the regulation of nonprofits. This chapter in particular highlights examples of why self-regulatory initiatives might founder, for example because of the dominance of the state regulatory regime or its control over access to resources, data, and information; the asymmetry of power between the statutory regulator and nonprofits; a lack of resources to fund self-regulation; and a lack of awareness and understanding of nonprofits toward regulatory activities.

Chapter 7 turns to an exploration of nonprofit regulation in Mexico. In this country case study Michael D. Layton identifies a state/sector regulatory relationship that is in transition from suppression to the creation of a more enabling legal environment. This has led to conflicting crosscurrents of nonprofit regulation: on the one hand, an impulse on the part of the tax authorities to tightly control and regulate the sector and limit tax expenditures and, on the other hand, a broad mandate to encourage the activities of nonprofits. Against this backdrop are high levels of public mistrust of nonprofits, and here self-regulation has arisen as a means by which the sector can achieve increased visibility and transparency, generating greater public trust, and thereby increasing public support.

A comparative analysis of the two jurisdictions of Brazil and Ecuador is provided by Susan Appe and Marcelo Marchesini da Costa in Chapter 8. These two countries share some characteristics as emerging democracies with initially fragmented nonprofit sectors, but they also demonstrate significant differences. For example, the development of state/sector partnerships has driven the agenda of regulation in Brazil and has resulted in a high level of dependency of the Brazilian nonprofit sector on the state. That, in turn, has allowed the state to exert pressure on nonprofits via regulation. This has not been a feature in Ecuador, where nonprofits have started to position themselves as explicitly self-regulatory, pointing to the new collective accountability reports as one way in which nonprofits are creating opportunities to be more accountable to government and the public.

Chapter 9 takes us to Australia, where Myles McGregor-Lowndes examines recent developments in relation to Australian nonprofit communities seeking to regulate their own collective behaviors. This country case study provides a prime example of the problems created when a nonprofit regulatory agenda is thrown backward and forward between regularly shifting political ideologies. It also illustrates policy learning, that is, how self-regulatory initiatives taking place in international nonprofit communities may prompt domestic nonprofits to develop their own self-regulatory codes.

The country case study of the United States in Chapter 10 has been chosen to provide a micro example of the sometimes limited role nonstate actors can play in pressuring for reforms to a state-dominated regulatory regime. In this chapter Putnam Barber and Megan M. Farwell provide an overview of the history of fundraising regulation in the United States, the ways that fundraising regulation has changed over the decades, the emergence of self-regulatory moves within the fundraising industry, and the rise of watchdog organizations and the role of the media in exposing fundraising abuses and calling for reforms. In so doing, they analyze the relationship between longstanding fundraising regulation and the newer self-regulatory, watchdog and media disclosure, and transparency developments.

Finally, in Chapter 11, the threads of these individual country case studies are drawn together in a conclusion, which also provides policy principles for nonprofit regulation.

Eddies and Tides

Statutory Regulation, Co-Regulation,
and Self-Regulation in Charity Law in Britain

ALISON DUNN

2.1 INTRODUCTION

Charity regulation and the bodies that enforce it in Britain have faced intense public, media, and political criticism in recent years. The criticism has focused on misuse of charity status as shelters for tax avoidance schemes, chief executive pay, poor fundraising practices, unethical investment policies, and overt political activities and has arisen from perceptions of weak governance within charitable organizations, inadequate oversight, or inadequate exercise of regulatory powers by charity regulators.[1] It has led to demands for charities and their regulatory bodies to be more robust in governance practices and in enforcement of charity law.

This is not the first time that British charities and their regulation have faced unfavorable scrutiny. But the timing of current criticism is noteworthy, arising at the end of two decades of intense regulatory development. Through a combination of state regulation, co-regulation, and self-regulation, British charities are now more closely regulated than ever before.

These recent regulatory developments have their genesis in a demand for greater accountability to secure public and donor trust and confidence and emphasize the importance of maintaining a strong charity "brand."[2] It is symbiotic with nonprofits' increased public service delivery role and their

---

[*] I am grateful to Dr. Ann Sinclair for her research assistance.

[1] Public Administration Select Committee (PASC), *The Role of the Charity Commission and "Public Benefit": Post-Legislative Scrutiny of the Charities Act 2006*, Third Report of Session 2013–2014 HC76 (June 6, 2013); National Audit Office (NAO), *The Regulatory Effectiveness of the Charity Commission* (London: Stationery Office, 2013); Committee of Public Accounts (PAC), *The Charity Commission*, 42nd Report of 2013–14, HC 792 (February 5, 2014).

[2] For example, Strategy Unit, *Private Action, Public Benefit: A Review of Charities and the Wider Not-for-Profit Sector* (London: Strategy Unit, 2001), para. 4.53.

presence at the policy table and sits alongside a demand for nonprofits to demonstrate legitimacy and credibility when delivering public services, applying for funding, or contributing to policymaking.

Increasingly the demand for accountability and good governance has been satisfied through the development of nonprofit self-regulatory initiatives. Self-regulation enables nonprofits to take ownership of sector regulation and is often more nuanced, flexible, and responsive than legislative regulatory instruments. The first code of governance created for the Welsh nonprofit sector, for example, was described as a "living document," with mechanisms embedded within it to enable development.[3] Self-regulation has not always been sufficient to satisfy calls for nonprofit accountability, however. In Scotland only state regulation has been able to meet the demand for comprehensive regulation, and the regulatory wave in that country has surged in a direction different from the one in England and Wales.

This chapter examines the different waves of charity regulation in Britain in recent years alongside the policy drivers that have triggered them. It argues that state regulation, co-regulation, and self-regulation fit together with their historical and political context as an evolving whole and that the British jurisdictions are at different places in an evolutionary cycle. We consider first the position in England and Wales, and second the position in Scotland, as two distinct jurisdictions of charity law in Britain. We shall see that the debate on co-regulation and self-regulation is more pronounced in England and Wales, whereas a demand for state regulation has dominated in Scotland. These different regulatory waves have been influenced by fiscal constraints, political imperatives, and broader regulatory trends driving a demand for better quality regulation.

Before proceeding it is worth noting the overarching regulation. Traditionally British charities have been regulated in the different jurisdictions through legislative instruments at the state level. The current operating legislation in England and Wales is the Charities Act 2011 and in Scotland the Charities and Trustee Investments (Scotland) Act 2005. The 2011 Act consolidates the latest wave of English and Welsh statutory legislation that, since the nineteenth century, has established a strong state regulatory framework. By contrast, the 2005 Act represents a nascent wave of statutory regulation specific to Scotland. A permanent charity regulator, the Charity Commission for England and Wales, has operated since the Charitable Trusts Act 1853. It is charged with maintaining an accurate and up-to-date register of charities and has extensive

---

3   First published in 2006, now WCVA, *Good Governance: A Code for the Third Sector in Wales*, 2nd ed. (Cardiff: WCVA, 2012), 5.

investigatory and enforcement powers. A specific Scottish charity regulator, the Office of the Scottish Charities Regulator (OSCR), was created in 2003 following devolution of powers to Scotland in 1999 and operates on principles similar to its English/Welsh counterpart. These distinct charity regulators are nonministerial departments of their respective governments.

2.2 ENGLISH AND WELSH CHARITY REGULATION: KEY REGULATORY TRENDS

Since the 1990s there have been three interconnected trends in English and Welsh charity regulation: the development of self-regulation, retrenchment by the Charity Commission, and most recently a move toward state/sector co-regulation. These trends have arisen in a charity sector that has strong state regulation and well-established umbrella/infrastructure bodies.

2.2.1 *Self-Regulation: A Developing Wave*

Nonprofit self-regulation has operated in England and Wales for some time, but its scope and development was initially ad hoc and underrated. This can be accounted for by the extensive provision of statutory regulation. With relatively comprehensive state provision the nonprofit sector did not need to fill a regulatory void or protect its public image, both traditional motivations for self-regulation. Indeed, registration with the Charity Commission has long been (mis)taken as a mark of governance standards and has doubled as determining a regulatory threshold.

In 1987 a government inquiry (the Woodfield Report) recognized the existence of nonprofit self-regulation but could not envisage it working at national level. Woodfield's view was that the sector's nature and diversity made it "impracticable to devise any internal regulatory body which would be accepted by charities as representative and to which even reserve powers of monitoring could be given."[4] Short of a decade later the sector's influential Deakin Commission promoted self-regulatory best-practice codes of governance but similarly dismissed the creation of a single central accrediting/regulatory body as burdensome, bureaucratic, and likely ineffective in raising standards.[5]

---

[4] Home Office and HM Treasury, *Efficiency Scrutiny of the Supervision of Charities* (London: HMSO, 1987) ("Woodfield Report"), para. 14.

[5] Commission on the Future of the Voluntary Sector, *Meeting the Challenge of Change: Voluntary Action into the 21st Century* (London: NCVO, 1996) ("Deakin Commission"), paras. 3.15.12, 4.4.10, 4.7.14.

Since then a quiet transformation has occurred. Impetus within the non-profit sector for self-regulation was recognized by the Government's Cabinet Office 2001 Strategy Unit report on charity law reform.[6] That impetus grew after umbrella bodies embraced Deakin's encouragement to develop national nonprofit governance standards. A concerted push for nonprofit involvement in promoting best-governance practices followed closely on the heels of the Strategy Unit report, which had recommended that the sector develop capacity in the area of governance and performance standards.[7] Work had already begun via a Quality Standards Task Group, an independent body formed in 1997 by the nonprofit umbrella organization the National Council for Voluntary Organisations (NCVO) to help build nonprofits' governance capacity.[8] Another sector umbrella body, the Association of Chief Executives of Voluntary Organisations (ACEVO), concerned at a lack of sector focus on governance, also launched a self-regulation governance agenda.[9] The intervening years between the Strategy Unit report and the Charities Act 2006 were an intense period in which self-regulation emerged strongly, with a plethora of codes of practice and self-accreditation schemes springing up across the sector.

The use of self-regulation by nonprofits is now so extensive it is an industry. In just one area of quality standards, for example, there are at least 130 standards in use by sector organizations.[10] Diverse self-regulatory schemes are utilized, from quality standards programs that use Kitemarks, for example, to externally validated accreditation schemes.[11] It encompasses codes of practice, such as the now well-established *Good Governance Code*.[12] Some of the self-regulation initiatives are activity focused, the most developed of which is a national fundraising self-regulatory scheme, but others exist too for areas such as charity retailing or advocacy.[13] Additionally, organizations that form coalitions or groups often set out common standards to be adhered to between

---

[6] Strategy Unit, n. 2, para. 8.1.   [7] Ibid., para. 6.38.
[8] Quality Standards Task Group, *A "White Paper" on Quality in the Voluntary Sector* (London: QSTG, 1998).
[9] Annie Kelly, "Governance framework show signs of old age," *Third Sector*, June 11, 2003, 12.
[10] Ellie Brodie et al., *Scoping Study: Quality Assurance in the Voluntary and Community Sector* (London: NCVO and Office for Public Management, 2012), 5.
[11] For example, *PQASSO Quality Mark for Efficiency and Effectiveness in Management and Governance of Organisations* endorsed by the Charity Commission, accessed July 1, 2015, www.ces-vol.org.uk/PQASSO/.
[12] *Good Governance: A Code for the Voluntary and Community Sector*, 2nd ed. (2010), accessed July 1, 2015, www.governancecode.org/about-the-code/.
[13] For example, the *Quality Mark for Advocacy*, accessed July 1, 2015, www.qualityadvocacy.org.uk/.

coalition/group partners,[14] and sector umbrella bodies lead in providing best-practice schemes and self-assessment tools for their membership.[15]

Most self-regulation schemes in use have been initiated by the nonprofit sector post-Deakin, although some have been prompted or promoted by government. Not all are sector exclusive. A range of schemes applied by nonprofits is designed for use by a variety of organizations or designed for specific fields, such as broadcasting.[16]

Although there has been extensive development of self-regulation in governance and quality standards, including sector-wide standards, Woodfield and Deakin's reservations about the feasibility of nonprofit national self-regulatory bodies have lingered. To date, just one comprehensive sector-wide self-regulation scheme has been created with an overarching regulatory body with enforcement and sanction powers. This is a voluntary membership–based self-regulation scheme for fundraising.[17] It was initiated and initially funded by the government (no doubt one reason why this self-regulatory body (and no other) got off the ground) but has faced severe criticism in recent times.

Development of this fundraising self-regulation scheme was prompted by the Strategy Unit's 2001 recommendations identifying this area as ripe for reform.[18] Fundraising regulation was complex, lacked clarity, and had a multiplicity of regulators, resulting in a poor record of compliance. A review investigating fundraising self-regulation followed, and in 2006 a finalized scheme was launched, overseen (until July 2016) by the Fundraising Standards Board (FRSB), the Institute of Fundraising (IOF), and the Public Fundraising Regulatory Association (PFRA).[19] Under the scheme members were bound by a "Fundraising Promise" and Codes of Practice set by

[14] For example, Disaster Emergency Committee developed an externally validated *DEC Accountability Framework* for its international humanitarian relief charity membership, accessed July 1, 2015, www.dec.org.uk/press-release/an-introduction-to-the-new-dec-accountability-framework.

[15] For example, British Overseas NGOs for Development, accessed July 1, 2015, www.bond.org.uk/effectiveness.

[16] For example, *Ofcom Broadcasting Code*, accessed July 1, 2015, http://stakeholders.ofcom.org.uk/broadcasting/broadcast-codes/broadcast-code/.

[17] It encompasses both British jurisdictions. The Institute of Charity Fundraising Managers and the Public Fundraising Regulatory Association had already developed codes of practice but without comprehensive adoption.

[18] Strategy Unit, n. 2; Strategy Unit, *Private Action, Public Benefit: The Regulation of Fundraising* (London: Strategy Unit, 2002).

[19] The Buse Commission undertook the initial review and the Charities Aid Foundation took its proposals forward. Coherence of roles between FRSB, IOF, and PFRA has remained an issue.

the IOF.[20] In return members were able to advertise compliance through the FRSB's "Give with Confidence" logo. The scheme's aim was to raise standards, alongside providing a complaints and sanctions process which included expulsion from the scheme for breach.

This fundraising self-regulation scheme included a reserve power, allowing the government to introduce statutory regulation if the scheme was not considered successful.[21] On its creation the Home Office set out twelve relatively flexible principles by which the scheme would be measured in a five-year review. These included encouraging scheme awareness and providing accessible, effective complaints procedures and fair, effective sanctions.[22] Lord Hodgson's subsequent review found the scheme had notably driven up standards and enjoyed a measure of sector support but, crucially, had not met two key interlinked principles for success, namely attracting sufficient membership (which had reached a "plateau") and monitoring compliance.[23] As a voluntary scheme, fundraising self-regulation has struggled to achieve levels of membership and secure sufficient sector buy in. This has an obvious impact on the scheme's resources, which, in turn, affects its capacity to develop sanctions. Without sufficient resources the scheme (over)relied on self-certification, one of the lowest levels of compliance monitoring.

Despite the concerns these failings raise there has been evident willingness within nonprofits and government to make the fundraising self-regulation scheme work, allowing it "more time to prove itself."[24] The government and nonprofits embarked on discussions as to how the scheme might be supported and developed. These discussions assumed greater importance following the death of ninety-two-year-old Olive Cooke in May 2015 amid allegations that she took her own life after being inundated with donation requests from charities and third parties fundraising on their behalf.[25] The ensuing public

---

[20] Members undertake to be honest and open, clear, respectful, fair, reasonable, and accountable and to comply with standards, accessed July 1, 2015, www.frsb.org.uk/what-we-do/fundraising-promise/.

[21] Charities Act 2006, s. 69; Charities and Trustee Investment (Scotland) Act 2005, s. 83.

[22] HC Deb (February 6, 2006), vol. 442, cols. 37WS–39WS, accessed July 1, 2015, www.publications.parliament.uk/pa/cm200506/cmhansrd/vo060206/wmstext/60206m02.htm.

[23] Lord Hodgson, *Trusted and Independent: Giving Charity Back to Charities. Review of the Charities Act 2006* (London: Stationery Office, July 2012), paras. 8.13–8.16, ch. 8.

[24] Cabinet Office, *Government Responses to 1) The Public Administration Select Committee's Third Report of 2013–14: The Role of the Charity Commission and "Public Benefit": Post-Legislative Scrutiny of the Charities Act 2006 2) Lord Hodgson's Statutory Review of the Charities Act 2006: Trusted and Independent, Giving Charity Back to Charities* Cm 8700 (London: Stationery Office, 2013), 16. A further review was set for 2017.

[25] FRSB, *Investigation into Charity Fundraising Practices: Interim Report* (London: FRSB, 2015).

and political storm, and parliamentary review, accused nonprofits of hounding vulnerable donors, and charities were warned that this is a "last chance for self-regulation."[26] This placed increasing pressure on the fundraising self-regulation scheme to prove that it and, by extension, self-regulation as a regulatory option, is fit for purpose.

The outcome of the government and sector discussions comprised a range of self-regulation, statutory regulation and co-regulatory changes.[27] These included content changes to the IOF's codes of fundraising practice; statutory requirements set out in the Charities (Protection and Social Investment) Act 2016 regulating agreements between charities and third-party fundraisers in order to protect vulnerable donors and prevent intrusion of privacy; and the creation of a new fundraising regulatory body, the Fundraising Regulator, which officially replaced the FRSB in July 2016. Rather than act as a membership body, this new regulator has a remit over all charities. It will be funded by a levy on organizations based on their fundraising expenditure, and it will put in place additional fundraising requirements, stronger monitoring measures and sanctions, and can refer to the Charity Commission any organization that fails to address its concerns. In this latter respect the new Fundraising Regulator demonstrates greater co-regulation, a regulatory trend considered further below. The scrutiny which led to the change of regulatory body should not be underestimated. It created an expectation on the part of the public and in political circles that the government should take action to better protect donors. In so doing, it also firmly placed on the political radar the question of the suitability of self-regulation as a workable regulatory tool. Fundraising served as a test case for how nonprofit self-regulation might develop at a national level, and until these most recent events that scheme was seen as having a positive impact on the self-regulation landscape in Britain. Self-regulation had been debated more seriously as a regulatory option, including developing more formal roles for sector umbrella bodies in dealing with complaints and internal disputes within charities.[28] It remains to be seen how, post–Olive Cooke, the new Fundraising Regulator performs and how the ongoing self-regulation debate develops. Despite the dismantling of the original FRSB self-regulation scheme, one positive outcome was that

---

[26] Public Administration Select Committee, *The 2015 Charity Fundraising Controversy: Lessons for Trustees, the Charity Commission, and Regulators*, Third Report of Session 2014–2015 HC431 (January 25, 2016), 3.

[27] The key report was Sir Stuart Etherington et al., *Regulating Fundraising for the Future: Trust in Charities, Confidence in Fundraising Regulation* (London: NCVO, 2015), which included the proposal for a new regulatory body.

[28] Hodgson, n. 23, 85, paras. 7.8–7.10, Recommendation 2.

the sector was fully engaged in reviewing fundraising self-regulation in an attempt to make it a stronger and more viable scheme and, by extension, to forestall the government exercising its reserve powers for statutory regulation.[29]

2.2.2 *Charity Commission Tidal Waves*

The second key regulatory trend in England and Wales concerns the charity regulator the Charity Commission. While not under ministerial control the Commission is subject to audit and parliamentary reporting.[30] Its statutory objectives include increasing public trust and confidence in charities, promoting legal compliance by trustees in the administration of charities, and enhancing charity accountability.[31] Its statutory functions include identifying and investigating misconduct/mismanagement in charity administration and taking protective action.[32] The Commission's roles have been categorized as advisory, administrative, supervisory, and quasi-judicial,[33] though the latter three fall under a broad regulatory compliance banner. In essence, the Commission advises and regulates.

The Commission has adopted two outwardly contrary approaches to regulation in recent times: a retrenchment of engagement activity with charities, followed by a move toward more "visible regulation." Each is prompted by different pressures.

The first regulatory development arose from implementation of the Commission's "risk framework," which emphasized risk-based regulation as the regulator's operating approach.[34] Risk-based regulation has been a regulatory trend across Britain, and its aim is to improve the quality of regulation and reduce regulators' administrative burdens by shifting responsibility for risk assessment onto organizations regulated.[35] The Commission used it strategically to rein in engagement with charity trustees and refocus instead on its core regulatory functions. It was supported in doing so by the government and the Hodgson Review.[36] As a result the Commission pulled back from its advice function and engagement activity with trustees at the same time as

---

[29] See generally Etherington, n. 27.   [30] Charities Act 2011, s. 13, sch. 1(11).   [31] Ibid., s. 14.
[32] Ibid., s. 15.
[33] *Report of the Committee on the Law and Practice Relating to Charitable Trusts*, Cmd 8710 (London: HMSO, 1952), para. 97.
[34] Charity Commission, *Risk Framework: Our Regulatory Approach to Protecting the Public's Interest in Charity* (London: Charity Commission, 2012).
[35] Pushed forward by Hampton Report, *Reducing Administrative Burdens: Effective Inspection and Enforcement* (London: HM Treasury, 2005).
[36] Cabinet Office, n. 24, para. 3; Hodgson, n. 23, 58–60, para. 5.9.

encouraging trustees to proactively ensure their regulatory compliance. The result was a regulatory shift toward greater trustee self-reliance.[37]

The second regulatory development was, in no small part, caused by this retrenchment and by a glut of negative inquiries by parliamentary committees and independent reports that fiercely criticized the Commission's operations. The criticism highlighted a reactive rather than proactive regulator, failure to utilize existing enforcement powers, and ineffectiveness and risk aversion in the Commission's operations. While the Public Administration Select Committee criticized the Commission's statutory objectives as "too vague and aspirational" and too ambitious,[38] the Public Accounts Committee was more caustic. It determined the Commission to be not fit for purpose and had "little confidence in the Commission's ability to put right its problems and failings."[39] The National Audit Office concluded the Commission was inefficient and ineffective, relied too heavily on the assurances given to it by trustees, and was not delivering value for money.[40] In a swipe at the Charity Commission's risk framework, it recommended the Commission be more proactive in investigating risk.[41] Much was made of the fact that the Commission had opened fewer than twenty statutory inquiries per year since 2009 and that its extensive powers and sanctions had been used sparingly.[42] The underlying premise of these inquiries was that to maintain public confidence the regulator should be more visible in its investigation of charities and more robust in its use of enforcement powers and sanctions.

The result was a scramble by the Commission toward more clearly evident exercise of its regulatory powers, demonstrated by a tougher stance on late filers of financial accounts, a stronger tone to its guidance, a request for more information in charities' annual returns, and a rise in serious case investigations.[43] The government too was keen to be seen to respond to the Commission's critics, principally via proposals to extend the Commission's statutory powers to "support public trust and confidence in charities, the regulator and the regulation of the charity sector."[44] The result was enaction of the Charities

---

[37] Alison Dunn, "Regulatory Shifts: Developing Sector Participation in Regulation for Charities in England and Wales," *Legal Studies* 34(4) (2014): 660–681.

[38] PASC, n. 1, para. 22.

[39] PAC, n. 1, 5–6; Commons Select Committee, "Charity Commission not fit for purpose," *Press Release* (February 5, 2014), accessed July 1, 2015, www.parliament.uk/business/committees/committees-a-z/commons-select/public-accounts-committee/news/publication-of-report-tax-reliefs-on-charitable-donations/.

[40] NAO, n. 1, paras. 24–26.   [41] Ibid., 10–11.   [42] Ibid., para. 3.8.

[43] Charity Commission, *Annual Report and Accounts 2013–2014* (London: Charity Commission, 2014).

[44] Cabinet Office, *Consultation on Extending the Charity Commission's Powers to Tackle Abuse in Charities* (London: Cabinet Office, 2013), 3.

(Protection and Social Investment) Act 2016 that increases the regulator's powers to investigate and tackle charity abuse. The sector's response has been mixed. While there has been broad support for the Commission and enhancement of its powers, concerns about proportionality and independence remain, alongside the view that the cause of the Commission's failings might be not lack of powers but the choices it makes over when and how to exercise them and the budget constraints under which it operates.[45]

2.2.3 Co-Regulation: A Building Swell

The third regulatory trend was triggered by the second. Retrenchment in Commission activity resulted in a shift toward the promotion of co-regulation with other bodies. Co-regulation already exists for charities with a principal regulator other than the Commission.[46] The current co-regulation trend, however, proposes utilizing sector umbrella/infrastructure bodies. These are well established in the nonprofit landscape, and the Commission has long run partnership schemes to draw on their knowledge and expertise. Following implementation of its risk-based framework, the Commission stepped up these partnership operations.

Recommendations to utilize sector umbrella/infrastructure bodies are not new. In 1978 the Wolfenden Committee emphasized the important functions they carry out, and this was reiterated by the Deakin Commission, which emphasized their role as advisors and standard setters.[47] Independently, some bodies forged ahead with a "professionalisation agenda," recommending co-regulation as a means to facilitate the sector taking greater responsibility and ownership of accountability and as a means by which the Commission could be freed to focus more efficiently on "high-impact" regulation.[48]

---

[45] NCVO, *Consultation on Extending the Charity Commission's Powers to Tackle Abuse in Charities: Response of the National Council of Voluntary Organisations* (London: NCVO, 2014); Stephen Bubb quoted in Vibeka Mair, "Proposed Commission powers 'must not turn it into some kind of Rambo,'" *Civil Society Online*, June 5, 2014, accessed July 1, 2015, www.civilsociety.co.uk/governance/news/content/17596/proposed_commission_powers_must_not_turn_it_into_some_kind_of_rambo.

[46] The principal regulator promotes charity law compliance, the Commission retains investigative powers.

[47] Wolfenden Committee, *The Future of Voluntary Organisations* (London: CroomHelm, 1978), ch. 7; Deakin, n. 5, paras. 2.4.1–2.4.2, 3.15.11, 3.16.11.

[48] ACEVO, *High Level Report of the ACEVO Taskforce on Better Regulation: Public Impact Centred Regulation for Charities* (London: ACEVO, 2010), 33–34.

Co-regulation was also recommended by the Hodgson Review as a means to balance Commission retrenchment and budget cuts.[49] For Lord Hodgson, co-regulation presents "a spectrum of possibilities" from signposting to delegation and is as much about size and scale as about regulatory expertise.[50] Existing partnerships focus on provision of Commission-endorsed guidance or best-practice governance systems and is co-regulation of the signposting variety. While Lord Hodgson was keen to see this practice extended independently or through such partnerships, his review countenanced a more formalized version of co-regulation with the sector taking on aspects of the Commission's work that were increasingly unfeasible for it to achieve, including, but not exclusively, advisory functions.[51]

To realize this vision, statutory powers to co-regulate will be required. Currently the Commission does not have delegation powers, and evidence to the Hodgson Review highlighted fears that delegation could lead to fragmentation of regulation.[52] Nonetheless, Hodgson recommended (and the government accepted) that the Commission be able to delegate functions in the future with the caveats that the Commission be satisfied that the co-regulator would provide equivalence in regulatory standard and the Commission retain investigatory powers along with the right of termination.[53]

While the Commission has welcomed the idea of a delegation as a "discretionary conditional power," the sector is not at one on the proposals.[54] Some have lauded the need to open up regulatory culture.[55] Others have expressed concerns about sector bodies' resourcing, capacity, and expertise to carry out regulatory functions.[56] Implementation of delegation will require enabling legislation. At present, then, co-regulation is embryonic but emerging strongly in the debate about the future regulation of the sector.

2.3 ENGLISH/WELSH POLITICAL AND REGULATORY CONTEXT

These trends in English/Welsh charity regulation do not exist in isolation. They are underpinned by a specific policy and political context.

---

[49] Hodgson, n. 23, ch. 6.
[50] Ibid., para. 6.12; Kaye Wiggins, "'We will study the technical detail – and the big picture,'" *Third Sector*, January 31, 2012, 10.
[51] Ibid., para. 5.12.   [52] Ibid., para. 6.13.
[53] Ibid., para. 6.16, Recommendation 5; Cabinet Office, n. 24, 30.
[54] Cabinet Office, n. 24, 30; Stephen Cook, "Perhaps it's time for a full rethink," *Third Sector*, April 24, 2012, 14.
[55] ACEVO, n. 48, 8, 15–16.   [56] PASC, n. 1, para. 18.

2.3.1 *Reform Waves*

Modern-day trends in English/Welsh charity regulation principally find their genesis in the sector's Deakin Report, the legacy of which was to cement the sector in the policy landscape. NCVO set up the Deakin Commission in 1995. It had a wide-ranging remit and sought an ambitious "new paradigm" for the sector.[57] Its state-level recommendations included proposals for:[58]

- A new legal form for nonprofit organizations
- An independent appeal tribunal against the regulator's decisions
- Consolidation of fragmented statutory regulation
- A "concordat" to set out good-practice principles and standardize government/sector relations
- Greater coherence within the government to promote the sector within the strictures of governmental power.

Although the incumbent Conservative government rejected many of Deakin's recommendations,[59] the fact that it responded to the report was significant in indicating the seriousness with which ministers took the nonprofit sector. As Nicholas Deakin, the report's author, later emphasized, it meant the sector had "crossed a frontier into the inside, the policy-making process."[60]

A year on and, after eighteen years of successive Conservative administrations, a Labour government came to power. The timing was propitious. It heralded the change in political ideology needed to make Deakin's vision a reality and started a period Deakin described as the sector's zeitgeist.[61] The nascent Labour government had developed policies toward the sector pre-election and was keen to cultivate a new political approach.[62] It found expression in Labour's vision for a "Third Way" that harnessed the nonprofit sector through partnerships in developing a mixed economy of welfare provision. Deakin's proposed concordat became a central feature of engaging sector organizations, and the now well-established Compact was born, setting standards of behavior for working relations between sector organizations and local

---

[57] Deakin, n. 5, para. 5.2.1.   [58] All came to fruition.

[59] Department of National Heritage, *Raising the Voltage: The Government's Response to the Deakin Commission Report* (London: Department of National Heritage, 1996).

[60] Quoted in Veronique Jochum and Colin Rochester, "An Interview with Nicholas Deakin," *Voluntary Sector Review* 3(1) (2012): 5–13, 8.

[61] Ibid., 9.

[62] Labour Party, *Building the Future Together: Labour's Policies for Partnership between Government and the Voluntary Sector* (London: Labour Party, 1997).

and national government departments.[63] An Office for the Third Sector was created in the government (which later became the Office for Civil Society) with a designated Minister, with responsibility for the sector. (In the summer of 2016 a government reshuffle moved the Minister for Civil Society's role to the Office for Culture, Media and Sport, with announcement awaited on the status of the Office for Civil Society.) Individual organizations and umbrella/infrastructure bodies played their part, too, forming a campaigning group, the Charities Bill Coalition, to ensure that momentum for regulatory reform was not lost.

Wholesale reform took longer to achieve. The Cabinet Office's 2001 Strategy Unit review into nonprofit regulation built on many of Deakin's recommendations. Underscored by a concern with accountability and linked to the sector's public service partnership role, it proposed statutory regulation alongside emphasizing that the sector should take responsibility for accountability and "have the courage to regulate itself."[64] This encouragement assisted the sector to develop self-regulatory codes of practice. By 2004, the Commission had published a good-governance guide, and in 2005, a partnership of sector bodies promulgated the sector's first good-governance code.[65]

Statutory reform came via the Charities Act 2006, a feature of which was a requirement for a five-year review. The subsequent Hodgson Review was alive to the need for balance in regulation and, as a whole, can be regarded as a litmus test as to where English/Welsh nonprofit regulation is headed. Alongside expected concerns with accountability and transparency, one of the Hodgson Review's key underlying themes was "judgment not process"; that is, ensuring that regulatory responsibility is shouldered by all rather than just the traditional regulatory agencies.[66] This underscores the interconnectedness of state regulation, self-regulation, co-regulation, and regulatory trends identified earlier in this chapter.

2.3.2 *Policy Waves*

At the heart of the post-1997 Labour government's push for a more robust regulatory and accountability nonprofit framework was a focus on service

---

[63] *Compact on Relations between Government and the Voluntary and Community Sector in England*, Cm 4100 (1998).

[64] Strategy Unit, n. 2, paras. 3.15, 8.1–8.2.

[65] Charity Commission, *Hallmarks of an Effective Charity* CC10 (London: Charity Commission, 2008). The sector *Good Governance code*, n. 13, was founded by ACEVO, Institute of Chartered Secretaries and Administrators, NCVO, Small Charities Coalition, and Wales Council for Voluntary Organisations.

[66] Hodgson, n. 23, paras. 2.18, 3.7, 5.29, appendix A.

delivery. Treasury and Home Office policy focused on enabling nonprofits to take on more public service roles alongside targets for them to do so.[67] The Welsh government similarly set out better services as an area in which the sector could partner with government.[68] Labour's move away from a traditional statist approach to welfare provision, heralded by its Third Way agenda, was significant. It offered opportunities (and costs) to the sector to contribute to policy and service development. But, as a Minister made clear at the time, "the sector cannot have its cake and eat it" but must "put its own house in order in terms of how it is organised and governed."[69]

Deakin too had recognized that the creation of an enabling legal and policy environment brought sector responsibility.[70] As nonprofits became more closely linked to government through service delivery partnerships it was important that the sector remained accountable to service users and other interested parties and independent of government. Adopting best-practice guides and codes of governance was one way of being able to demonstrate nonprofit legitimacy as policy partners as well as independence of government. With this the plethora of self-regulatory codes was born.

The flipside of expanding toward a mixed economy of welfare provision is shrinking of the state. State retrenchment had been the approach of successive Conservative governments in the 1980s–1990s that kickstarted the contracting agenda. The Conservative/Liberal Democrat coalition government that came to power in May 2011 after fourteen years of Labour administrations took up the same "small-state" mantle. It adopted the Conservative Party's "Big Society" agenda, which promoted moving "from state action to social action" and followed in the tradition of seeking small government by transferring responsibility to communities.[71]

Whatever opportunities this might have offered nonprofits in shifting power away from the state, the Big Society agenda was undermined by austerity measures brought in to respond to the 2008 economic crisis, a coalition

---

[67] HM Treasury, *The Role of the Voluntary and Community Sector in Service Delivery: A Cross Cutting Review* (London: HM Treasury, 2002); Home Office, *SR2004 PSA Targets, Technical Notes* (London: Home Office, 2004).

[68] Welsh Assembly, *"The Third Dimension": A Strategic Action Plan for the Voluntary Sector Scheme* (Cardiff: Welsh Assembly, 2008), 6–7.

[69] Alan Milburn MP quoted in Mathew Little, "Milburn: charities 'new third way,'" *Third Sector*, May 12, 2004, 1.

[70] Deakin, n. 5, para. 5.2.1.

[71] David Cameron, "The Big Society," *Hugo Young Memorial Lecture* (November 10, 2009); HM Government, *The Coalition: Our Programme for Government* (London: Cabinet Office, 2010); HM Government, *Making It Easier for Civil Society to Work with the State: Progress Update* (London: Cabinet Office, 2012).

government not wholly committed to the policy, and a lack of understanding on what Big Society meant in practice. As a policy agenda, Big Society became too nebulous a concept to be implemented successfully. It has, quietly, slipped off the political agenda and was not formally revived by the Conservative government elected in 2015. Nonetheless the small-state ideology had a clear impact on the regulatory trends currently at play. The retrenchment in the regulator's operations, for example, was caused in large part by a drastic budget cut resulting from government's wider financial austerity measures. Crucially, those cuts were implemented by a government whose operating ideology was to push for greater devolved power to community groups. In that context a Charity Commission operating at a reduced level made space for the community to take responsibility for its regulation.

Although sharing regulation, Wales has specific policies toward the nonprofit sector that differ from those in England.[72] Devolution brought Wales its own executive, the National Assembly for Wales, and autonomy over policymaking in areas of health, education, environment, housing, and social policy. At its inception in 1999 the Welsh Assembly set up a "Voluntary Sector Scheme" by which partnership between the sector and the Welsh Assembly (later the Welsh government) is facilitated.[73] This Scheme was revised in 2014 as the *Third Sector Scheme*.[74]

The Scheme can be read on different levels. At one level, it is a formalized version of the Compact, setting out principles of operation, rights, and responsibilities between nonprofits and the Welsh Assembly government. The scheme's distinctiveness is that, unlike its English and Scottish counterparts, it has statutory force. At another level, however, this Scheme has not just regularized Welsh government/sector working relationships. It has guaranteed the nonprofit sector a place at the policy table, enabling the sector to contribute directly to Welsh Assembly policies and programs, have an equal say in how the sector works with government, and have access to capacity-building

---

[72] The Welsh nonprofit sector comprises approximately 33,000 organizations, with 9,221 registered as charities: WCVA, *Third Sector Statistical Resource* (Cardiff: WCVA, 2013), 1. The Commission has a separate Welsh office.

[73] Government of Wales Act 2006, s. 74. A *Code of Practice for Funding the Voluntary Sector* was also issued (2009, revised 2014). See Mark Drakeford and Carol Green, "The Voluntary Sector in Wales," in *Next Steps in Voluntary Action*, ed. Centre for Civil Society and NCVO (London: NCVO, 2001).

[74] Welsh Government, *Third Sector Scheme* (Cardiff: Welsh Government, 2014); *Welsh Government, Continuity and Change: Refreshing the Relationship between Welsh Government and the Third Sector in Wales* (Cardiff: Welsh Government, 2013); Welsh Government, *Consultation – Summary of Responses: Continuity and Change* (Cardiff: Welsh Government, 2013).

resources. Additionally, the Scheme requires the Welsh Assembly to promote the sector, and the Welsh government's 2008 Strategic Action Plan set out to do so through "better regulation," including governance self-regulation.[75]

In practice there are suggestions that the Scheme's responsibility across all aspects of the Welsh Assembly government has "defused" the creation of a "strong policy steer."[76] To that may be added the view that it has effectively created a tiered system of sector organizations: a smaller group within the policy circle with influence and a larger group without.[77] Howsoever it works in practice, in comparison with their English counterparts Welsh nonprofits have a clear role within the policymaking process, and one that finds expression in the development of self-regulation.

2.3.3 *Fiscal Waves*

A third wave affecting charity regulation is fiscal in origin. The 2008 recession led to severe cuts and terminations of government funding of a range of nonprofit sector programs. This had a direct impact on sector bodies and puts in doubt their capacity to take on co-regulatory roles. Cuts to regional agencies and local authorities had a knock-on effect too, with cuts in funding and a fall in donations placed alongside greater demand for services as a double resource squeeze.[78] A government Transition Fund was launched for charities facing financial hardship as a result of the financial cuts, but it did not get close to addressing the shortfall.

Severe budget cuts also led to the hollowing out of the Charity Commission, making it difficult for the regulator to deliver on its objectives. The Commission was spared in the 2010 "bonfire of the quangos" that led to the demise of the Commission for the Compact and a raft of other sector bodies, but it nonetheless received budget cuts of one third in real terms over a four-year period to 2015.[79] These cuts were so significant that the Commission was unable to make efficiency savings without reducing one third of its staff, directly impacting its expertise and capacity to carry out its functions. This led the Commission to reprioritize its core regulatory functions and retrench

---

[75] Welsh Assembly, n. 68, 45, 50.

[76] Pete Alcock, "Devolution or Divergence? Third Sector Policy Across the UK since 2000," *Third Sector Research Centre Working Paper* 2 (2009): 11.

[77] Graham Day, "The independence of the Voluntary Sector in Wales," in *The First Principle of Voluntary Action*, ed. Matthew Smerdon (London: Baring Foundation, 2009), 133.

[78] David Kane and James Allen, *Counting the Cuts: The Impact of Spending Cuts on the UK Voluntary and Community Sector* (London: NCVO, 2011).

[79] HM Treasury *Spending Review 2010* Cm 7942 (London: Stationery Office, 2010), 88, table A12.

in overall regulatory activity. Those bodies that criticized the Commission were alive to its budget cuts but saw the regulator's inefficiency as more endemic. The Hodgson Review was more forgiving in this regard, rationalizing its proposal for greater sector self-regulation and co-regulation in light of the Commission's budget constraints. Although self-regulation had been building within the sector post-Deakin and the Strategy Unit review, the Commission's financial position added incentive to the debate on how self-regulation and co-regulation might be further developed.

2.3.4 *Regulatory Waves*

A final driver originates in wider government policy toward improving the quality of regulation. Bodies exercising regulatory functions, including the Commission, must bear in mind the independent advisory body Better Regulation Task Force's principles of good regulation, which include proportionality, accountability, consistency, and transparency. These are incorporated into statute and promulgated through a Regulator's Code.[80]

Of relevance to self-regulation and co-regulation, the Task Force had a deregulatory focus. It recommended the benefits of self-regulation for the nonprofit sector (coinciding with the development of fundraising self-regulation) as well as recommending the Commission lighten the burden of regulation on trustees.[81] A Red Tape Challenge for Civil Society followed, focusing on how to simplify charity regulation.[82] This deregulatory focus can be placed alongside a wider regulatory movement in the corporate and public sectors, developing governance codes of good practice for for-profit organizations and standards in the public sector. This had a knock-on impact on nonprofits as the trend for self-regulatory codes extended outward.

2.4 SCOTTISH CHARITY REGULATION: KEY REGULATORY TRENDS

Scotland is a jurisdiction separate from England and Wales. Decision-making powers were devolved to Scotland by the Scotland Act 1998, leading to the creation of a Scottish Parliament and the Scottish Executive (which later

---

[80] Legislative and Regulatory Reform Act 2006; Better Regulation Task Force, *Principles of Good Regulation* (London: Better Regulation Task Force, 1998 and 2003); Department for Business Innovation and Skills, *Regulators' Code* (London: BIS, 2014); Charities Act 2011, s. 16(4).

[81] Better Regulation Task Force, *Better Regulation for Civil Society: Making Life Easier for Those Who Help Others* (London: Better Regulation Task Force, 2005), 5, 47–49; Better Regulation Task Force, *Self-Regulation Interim Report* (London: Better Regulation Task Force, 1999).

[82] Red Tape TaskForce, *Unshackling Good Neighbours* (London: Cabinet Office, 2011).

became the Scottish Government). Unlike Wales, Scotland has devolved power in relation to charity law. Not all legal matters are devolved to Scotland, however, and some aspects of taxation are (currently) reserved to the UK government (although Scotland will receive greater income tax powers by April 2017).

After years of neglect, the principal nonprofit regulatory trend in Scotland has been to achieve workable, comprehensive statutory regulation.[83] Following Woodfield's recommendations,[84] statutory provisions for Scottish charity law were first set out in the Law Reform (Miscellaneous Provisions) (Scotland) Act 1990. While an improvement on what had gone before, the 1990 regime and wider legal framework were still too "fragmented" to operate effectively.[85] A key provision had been to compel Scottish charities to prepare accounts accessible on request (though it was not a requirement to file accounts).[86] A major regulatory deficit was that the Act did not provide for a Scottish test of charity or for a single charity regulator.[87] As the Scottish Executive later admitted, the "main deficiencies" of the prereform law were "[g]aps in responsibility, fragmentation of advice and support systems, and a lack of routine monitoring."[88] Wholesale reform was needed.

Impetus for legislative reform came first from a series of charity fundraising and governance mismanagement scandals that drew media attention and public/political concern. Although charity mismanagement had been evident in the previous decade,[89] it was the conjunction of two high-profile miscon-duct cases in 2003 alongside the investigation of fifty others for fraud that prompted the Scottish Executive to act.[90] Public trust was at an all-time low; donations dropped by one third in the immediate aftermath and continued to flatline some two years later. The scandals emphasized the lack of publicly accessible information. Although from 1992 the Inland Revenue kept an index

---

[83] Approximately 45,000 nonprofits operate in Scotland (SCVO, *State of the Sector Report April 2014* (Edinburgh: SCVO, 2014), 2), and 23,637 are charities. Charities operating in Scotland must register with the regulator, the Office of the Scottish Charity Regulator (OSCR).

[84] Woodfield, n. 4, paras. 134–144.

[85] Scottish Charity Law Review Commission, *Charity Scotland* (Edinburgh: Scottish Executive, 2001) ("McFadden Commission"), 7, para. 3.12.

[86] Law Reform (Miscellaneous Provisions) (Scotland) Act 1990, s. 1(4), s.5(7).

[87] McFadden, n. 85, para. 1.26.

[88] Scottish Executive Justice Department, *Charity Regulation in Scotland: The Scottish Executive's Response to the Report of the Scottish Law Review Commission* (Edinburgh: Scottish Executive, 2002), para. 3.

[89] A. Thompson, "Charitable trust," *Community Care* 1103 (1996): 25–31.

[90] Scottish Government, *Charities and Trustee Investment (Scotland) Act 2005: Proposals for Minor Amendments to the Act and to the Charities Accounts (Scotland) Regulations 2006, Consultation Paper* (Edinburgh: Scottish Government, 2009), para. 21.

of Scottish tax-exempt charities, it was no more than a list of contact information, some of which was out of date, with no active monitoring of organizations' activities or accounts.[91] The announcement of a new Scottish charity regulator, the OSCR, as an executive agency of the Scottish Executive, followed on the heels of a court order freezing the assets of one of the charities at the center of the financial mismanagement allegations. OSCR was put on a statutory footing as a single charity regulator with monitoring and enforcement powers by the Charities and Trustee Investment (Scotland) Act 2005, an act that carried through major reform of charity law in Scotland. OSCR replaced the Scottish Charities Office, which had previously supervised Scottish charities but did not have extensive powers. In enacting these reforms and providing for a Scottish charity test, the 2005 Act aimed to raise public confidence in charities and protect the "charity brand."[92] These purposes were not dissimilar to the ones emphasized by charity law reform in England and Wales.

The second trigger for legislative reform was a push from the Scottish nonprofit sector. The umbrella body the Scottish Council for Voluntary Organisations (SCVO) was instrumental. It set up the independent Kemp Commission on the Future of the Voluntary Sector in Scotland (1995), a counterpart to the English Deakin Commission. The resulting Kemp Report prompted the Scottish Executive to found the McFadden Commission to review Scottish charity law.[93] Although Kemp found that there was "low political salience and little political leverage" in the Scottish sector as a whole,[94] SCVO lobbied to keep reform on the agenda and, once the plan for a reform bill (subsequently the 2005 Act) was announced, lobbied on its content.[95] In the face of a lack of overarching regulation, SCVO had already promulgated a *Scottish Code of Fundraising Practice* as a means of promoting and setting standards for fundraisers in their internal governance[96] and a *Code of Conduct Governing Contracts* to help set standards in contracting relationships.[97] It had also established a "register" of Scottish charities in 1996 as an

---

[91] Commission on the Future of the Voluntary Sector in Scotland, *Head and Heart: The Report of the Commission on the Future of the Voluntary Sector in Scotland* (Edinburgh: SCVO, 1997) ("Kemp Commission"), para. 7.9.3.

[92] *Charities and Trustee Investment (Scotland) Bill Policy Memorandum*, SP Bill 32-PM, Session 2 (2004).

[93] Kemp, n. 91; McFadden, n. 85. [94] Kemp, n. 91, 4.

[95] For example, SCVO, *The Draft Charities and Trustee Investment (Scotland) Bill: A Response from the Scottish Council for Voluntary Organisations* (Edinburgh: SCVO, 2004).

[96] Published in 1995 with the Institute of Charity Fundraising Managers.

[97] Kemp, n. 91, para. 6.8.6.

attempt to bring together information and accounts on sector organizations and "plug a gap and strengthen public trust in charities."[98] By no means comprehensive, SCVO's register was still effective in revealing the proportion of Scottish charities unaware of or noncompliant with their legal duty to provide accounts to the public.[99] SCVO lobbied for both statutory regulation and self-regulation. Martin Sime, chief executive of SCVO, argued at the time, "If the two aspects can work together, we will have created the right regime in Scotland."[100]

Devolution was the third trigger in the push for legislative reform. Devolution opened up a space enabling the Scottish polity to make its own determinations on laws governing its organizations and institutions. This shift in power created a new legal forum in which reform could be conceived and delivered. It created a new policy environment too, enabling a Scottish government to develop its own Scotland-centric policies. It also created a new forum for nongovernmental groups to lobby or enter into government partnerships. This constitutional change, and the creation of a closer, more proximal policy environment, had obvious implications for the nonprofit sector in government policies toward it and in the evolution of a state/sector relationship.

Devolution also unleashed an added ingredient of community spirit (broadly speaking) toward nation building, without which devolution would not have flourished. There was willingness to make this new policy environment work. To do so the experience and expertise of many groups within Scottish society, the Scottish voluntary sector among them, had to be harnessed to enable the new Scottish government to achieve its aims. This proved significant in spurring on nonprofit regulatory reform, since the sector was now "sewn into the political and policy process."[101]

Given the Scottish regulatory wave focused principally on designing and implementing a strong statutory regime, the potential for nonprofits to develop self-regulatory initiatives was sidelined to limited aspects of organizational governance. The McFadden Commission indicated a fair degree of sector support for fundraising self-regulation, but it did not make self-regulation one

---

[98] Martin Sime, SCVO Chief Executive, quoted in Thompson, n. 89.

[99] SCVO, "Charity Scotland: What Happened to Charity Law Reform?," *Policy Paper Series* No. 2 (2003): 2; Louise Crawford et al., *An Exploration of Scottish Charities' Governance and Accountability* (Edinburgh: ICAS, 2009), 190–191.

[100] Scottish Parliament Official Report, Communities Committee, Session 2, (December 15, 2004), col. 1550.

[101] Martin Sime, SCVO chief executive, quoted in Kaye Wiggins, "'The sector is sewn into the political and policy process,'" *Third Sector*, April 10, 2012, 10.

of its recommendations.[102] It was events in England and Wales that triggered a sea-change. The Scottish Executive recommended allowing a fundraising self-regulatory scheme to "prove its worth,"[103] with implementation as an extension to the scheme proposed in England and Wales.[104] It sits alongside a reserve power to introduce legislation if the self-regulatory scheme does not work.[105] (The recent 2016 changes to the scheme and the replacement of the fundraising regulatory body have resulted in a difference of approach between England and Wales and Scotland, with Scotland opting out of the new Fundraising Regulator. In its place there will be a new self-regulation scheme in Scotland overseen by a new body, the Independent Panel, working with OSCR.)

Fundraising aside, the Kemp Report recognized the sector's responsibility to improve accountability and governance standards. Initiatives spearheaded by SCVO were already in operation, but they were disparate and not widely implemented. Kemp recommended the introduction of a nonprofit governance code of practice, part of which was to include a code of practice for volunteers.[106] That sat alongside the Scottish Compact setting standards of best practice for state/sector partnerships.[107] SCVO had been lobbying to retain a governance role for the sector, specifically for OSCR's advice function to be removed or limited, arguing that the sector, not the regulator, was best placed to offer advice on charity governance.[108] The Scottish Executive responded by giving OSCR a "signpost and facilitator" role to sources of best practice promoted by and within the sector.[109]

In sum, the regulatory wave in Scotland, supported by the sector, was toward securing a workable legislative framework as the foundation upon which nonprofit regulation could be built. This was not to the exclusion of self-regulation, but self-regulation and co-regulation were lesser alternatives. Although self-regulation held nonprofits together at a time when state regulation was fragmented, it was disparate, inadequately implemented, and unable to resolve major issues of accountability. It is unsurprising that as the move toward legislative reform progressed, self-regulation assumed lesser

[102] McFadden, n. 85, para. 5.55.
[103] Scottish Executive, *Draft Charities and Trustee Investments (Scotland) Bill: Consultation* (Edinburgh: Scottish Executive, 2004), 24, 25; Bill Policy Memorandum, n. 92, para. 77.
[104] Scottish Executive Justice Department, n. 88, paras. 60–61.
[105] Charities and Trustee Investment (Scotland) Act 2005, s. 83.   [106] Kemp, n. 91, 5.
[107] Scottish Office, *The Scottish Compact: The Principles Underpinning the Relationship between Government and the Voluntary Sector in Scotland* Cm 4083 (Edinburgh: Scottish Office, 1998); Scottish Executive, *The Scottish Compact* (Edinburgh: Scottish Executive, 2003).
[108] SCVO, n. 95, 10.   [109] Scottish Executive Justice Department, n. 88, paras. 57–58.

importance than it had during the same time period in England and Wales. Post legislative reform, self-regulation is beginning to assume greater prominence and is expected to develop in the coming years.

2.5 SCOTTISH POLITICAL AND REGULATORY CONTEXT

During this reform period the policy drivers in Scotland and the political framework in which they sat were remarkably similar to those in England and Wales. Even with devolution there remained a significant degree of policy convergence between the jurisdictions. Some aspects of policy, such as the Better Regulation Task Force's drive for better quality regulation, understandably cut across the jurisdictions. There were also points of resonance in political ideology. Initial Scottish executive bodies in power at Holyrood found congruence in policy with the UK Labour government in power at Westminster and the Welsh Assembly government in Cardiff. All three recognized the value of the nonprofit sector's contribution to a mixed economy of welfare provision and its role in strengthening communities through developing civic engagement, reducing inequality, reaching out to disenfranchised groups, and improving citizen participation. Even with the political change wrought by the removal of the Labour government and the rise of the Scottish National Party to minority and then majority power in Scotland, there has not been any significant alteration in policy affecting the nonprofit sectors in either jurisdiction. Recognition that nonprofits are needed to deliver on public services and civic engagement agendas pervades with active "mainstreaming"[110] of state/charity sector partnerships for the delivery of public services north and south of the border.

Infrastructure was instigated within the organs and levels of the respective governments, too. In Scotland this comprises the Third Sector Unit, a Cross Departmental Group of the Voluntary Sector, and a Third Sector Research Forum drawn from the government, umbrella bodies, OSCR, and academics. This appears to be more widespread and consensual than the equivalent in England (and compares well to Wales), and that might be symptomatic of Scotland's smaller size and the closer involvement of the sector in nation building.

Full Scottish independence has loomed large on the policy agenda. Although it was rejected by referendum in 2014, the 2016 UK referendum

---

[110] Jeremy Kendall, "The UK: Ingredients in a Hyper-active Horizontal Policy Environment," in *Handbook on Third Sector Policy in Europe*, ed. Jeremy Kendall (Cheltenham: Edward Elgar, 2009).

decision to exit the European Union has put the question of Scottish independence from the rest of the United Kingdom (but remaining within the European Union) back on the agenda. Independence for Scotland would bring with it potential for significant legal, cultural, and social change, although prior to the 2014 independence referendum the Scottish government had pledged not to change its vision for the nonprofit sector, emphasizing the sector's role as a "key partner" in the economy and public services.[111] If independence does occur in the immediate future and that policy remains, the impact on charity law will be limited in light of the fact that charity regulation is already a devolved matter in Scotland.

There are wider and more uncertain economic factors that might impact on nonprofits if Scottish independence is revisited in the future. Although the 2008 economic downturn affected the nonprofit sector in Scotland as it did in England and Wales, OSCR's budget was more insulated.[112] It is impossible to estimate how the Scottish government's operating budget would change in light of independence, but such issues might still become relevant if fiscal autonomy, including full taxation powers, is devolved to Scotland.

2.6 CONCLUDING THOUGHTS

It is evident in the British context that state regulation, self-regulation, and co-regulation are not independent but fit together as an evolving whole. Where the regulator's budget is cut as part of wider austerity policy and it has to retrench activity, the nonprofit sector has stepped forward to co-regulate. Where state regulation is fragmented, the sector has initiated self-regulation to fill the gap. It is also evident that the regulatory balance is directly influenced by political policy. In both British jurisdictions nonprofit regulatory reform occurred at propitious moments when the sector's push for reform aligned with a new government seeking to harness the sector in its own vision of governance. This can have unintended consequences, such as changing the underlying rationale of regulation or blurring the boundaries between types of regulation.

While changes in the sources of British nonprofit regulation are not seismic, they have nonetheless started a process of reworking the regulatory balance overall. These regulatory shifts have initiated a nascent debate on

---

[111] Scottish Government, *Scotland's Future: Your Guide to an Independent Scotland* (Edinburgh: Scottish Government, 2013), 368–370.
[112] The 2010 Scottish Comprehensive Spending Review reduced OSCR's budget by 10 percent: OSCR, *Corporate Plan 2011–2014* (Dundee: OSCR, 2011), 27.

the nature and role of nonprofit regulation, which may well lead to the unpicking of traditional working practices. It is inevitable in England and Wales, for example, that if self-regulation and co-regulation are to work well they will involve some dismantling of a well-established system of state regulation that has traditionally held sway, as well as requiring a change in attitudes toward regulation on the part of those regulated and the public.

Taking a broader comparative look, it might be argued that nonprofit regulation in the British jurisdictions is surging in different directions. In England and Wales, with strong state regulation in place, there is government encouragement for nonprofits to take greater responsibility via self-regulatory and co-regulatory practices. In Scotland, where the state framework was neglected, self-regulation was sidelined in the push for a comprehensive and cohesive statutory regime. However, rather than flowing in different directions, it might be argued that the regulatory waves are simply at different points in a progressively evolving cycle. Thus, England and Wales is evolving toward co-regulation against the bedrock of a well-established state regime, but Scotland needs first to establish that strong statutory framework before it can develop self-regulation and co-regulation to its full potential. Either way, the regulatory directions toward which the two British jurisdictions are moving are a clear product of their direct historical and policy context.

3

Waiting for the Big Wave

A Fifty-Year Retrospective on the Ebb and Flow of Irish Charity Regulation

OONAGH B. BREEN

3.1 INTRODUCTION

In common with many nations, Ireland has been subject to a perennial cycle of statutory and nonstatutory regulation of the nonprofit sector. One can identify with ease the major waves of statutory regulation that occurred in 1844, 1961, and 2009, with the gap between regulatory bouts shortening in each successive wave. The stated purpose of these statutes remains remarkably consistent and aligned, implying either the continuation of a clear policy objective or a marked failure to attain the goal on the previous occasion such that the task must be tackled de novo. Thus, the Preamble to the Charitable Donations and Bequests Act (Ireland) 1844 declares:

> ... it is expedient that the pious intentions of charitable persons should not be defeated by the concealment and misapplication of their donations and bequests to public and private charities in Ireland ... and it is expedient and necessary that provision should be made for the better management of such charitable donations and bequests as have been heretofore made ...

One hundred and seventy years on, the desire to better regulate charitable organizations resonates as strongly. The long title to the Charities Act 2009 expressly provides for the regulation and protection of charitable organizations and trusts. On its commencement in 2014, the act replaced the Commissioners of Charitable Donations and Bequests, as reimagined by the 1844 act, with a new statutory body, the Charities Regulatory Authority (CRA). Bookended between these two important waves of statutory regulation one finds the Charities Act 1961, which prior to the commencement of the 2009 act constituted the primary charity legislation. Described simply as "as Act to amend the law relating to charities," this statute was the mainstay of charity regulation for more than fifty years. A creature of its time, and in

common with similar enactments elsewhere,[1] it eschewed a statutory definition of "charitable purpose," devoting its efforts to enhancing the commissioners' powers. These enhancements, however, fell short of empowering the
commissioners to curtail or preempt charitable maladministration.

Turning from formal statutory regulation, there are also identifiable waves
of self-regulation in which the nonprofit sector has sought, at various stages, to
improve its own conduct by developing codes of good practice. Somewhat
paradoxically, the subject areas of self-regulation have been those normally
viewed as central to a statutory regulatory regime, namely, charity governance,
public registration and reporting, and fundraising.

Interpreting the interplay between these statutory and nonstatutory waves is
difficult. The timelines do not flow successively from one form to the other,
and yet one must suspect that the challenges, successes, and failures of these
regimes are closely interlinked. To fully appreciate the influence of one on
the other, we must look below the waves at a strong undercurrent that influences and ultimately shapes both the expectations and the realities of the
relationship between the Irish state and the charity sector. Political with a
small "p," this third strand weaves its way between statutory and nonstatutory
regulation, at times bringing state and sector into relationships of partnership,
at other times comprising a relationship in which the state and sector, in turn,
are dominant or dependent. Borne of interstitial conversations between government and nonprofit actors on the periphery of formal government – in the
corridors rather than the rooms of power – these exchanges take stakeholders
outside their express spheres of authority, giving rise to nonbinding commitments that nevertheless determine stakeholders' future actions. In a similar
fashion to the regulatory waves, this third strand occurs and recurs on a small-
scale episodic basis, experiencing slow but incremental growth, resulting in
significant, albeit sometimes short-lived collaborations that have the power to
change the state/sector relationship dynamic.

Recent inclusions in this third strand would be the Community and
Voluntary Pillar of Social Partnership (1996–2006) and the Implementation
and Advisory Group (IAG) for the White Paper on a Framework for Voluntary
Action (2000–2004). Older examples of this state/sector dynamic comprise the
Combat Poverty Agency (CPA) (1975–2011) and the National Social Service
Council (NSSC)/Comhairle (1970–2000).

This chapter argues that to truly understand how the Irish nonprofit sector
works and to predict the future direction of nonprofit regulation, one must be
fully familiar with all three strands – the waves of both statutory and

---

[1] See English Charities Act 1960; Charities Act (Northern Ireland) 1964.

nonstatutory regulation and the undercurrent of state/sector dialogue and collaboration – and how they interact with each other. Viewing any one strand in isolation not only gives a distorted picture of the regulatory framework, but also inhibits a policymaker from taking proper account of important factors that continue to influence regulatory outcomes.

Section 3.2 reviews the pace of legislative reform in the charity sector, identifying key measures and trends and setting the context for Section 3.3's discussion of the nonstatutory measures of importance that influence the regulatory space. Section 3.4 explores the state/sector relationship, identifying key state/sector engagement, analyzing where the balance of power lies, and examining how this engagement has impacted on subsequent regulatory efforts. Section 3.5 brings these different strands together by exploring the causal links between them and the extent to which historical and political context dictates outcome before offering some conclusions on the nature of the cyclical relationship between statutory and nonstatutory Irish charity regulation.

3.2 THE PACE OF LEGISLATIVE CHANGE: KEY MEASURES AND TRENDS IN CHARITY LAW

Legislative change comes slowly in Ireland and nowhere is this truer than in charity law reform. The waves of charity legislation over the past three centuries have been well spaced and surprisingly consistent in the quest for better regulation of charitable institutions. King George III tackled the matter in the 1763, introducing An Act for the Better Discovery of Charitable Donations and Bequests, subsequently amended in light of the Act of Union 1800.[2] The 1763 act provided for the first national inquiry into charities. It focused on tackling fraud, introducing a mandatory register of charitable donations, and requiring heirs, executors, or trustees to "publish in the Dublin Gazette three times successively every charitable donation or bequest."[3] The Irish House of Lords' establishment of a committee of inquiry to examine charities in 1764 reinforced this scrutiny.[4]

---

[2]   3 George III c.18, amended by 40 George III c. 75. See Leonard Shelfer, *A Practical Treatise of the Law of Mortmain, and Charitable Uses and Trusts* (London: S. Sweet, 1836).

[3]   Ibid.

[4]   40 George III, c. 75, dissolved the Irish House of Lords Committee of Inquiry into Charities, first established in 1764, then continued on a year-to-year basis. It replaced it with the Commissioners of Charitable Donations and Bequests. Drawn from the Protestant faith, the commissioners had power to recover all property belonging to charities withheld, concealed, or misapplied and to apply all charitable funds according to charitable and pious purposes. F.A.P. Hamilton, *The Law Relating to Charities in Ireland* (Dublin: E. Ponsonby, 1879), 124.

Forty years later, Queen Victoria signed into law the Commissioners and Charitable Donations and Bequests Act (Ireland) 1844, introducing a revised statutory committee that endured in the facilitation of charities and their operation until 2014.[5] The act's purpose was to centralize responsibility for charity law.[6] It is noteworthy that the preamble expressly referenced the insufficiency of the 1763 act, which it repealed, to protect charitable donations and bequests. Not without its own shortcomings, the 1844 act was amended in 1867, 1871, and 1955, enactments that enlarged the commissioners' powers.[7] The Charities Act 1961 repealed all of these earlier acts but preserved the role and powers of the commissioners, powers that were then subsequently enlarged in the Charities Act 1973. Apart from some miscellaneous amendments,[8] no further statutory reform followed until the enactment of the Charities Act 2009, more than forty years later.

Despite Ireland's early foray into public accountability for charitable donations received, the mandatory register did not survive into the nineteenth century, and the commissioners, as empowered in 1844, had no statutory role regarding the register's maintenance. Unlike the English Charities Act 1960, the Irish Charities Act 1961 did not establish a register of charities. However, the 1763 statutory obligation on executors to publish three times successively information on charitable bequests lives on in section 52 of the 1961 act. Although the 1961 act charged the commissioners to protect charitable donations and bequests with powers to compromise claims; to sue for the recovery of charitable property withheld, concealed, or misapplied; and to certify cases to the Attorney General, these powers were little used.[9] The act did not define an investigatory role for the commissioners nor were they provided with sufficient resources to enable them to uncover instances of misapplied charitable property.[10]

In summary, then, we have come full circle, from the introduction of a statutory register and a requirement of accountability subject to public inquiry

---

[5] 7 and 8 Vic. c. 97. Unlike its predecessor 40 George III, c. 75, the commissioners under the 1844 act were comprised equally of Protestants and Catholics and lasted until the Charities Act's commencement in 2014 – SIs 456/2014 and 457/2014.

[6] Nicholas Acheson et al., *Two Paths, One Purpose: Voluntary Action in Ireland, North and South: A Report to the Royal Irish Academy's Third Sector Research Programme* (Dublin: Institute of Public Administration, 2004), 156.

[7] Charitable Donations and Bequests Act (Ireland) 1867, 30 and 31 Vic. c. 54; Charitable Donations and Bequests Act (Ireland) 1871, 34 and 35 Vic. c. 102; and the Charitable Donations and Bequests (Amendment) Act 1955.

[8] Social Welfare (Miscellaneous Provisions) Act 2002, Pt. 2.

[9] Kerry O'Halloran and Oonagh Breen, "Charity Law in Ireland and Northern Ireland: Registration and Regulation," *Irish Law Times* 18(1) (2000): 6–14.

[10] Ibid.

in 1763 to the subsequent replacement of the committee of inquiry with a statutory body of commissioners in 1800 and the loss of the public register thereafter, from a shoring up of the commissioners' facilitative role over a hundred-year period until 1961 to a further rethinking of the need for greater transparency and accountability with the 2009 act's (re)introduction of a new register of charities and the establishment of a new statutory body with investigative and enforcement powers. The cyclical nature of legislation sees us once more attempting to tackle problems in 2014 first identified in 1763 and resorting to the very same tools of accountability and greater transparency.

3.3 NONSTATUTORY REGULATION: A LATE BUT WELCOME ENTRANT TO THE NONPROFIT ARENA

If one were to judge solely by the dates of the nonprofit self-regulatory initiatives in Ireland, one might summarily conclude that nonstatutory regulation is merely a belated afterthought. Sectoral mobilization around self-regulation is predominantly absent before the year 2000, attributable to the lack of peak representative bodies, an absence of sector capacity to create self-regulatory regimes, and a sectoral focus on supporting the development of statutory regulation. The post-2000 picture, however, sees not only the emergence of nonstatutory regulation but its impact in areas of core regulatory interest, namely, fundraising regulation, governance, and accountability.

3.3.1 *Fundraising*

The first of these twenty-first-century self-regulation models to emerge was the establishment of the Irish Fundraising Forum for Direct Recruitment (IFFDR) in 2003. The forum developed a best-practices code on person-to-person fundraising ventures to increase public confidence in this new fundraising method, learning greatly from the UK experience in this regard.[11]

With the 2006 publication of the Heads of Bill for the Charities Act, the government proposed to extend the scope of nonstatutory regulation of public collections fundraising. The government commissioned Irish Charity Tax Research (ICTR), at the charity representative body's prompting, to carry

---

[11] Correspondence with Mark Mellett, founding IFFDR member, July 21, 2015. See IFFDR, *Code of Practice of Irish Fundraising Forum for Direct Recruitment* (2003), reprinted in ICTR, *Feasibility Study* (2008), 29, accessed January 6, 2016, www.ictr.ie/files/R1.%20Regulation%20of %20Fundraising%20Report%20-%20May%202008.pdf.

out a public consultation[12] and a feasibility study on forms of fundraising regulation,[13] the results of which, after much consultation with the sector,[14] engendered a *Statement of Guiding Principles on Fundraising*.[15] The Charities bill's Explanatory Memorandum acknowledged the development of this code and made provision for self-regulation efforts, if effective, to replace the need for statutory intervention.[16] Described by the European Centre for Not-for-Profit Law (ECNL) in its 2009 Report to the European Commission as "an innovative and flexible system for fundraising regulation, combining elements of both public and self regulation," ECNL commended Ireland's attempt at hybrid regulation as an outstanding example.[17]

The statement's subsequent rollout and the rate of nonprofit signup, however, have been disappointing. Officially launched in 2010, delays in commencing and fully realizing the code's potential are directly attributable to the entanglement of state and sector in this area of regulation. To date, there are just 230 signatories to the statement, a tiny percentage of the 8,170 tax-exempt charities and a fraction of the 4,828 active fundraising charities that enjoy "eligible charity" tax status.

Contributing factors to this malaise have been fourfold: first, the lack of government funding (and no provision for membership subscriptions) to publicly promote the code has greatly inhibited public awareness. Second, the nonrealization of state funds to develop the originally promised detailed codes of conduct has left the ethical *Statement of Guiding Principles* without the necessary support it requires for successful implementation. Third, delays in the appointment of the promised Monitoring Group to oversee signatories' compliance and to investigate donor complaints against charities has further crippled the regime's effectiveness. Finally, there is a misplaced assumption

---

[12] ICTR, *Regulation of Fundraising by Charities through Legislation and Codes of Practice: Consultation Paper* (2006), accessed January 6, 2016, www.ictr.ie/files/R5.%20Regulation%20of%20Fundraising%20Consultation%20Paper%20-%20Sept%202006.pdf.

[13] ICTR, n. 11.

[14] The consultation led to draft proposals and a draft statement of guiding principles in 2007; see ICTR, *Regulation of Fundraising by Charities through Legislation and Codes of Practice: Draft Proposals* (2007), accessed January 6, 2016, www.ictr.ie/files/R4.%20Regulation%20of%20Fundraising%20Draft%20Proposals%20-%20Apr%202007.pdf.

[15] ICTR, *Statement of Guiding Principles on Fundraising* (2008), accessed January 6, 2016, www.ictr.ie/files/R2.%20Guiding%20Principles%20of%20Fundraising%20-%20Feb%202008.pdf.

[16] *Charities Bill 2007 Explanatory Memorandum* (2007), 14, accessed January 6, 2016, www.oireachtas.ie/documents/bills28/bills/2007/3107/b3107d.pdf.

[17] ECNL, *Study on Recent Public and Self-Regulatory Initiatives Improving Transparency and Accountability of Nonprofit Organisations in the European Union* (Brussels: European Commission, 2009), 24.

among certain charities that not signing up to the statement frees them of ensuing responsibility for bad fundraising practices.

Applications for the Monitoring Group closed in April 2011. Intended to comprise an Independent Chair, three independent members, two charity sector members, and one Government Department representative, the group remains unconstituted following a Department of Justice request to defer establishment pending the introduction of the Charities Act 2009. This direction has affected both signup to and enforcement of the code, making ICTR's role untenable. In 2015 ICTR filed a report with the Department of Justice outlining the project's achievements and challenges and expressing its desire to relinquish its secretariat role if the Department of Justice was willing to transfer the project to Fundraising Ireland as a more natural self-regulatory home.[18] Media focus on fundraising scandals,[19] however, may have preempted matters with the Minister's recent announcement of her intention to convene a statutory consultative panel on charity fundraising to review regulatory oversight.[20]

3.3.2 *Governance*

Prior to the Charities Act 2009, there was little statutory guidance for charities on probity and accountability matters. The act introduces a necessary regulatory framework, but many of the important substantive details require further delegated legislation. Legislative vacuums can lead to poor governance practices, a concern charities readily acknowledge.[21] Charity leaders have been mindful of the need to encourage better governance. Beginning with overseas development charities in 2009, Dóchas (an umbrella representative body) in conjunction with the Corporate Governance Association of Ireland developed a *Governance Code for Development Organizations*. Dóchas requires its sixty member organizations to adhere to the governance code along with its *Code on Images and Messages*.[22]

---

[18] Correspondence with Sheila Nordon, ICTR CEO, June 2015.

[19] Michael O'Farrell, "Charity Muggers' Dirty Tricks," *Irish Mail on Sunday*, October 18, 2015, 1.

[20] Department of Justice Press Release, "Minister of Justice Addresses International Charity Regulators Conference," November 26, 2015, accessed January 7, 2016, www.justice.ie/en/JELR/Pages/PR15000611.

[21] Institute of Directors in Ireland, *Governance in the Charity and Not-for-Profit Sector in Ireland* (Dublin: Institute of Directors in Ireland, 2014). Of the 229 charity respondents to this survey, 75 percent rated governance levels in the Irish nonprofit sector generally as average or poor.

[22] Codes are set out on the Dóchas website, accessed January 6, 2016, www.dochas.ie/standards-excellence-codes-anad-guidelines.

Building on the *Dóchas Code*, a broader collaboration of nonprofit interests developed a more sophisticated governance code model to tackle areas of common concern across the Irish nonprofit sector.[23] Developed between 2009 and 2011 and launched in 2012, the *Nonprofit Governance Code* boasts 288 signatories with a further 917 organizations on the journey toward full compliance.[24] The code focuses on five key areas: organization leadership, exercise of control, accountability and transparency, working effectively, and behaving with integrity. It caters for three different organizational types that vary according to size, turnover, and staffing levels. Developed on a "comply or explain" basis, the code drills down to specific requirements from ensuring proper internal financial and management controls are in place to encouraging review of all organizational policies, from volunteer policies to conflict of interest policies. Of the self-regulatory codes discussed in this chapter, this governance code is the best known in the sector with the highest signup rates, although the number remains a small fraction of tax-exempt charities.

Two cautionary notes must be sounded. The first relates to oversight. Signatories to the code self-assess their own compliance and renew their adherence to the code annually, but the code makes no provision for any external monitoring or enforcement. The Wheel, a network organization for the voluntary sector, acts as the Working Group's secretariat. The Working Group's responsibility is expressed in the following terms: "The organisations involved in the Working Group share the responsibility for guarding the standards in this Code. They have a written agreement on this. They have committed to reviewing the Code within three years in light of the experience organisations have in adopting it."[25]

How this experience will be gathered or analyzed is unexplained, and whether the numbers of signatories will drop dramatically when the list is reset after the twelve-month time period to include only those who have recommitted remains to be seen.[26] The biggest challenge, particularly in the absence of a clear oversight mechanism, will be in proving that signatories have gone further in self-reflective practices than merely signing and returning the Principles Statement signup sheet.

The second cautionary note concerns the current public mistrust of charities arising from recent charity scandals that highlighted exceptionally poor

---

[23] *Code of Practice for Good Governance of Community, Voluntary and Charitable Organisations in Ireland*, accessed August 11, 2016, www.governancecode.ie/about.php.
[24] Ibid.   [25] Ibid.
[26] Correspondence with Diarmuid O'Corrbui, Chair of Code Working Group, alluded to plans to extend the sign-up period of validity from one to three years (October 9, 2014).

governance and accountability practices of some leading charities.[27] Following these governance scandals, public donations to many charities in 2014 fell significantly.[28] The public may not therefore view self-regulation as sufficient in an area as important as governance, encompassing as it does matters relating to mission delivery, stewardship, and financial probity. Moreover, the 2014 Institute of Directors Governance Survey notes that "it is extremely concerning that ... two-thirds [of charity respondents] believe that organizations in receipt of State funding are not adequately monitored or held to account for the appropriation of these funds. This is particularly worrying given that a majority of the respondents indicated that their organisations are in receipt of State funding."[29]

3.3.3 *Reporting and Accountability*

The final nonprofit sector initiative of note is the Irish Nonprofits Knowledge Exchange project (INKEx), which set out to create an authoritative source of statistical data on Irish nonprofits for a wide variety of users in the public, private, and third sectors.[30] The main purpose of this initiative was information disclosure rather than self-regulation. Piloted with European Union (EU) funding in 2007, the initial objective of the project was to explore whether a GuideStar model could work in a number of countries, including Ireland. Developed as a nonprofit entity and funded by the Irish government and other philanthropic sources, INKEx undertook a three-year project to design, test, build, and launch a free, searchable website with extensive regulatory data on Irish charities and nonprofits, on a new custom-built database.

The database went live in November 2011, with a medium-term plan to use a mixture of grants and service fees to fund its operations. It was originally envisaged that the database could provide the "back office" for the CRA on its establishment.[31] Following national elections in 2011 and the reallocation of

---

[27] Oonagh B. Breen, "Recent Developments in Irish Charity Law: Tsunami or Rising Tide to Lift All Boats?," *Nonprofit Law Yearbook* (2014) 105–123; Oonagh B. Breen, "Long Day's Journey: The Charities Act 2009 and Recent Developments in Irish Charity Law," *Charity Practice and Law Review* 17 (2014): 91–112.

[28] Marie O'Halloran, "€1.6 Million Charity Donations Drop Shows Transparency Need – McGrath," *The Irish Times*, February 14, 2014; Mark Hilliard, "Majority of Charities Report Drop in Donations Following Scandals," *The Irish Times*, May 15, 2014.

[29] Institute of Directors in Ireland, n. 21.

[30] See the Benefacts website, accessed January 6, 2016, http://benefacts.ie/history/.

[31] A government amendment to the Charities bill sought "to ensure there will be no impediment preventing the authority, under direction of the Minister, from engaging with an external data provider such as a future GuideStar Ireland with regard to the provision of material to assist in

responsibility for charity regulation to the Department of Justice, the Minister declared that the CRA's establishment was not an immediate priority in recession-hit Ireland and he withdrew government funding of INKEx, forcing it into voluntary liquidation.

In many ways, the life cycle of INKEx parallels the life cycle of nonstatutory initiatives more generally in Ireland. Prompted by the lack of a publicly available, consistent source of comparably presented, regulatory disclosure information for charities, INKEx sought to fill that gap. Devising an information collection and management system, INKEx reused existing public domain regulatory disclosures by Irish nonprofits, classifying them according to internationally recognized norms and storing them in a harmonized way.[32] Collation of this information created a rich data source that then could be used by government departments in reviewing and assessing grants, by charities in benchmarking their own performance against those of their counterparts, and by the general public, seeking a better understanding of how charities manage and spend their charitable assets.

The sustainability of the project, in the short term, was overly dependent on government funding. Given its statutory mandate to create a register of charities the state had a vested interest in the development of a comprehensive charities database, making its €1.1 million (US$1.9 million) project investment an effective use of resources. Despite this apparent alignment of interests, political and financial priorities within the Department of Justice resulted in the project's abandonment at a crucial stage in its development.[33] In this context, the Department of Public Expenditure and Reform's 2014 decision to invest in the reactivation of the INKEx database and to reestablish a single digital repository of nonprofit financial, governance, and other relevant data and documents is noteworthy.[34] How this nonstatutory reporting mechanism will sit alongside the separate and evolving Charities Register remains to be determined.[35]

---

maintaining the register of charities," *Dáil Eireann Debates* (February 11, 2009), vol. 674, no. 2, 452, accessed January 6, 2016, http://oireachtasdebates.oireachtas.ie/debates%20authoring/debateswebpack.nsf/takes/dail2009021100022?opendocument.

[32] INKEx, *Irish Nonprofits: What Do We Know?* (Dublin: INKEx, 2012).

[33] Sara Burke, *Case-Study of INKEx* (Dublin: INKEx, 2013), accessed January 6, 2016, http://openknowledge.ie/wp-content/uploads/2015/01/INKEx-Case-Study-Sara-Burke-February-20131.pdf.

[34] Secretary General Robert Watt, "Future Trends in Community and Voluntary Funding," *Conference on Social Investment – Common Cents 2014 Aligning Capital with Economic and Social Justice*, Dublin, October 16, 2014. INKEx was relaunched in June 2015 as "Benefacts," accessed June 17, 2015, http://benefacts.ie/.

[35] The CRA Register, accessed January 6, 2016, www.charitiesregulatoryauthority.ie/Website/CRA/CRAweb.nsf/page/publicregister-reg-of-charities-en. An interdepartmental steering group

3.3.4 *Self-Regulatory Outcomes*

The trend of nonprofit self-regulation in Ireland has been to focus on important areas that normally fall within the statutory regulatory space. Although coming late to the scene, with nonstatutory regulation first emerging in the early 2000s, certain nonprofit leaders invested much time and effort in the development of codes and nonstatutory approaches that have garnered praise internationally for their innovative and consultative form. To date, implementation success rates have not mirrored the level of effort invested. Common causes include the thwarting of the planned schemes either by a lack of resources for implementation (revealing an unhealthy level of state dependency) or by the direct intervention of the state (as in the case of fundraising regulation), lack of effective enforcement and sanction mechanisms, and a reticence by nonprofits to participate for fear that engagement will expose them to liability for subsequent shortcomings in a way that nonparticipation will not. With the Irish public beginning to seek greater evidence of good governance arrangements, nonstatutory regulation will need to prove its effectiveness and capacity to self-enforce in the medium term in order to be an adequate supplement or alternative to statutory measures.

3.4 UNDERCURRENTS INFLUENCING THE RELATIONSHIPS BETWEEN STATE AND SECTOR

Unlike other common law jurisdictions,[36] Ireland does not have a grand scale policy document that purports to frame the relationship between the state and the sector. To date, Irish efforts to develop such a charter and to implement its principles have been less successful. Thus, Irish state/sector engagement currently functions without a strong ideological exposition of the parties' rights and obligations. If anything, Ireland's approach to voluntary sector/state engagement has been pragmatic rather than theoretical.[37] The nature of

---

has been established to explore the Benefacts database potential and how it might assist in reducing dual reporting and regulatory red tape.

[36] See, for example, *Compact on Relations between Government and the Voluntary and Community Sector in England* (London: Cabinet Office, 2010); *Accord between the Government of Canada and the Voluntary Sector* (Canada: Voluntary Sector Taskforce, 2001); *Australian Government, National Compact: Working Together* (Canberra: Commonwealth of Australia: 2011).

[37] Michael Doherty, "It Must Have Been Love ... but It's over Now: The Crisis and Collapse of Social Partnership in Ireland," *Transfer: European Review of Labour and Research* 17(3) (2011): 371–385.

state/sector collaboration has, in turn, influenced the form of charity regulation imposed: at times, creating a relationship of complacency such that
statutory scrutiny was thought less necessary; at other times, opening the eyes
of nonprofits to the need for good governance standards, whether self-imposed
or otherwise.

3.4.1 *Early Examples of Religious Collaboration and the Emergence of Community Development: 1950–1970*

A common feature in the late nineteenth- and early twentieth-century political
landscape was the clear separation between the activities and responsibilities
of the state and those of the nonprofit sector. These parallel, if separate,
existences were driven by Ireland's predominantly Roman Catholic culture
and Catholic social thought, the foundations of which were widely considered
to have been laid by Pope Leo XIII's 1891 encyclical letter *Rerum Novarum*,
which advocated economic distributism and condemned both capitalism and
socialism.[38] Thus, in the areas of health, education, and social rights, the
Catholic Church played a leading role, using the principle of subsidiarity to
sideline state involvement.[39] Throughout the nineteenth and twentieth centuries, Catholic social service provision operated as an independent alternative
to a nonexistent or very poor state service.

A combination of weak central government[40] in the first instance and
limited state capacity to provide universal social welfare services in the
second[41] meant that the Church's occupation of this space and its associated
charitable endeavors were relatively uncontested until the 1960s. The innate
conservatism of the Church and its resistance to broader social provision led to
political conflict,[42] and it took time for the state to carve out a national space
for universal social service provision.[43] Delivery of these services, however, still

---

[38] *Rerum Novarum: Encyclical of Pope Leo Xiii on Capital and Labor* (1891), accessed June 25,
2014, www.vatican.va/holy_father/leo_xiii/encyclicals/documents/hf_l-xiii_enc_15051891_
rerum-novarum_en.html.

[39] Pope Pius XI, *Quadragesimo Anno* (Rome: The Holy See, 1931), 1–34, 16.

[40] Acheson et al., n. 6, 158.

[41] Tony Fahey, "The Catholic Church and Social Policy," in *Social Policy in Ireland: Principles,
Practice and Problems*, ed. Seán Healy and Brigid Reynolds (Dublin: Oak Tree Press, 1998),
146.

[42] See Noel Browne, *Against the Tide* (Dublin: Gill & Macmillan, 1986). Compare Eamonn
McKee, "Church–State Relations and the Development of Irish Health Policy: The Mother-
and-Child Scheme, 1944–53," *Irish Historical Studies* 25 (1986): 159–194, 166.

[43] The Health Act 1953; Department of Health, *Cúrsaí Sláinte: Health Progress Report 1947–1953*
(Dublin: Stationery Office, 1953), 21.

required partnership with the Church since the latter retained ultimate control through its ownership of schools and hospitals.[44]

The passing of the Health Act 1953, with the state's express acceptance of responsibility for citizens in need of assistance, represented an important shift in public policy toward statutory responsibility for social services provision.[45] The act enabled state funding of voluntary organizations providing "ancillary or similar services" to those of the health authority, opening the door to state support of secular nonprofits.[46] Thus Ireland moved from laissez-faire dependence on religious organizations to state responsibility for social provision with an ability to fund nonprofits to deliver such services. Notwithstanding funding availability, the act of "relationship building" between the state and the voluntary sector continued on an ad hoc basis and lacked a clear policy direction.

3.4.2 *First Forays into Building and Supporting a Sector: 1970s–2000s*

By the 1970s with Ireland's accession to the European Economic Community (EEC) in 1973, access to external funding grew and community development organizations began to emerge among the predominantly religious-based charities of the 1940s and 1950s. A new voice of dissent was born and the state now had to grapple with secular organizations focused on issues of social exclusion, a domain the state viewed as extremely political and off limits. A new regulatory framework was thus necessary to contain, as much as to manage, these actors.

3.4.2.1 From NSSC to Comhairle: 1971–2000

In 1971 the government established the National Social Services Council (NSSC) to stimulate and encourage the development of voluntary bodies in the area of social services provision and to promote liaison between central and local authorities and voluntary organizations providing social

---

[44] Today, 96 percent of Irish primary schools are owned and under the patronage of religious denominations, of which the Catholic Church accounts for 90 percent; see John Coolahan, Caroline Hussey, and Fionnaula Kilfeather, *Report of the Forum Advisory Group on Patronage and Pluralism in the Primary Sector* (Dublin, 2012), accessed January 8, 2016, www.education .ie/en/Press-Events/Events/Patronage-and-Pluralism-in-the-Primary-Sector/The-Forum-on-Patronage-and-Pluralism-in-the-Primary-Sector-Report-of-the-Forums-Advisory-Group.pdf.

[45] Pauline Connolly, "The Public Funding of the Nonprofit Sector in Ireland: The Muddy Waters of Definitions," *Administration* 54(2) (2006): 85–96, 90.

[46] Health Act 1953, s. 65.

services.[47] Never fully reaching its potential, the NSSC was reconstituted as the National Social Services Board (NSSB) in 1984 with responsibility for encouraging voluntary community action.[48] Even this narrower outreach role of NSSB's development officers caused conflict with the Health Boards, and in 1987 the government decided to abolish the NSSB and reintegrate its functions within the Department of Social Welfare, much to the consternation of voluntary organizations.[49] Although ultimately surviving the threat of abolition, the government further pared down the NSSB's responsibilities, removing its community development role and confining it to information-giving functions and the support of citizen's information centers alongside the promotion of volunteering and the provision of a social mentoring scheme.[50]

The NSSB's role was further diluted in 2000 when it was merged with the National Rehabilitation Board to form Comhairle, an agency tasked with combining the NSSB's citizen information role with assisting and supporting disabled individuals to identify their needs and access their social service entitlements.[51] The twenty-year mutation of NSSC to NSSB and ultimately to Comhairle did little to achieve the initial aims of the agency. With each successive transformation the ability to act as a coordinating hub for nonprofit action was reduced or lost. The political landscape throughout most of this period was one in which the state had no clear defined relationship with the nonprofit sector despite repeated government commitments to review how the state and the sector might better work together.

3.4.2.2 The Combat Poverty Agency: 1975–2011

In many ways, the story of the CPA provides an interesting contrast to that of the NSSB and throws up the inherent conflicts and tensions existing in the state/sector relationship between 1975 and 2011, which provide further insights into the effects of this relationship on the regulatory state that subsequently emerged. Conceived and funded as part of a €20 million European pilot program in 1975, the CPA's objective was to eradicate poverty. Recognizing

---

[47] Ray Mulvihill, *Voluntary-Statutory Partnership in Community Care for the Elderly* (Dublin: National Council of the Elderly, 1993).

[48] National Social Service Board Act 1984. S.4(1)(e) tasks the NSSB to "to promote … co-operation in relation to social services between boards, and other bodies, established by or under statute and voluntary organisations."

[49] Acheson et al., n. 6, 91.   [50] Ibid.   [51] Comhairle Act 2000.

the central role of nonprofits in the fight against poverty, the CPA carried out research on community and voluntary activities, funded resource centers, and began to adopt a programmatic response to social inclusion issues, which focused on the role of NGOs.[52] The CPA built nonprofit sector capacity in Ireland and opened the door to European funding for NGOs for the first time.

The 1980s proved to be a precarious time for the CPA. The center-right Fianna Fáil government allowed the poverty scheme to lapse in 1981, passing legislation in 1982 to abolish the CPA.[53] It proposed its replacement by a new body, the National Community Development Agency (NCDA), which would support the seemingly less radical concept of community development over voluntary organizational involvement in poverty relief, which Fianna Fáil viewed as unacceptably political.[54] A change of government in 1982 reversed this decision, subsequently abolishing the NCDA and reestablishing the CPA, although it took a further four years for it to gain a statutory basis.[55]

The CPA's significance for the nonprofit sector was more inspirational than financial. According to Acheson, its importance "lay in the agency's support for community based and voluntary sector action that confronted social policy issues … The agency helped to form, in the public mind, a strong connection between 'voluntary action' and the new battleground of 'social inclusion.'"[56] In addition to channeling EU funding to Irish nonprofits through Structural Funds and programs such as EQUAL, HORIZON, and PEACE I-III, the CPA's research capacity empowered many voluntary organizations in ways not always comfortable for the state and which, at times, led the state to classify the CPA as part of the nonprofit sector, despite its state agency status.[57] In July 2009, the CPA was reintegrated into the Department of Social Protection.[58]

---

[52] The CPA's research working papers are set out on its website, accessed July 8, 2014, www.combatpoverty.ie/publications/workingpapers.htm.

[53] National Community Development Agency Act 1982.   [54] Acheson et al., n. 6, 92.

[55] Combat Poverty Agency Act 1986.   [56] Acheson et al., n. 6, 92.

[57] Department of Social, Community and Family Affairs, *Supporting Voluntary Activity: A Green Paper on the Community and Voluntary Sector and Its Relationship with the State* (Dublin: Stationery Office, 1997) ("Green Paper"); Freda Donoghue, Helmut K. Anheier, and Lester M. Salamon, *Uncovering the Nonprofit Sector in Ireland: Its Economic Value and Significance* (Baltimore, MD, and Dublin: Johns Hopkins University/National College of Ireland, 1999), 1–61, 13.

[58] *Report of the Inter-Departmental Review of the Combat Poverty Agency* (2008), accessed October 31, 2014, www.combatpoverty.ie/aboutus/2008-09_ReviewOfCombatPovertyAgency_Report.pdf.

3.4.3 *From Implementation Advisory Groups to Partnership and Back Again: 2000–2010*

3.4.3.1 White Paper and the Implementation Advisory Group: 1976–2004

The absence of a clear policy on statutory and nonprofit organization engagement marred the state/sector relationship. First mooted in 1976 by Health Minister Brendan Corish, the promised policy on the respective roles and relationships of statutory and nonprofit organizations in social welfare service planning and provision never materialized.[59] Similarly, the 1981 Programme for Government's commitment to the production of a charter framework for the state/nonprofit relationship remained unfulfilled.[60] Another decade passed before the Minister for Social Welfare announced plans for a White Paper to examine the relationship between the state and voluntary organizations, renewing the commitment for a voluntary social services charter in Ireland.[61] Despite the 1992 establishment of an eighteen-member expert committee, unspecified difficulties with the Departments of Justice and Health stalled the promised White Paper for five years before it eventually emerged as a Green Paper in 1997.[62] Its belated appearance was prompted more by EU developments than any domestic initiative to define the state/voluntary sector relationship.[63] Among its objectives the Green Paper sought to:

- Clarify the responsibilities of different departments to the nonprofit sector
- Examine the effectiveness of existing programs and support structures
- Introduce Customer Charters in relation to specific social services and provide training for the statutory sector
- Develop statements of good practice for both statutory and voluntary sectors.[64]

The subsequent White Paper on Supporting Voluntary Activity in 2000 gave formal recognition to the sector's role in "contributing to the creation of a vibrant, participative democracy" and provided for the establishment of a joint IAG, comprising both state and nonprofit sector representatives, to

---

[59] John Curry, *Irish Social Services*, 4th ed. (Dublin: Institute of Public Administration, 2003), 201.
[60] Ibid.   [61] Acheson et al., n. 6, 106.   [62] Green Paper, n. 57.
[63] See *Communication of the Commission on Promoting the Role of Voluntary Organisations and Foundations in Europe* (COM(97) 241 Final).
[64] Address by Dermot Ahern, Minister for Social, Community and Family Affairs, *Combat Poverty Agency Conference on Supporting Voluntary Activity*, Dublin Castle, February 23, 1998.

oversee its implementation.[65] In broad terms, the IAG was an experiment in "blue skies thinking" – inviting state and sector representatives to work together to improve state/sector relations in a mutually beneficial way. To this extent, the IAG process differed from Social Partnership (discussed below) because the IAG process was a vested interest process. It concentrated solely on improving the relationship between the state and voluntary sector. By common consensus, however, the IAG experience was not a happy or productive one.

The White Paper set out a bold agenda for the IAG: to advise the government generally on voluntary sector policy matters and to participate with relevant statutory bodies in the implementation of the White Paper's specific policy recommendations relating to state/sector consultation and funding.[66] For the first time in the history of Irish nonprofit sector/state relations, the White Paper envisaged a forum bringing together statutory representatives and nonprofit sector members, elected as representatives not of their own organizations but of "the sector." This crosscutting approach to voluntary and community activity was a groundbreaking development in Ireland at the time.[67]

Four years after its inauguration, the IAG process reached a state of impasse. The mandate of the voluntary sector representatives, known as the CV 12, expired in 2004. Pending a departmental review of the IAG process by the Department of Community, Rural and Gaeltacht Affairs, no new mandates were sought. Officially, the group still had an important role to play in overseeing the implementation of the White Paper, which, according to government sources, remained government policy.[68] Unofficially, all parties conceded that the IAG process was not working and that, if anything, the experience had deepened the distrust between statutory bodies and the nonprofit sector by reinforcing a perception of "them" and "us."

It is hard to identify policy changes toward the state/sector relationship directly attributable to the IAG. Government officials claimed that the White Paper (and implicitly the IAG) achieved greater state funding of the sector, although it would be difficult to draw a causal connection in this regard. On

---

[65] Department of Social, Community and Family Affairs, *White Paper on a Framework for Supporting Voluntary Activity and for Developing the Relationship between the State and the Community and Voluntary Sector* (Dublin: Stationery Office, 2000), 3.

[66] Ibid., ch. 6.

[67] Correspondence with Deirdre Garvey, CEO, The Wheel, Dublin (January 10, 2005).

[68] Parliamentary Question 63 to Minister of State for the Department of Community, Rural and Gaeltacht Affairs, *Dáil Debates*, vol. 592, December 14, 2004 (Minister Ahern responding that "the White Paper remains Government policy. However, the context in which the White Paper policy is to be implemented has clearly changed with time").

the contrary, CV 12 members were quick to list the IAG's wasted opportunities to influence policy change. With regard to supplementary outcomes, such as enhanced interaction between stakeholders or the nurturing of ideas for future cooperation, the IAG offered little collaborative benefit. Rather, relations between IAG partners deteriorated toward the end to one of ambivalence, if not quite hostility. Evaluating the IAG's achievements against its initial terms of reference, it achieved little in its research and funding role. Government cuts eliminated the IAG's budget for sector research and reduced the training budget. The IAG's poorly run adjudication process for awarding training grants damaged state/sector relations. The IAG also failed to produce any codes of practice or manuals on funding.

The IAG's involvement in advising government on regulatory matters fared equally badly. Early on in the IAG's lifetime, the government transferred the charity regulatory reform brief from the IAG to a departmental charities regulation unit. In those regulatory areas left to the IAG, little progress was made. No agreement was reached on standard protocols for financial accountability for state funding of the sector. With regard to policy matters affecting the broader state/sector relationship, apart from limited progress on support of volunteering, the dearth of IAG meetings prevented regular monitoring or reform of the administrative mechanisms that were meant to underpin the functioning of the voluntary sector/state relationship. Partnership paralysis set in.

3.4.3.2 Recent Rounds of Partnership: 1996–2010

Social partnership describes a national deliberative and bargaining process conducted between the government and four Social Partner groupings (known as "pillars"): the trade unions, the employers' confederations, the farming bodies, and, from 1996 onward, the community and voluntary sector. The purpose of Social Partnership was to negotiate an agreement between the parties that set out a socioeconomic strategy for Ireland for the subsequent three years. This strategy addressed not only economic concerns relating to taxation, worker productivity, and wage levels, but also social concerns relating to the reduction of long-term unemployment, poverty, and social exclusion.

Social Partnership existed as a process for more than ten years without the participation of the nonprofit sector. Admission to the process, which was by government invitation only, did not initially extend to nonprofits because the existing players (the business, union, and farming pillars) and government viewed Ireland's problems as economic problems requiring an economic solution. The definition of the problem and the shape of the solution changed over time. Measurement of societal success as something broader than just economic prosperity achievable through collective wage bargaining forced the social partners to tackle structural issues relating to social exclusion, namely, the challenges presented by disadvantaged communities and the problems of long-term unemployment.[69] Acceptance of this agenda, however, opened the door to nonprofit sector participation.[70]

Prior to joining social partnership in 1996, nonprofit participation in policy-making ranged from direct political access for elite players to outside lobbying by less well-connected nonprofits. The policy impact achieved in both cases tended to be ad hoc and limited. Significant changes in the ways that government reached out to the sector at national and local levels occurred in the 1990s with the creation of National Economic and Social Forum (NESF) and Area Based Partnerships (ABPs). Both vehicles offered nonprofits a formal, if still limited, role in policymaking. By making nonprofit representatives equal players alongside business, union, and government officials, NESF and the ABPs raised the sector's profile. This greater role for the sector in policy deliberation gave rise to tensions with other established players, tensions reflected in local councilors' mistrust of nonprofits at the ABP level and the lack of priority placed by unions and employers on the NESF at a national level.

In 1996, following ten years of informal involvement and lobbying for admission, the Irish government created a new Social Partnership interest group – the Community and Voluntary (CV) pillar – and invited a select number of CV organizations to join.[71] Of the eight initial invitees, at least four had been actively involved in public policy debates for years and in outer policy circles and at NESF,[72] while one group (the Community Platform) was a new composite group representing twenty-two smaller CV organizations.[73] Over the ten-year period of its existence the composition and structure of the pillar changed as some parties departed the Social Partnership process when they failed to sign up to negotiated agreements and the government took the opportunity to revise the areas represented. Although there was no express mention of charities as public policy collaborators, a majority of the organizations in the CV pillar (ten out of fifteen) were charities.

---

[69] Rory O'Donnell and Colm O'Reardon, "The Irish Experiment," *New Economy* 3(1) (1996): 33–38, 34.

[70] Niall Crowley, "Partnership 2000: Empowerment or Co-Option?," in *In the Shadow of the Tiger*, ed. Peadar Kirby and David Jacobson (Dublin: Dublin City University Press, 1998), 74.

[71] Department of An Taoiseach, *Partnership 2000* (Dublin: Stationery Office, 1996), para. 11.6.

[72] Conference of Religious in Ireland, Society of St. Vincent de Paul, National Youth Council of Ireland (NYCI), and the Irish National Organization for the Unemployed.

[73] Current Community Platform members are set out on the platform's website, accessed January 6, 2016, http://communityplatform.ie/membership.html.

The advantages of pillar membership included access to the National Economic and Social Council (NESC) where longer-term social and economic strategies are developed,[74] constant information updates on projects falling within the partnership remit,[75] and raised profiles of CV representatives among government departments and agencies, leading to increased invitations to participate in policy working groups and interdepartmental committees. A final procedural advantage of CV pillar membership was the political access enjoyed by CV pillar representatives. Through Social Partnership, CV pillar members formed valuable relationships with senior civil servants, raising their profile and credibility and giving them direct access to relevant Ministers when matters affecting their funding or remit arose.[76] Proponents argued that Social Partnership enabled CV representatives to make a substantive difference to policy design and policy outcomes.[77] Housing policy, child poverty, and national performance indicators were three areas in which CV pillar interviewees claimed that nonprofit stakeholders had successfully converted moral pressure into political leverage.[78] This political leverage, it is claimed, enabled the CV pillar to obtain policy outcomes through Social Partnership collaboration that individual organizations could not achieve through bilateral negotiation with government. Yet Social Partnership, no more than the experiences of the IAG, did not lead to any direct collaboration on the reform of charity regulation. Government commitments in the final Social Partnership Agreement, signed by all pillars in June 2006, recognized that:

> [C]ommunity and voluntary activity forms the very core of a vibrant and inclusive society. The great strength of voluntary activity is that it emerges organically from communities. While the Government should not seek to control and be involved in every aspect of voluntary activity, it does have a responsibility to provide an enabling framework to help the sector. Where this involves direct supports, a delicate balance must be struck between having a relatively light regulation and maintaining proper accountability.[79]

---

[74] The CV pillar strategically used its five seats on NESC to commission studies to support its policy agenda.

[75] Parties departing social partnership expressed frustration over their exclusion from the information circle by remaining CV pillar representatives, illustrating the value of shared information within the pillar process. See Oonagh B. Breen, *Crossing Borders: Comparative Perspectives on the Legal Regulation of Charities and the Role of State-Nonprofit Partnership in Public Policy Development* (New Haven, CT: Yale Law School, 2006), 422.

[76] Interview with Dónall Geoghegan, Policy Officer with NYCI, Dublin (June 22, 2005).

[77] Ibid.   [78] Breen, n. 75, 424–428.

[79] Government of Ireland, *Towards 2016: Ten Year Framework Social Partnership Agreement 2006–2016* (Dublin: Stationery Office, 2006), para. 34.1.

3.5 CONTEXTUALIZING THE THIRD STRAND:
THE GLUE THAT HOLDS THE PROCESS TOGETHER OR THE
QUICKSAND IN WHICH IT IS STUCK?

The value of these various forms of collaboration through the IAG, the CV pillar of Social Partnership, NESF, and NESC – whether viewed as partnership, consultation, or cooption – lay in the opportunities presented to CV representatives to gain new negotiation skills, to participate in the decision-making process, and to be part of a political process beyond the lobbying threshold. For the first time, the tangibility of the sector began to emerge through the necessary processes of selecting representatives for both IAG and Social Partnership processes. Political experiences taught the parties of the need to bring your constituents with you and the importance of good personal relations with your counterparts and not just your colleagues. Experience in not reaching agreement, particularly in the Social Partnership process, brought home to nonprofits the value and challenges inherent in dissent. The rediscovery of the dissenting voice toward the end of Social Partnership in many ways laid the groundwork for the subsequent research of the Advocacy Initiative.[80]

Another important lesson that emerged from the collaborative experiences was the nonprofit realization that the first party to fill a policy vacuum gains the upper hand in influencing, if not dictating, the shape of the future policy solution. ICTR used this lesson to its advantage in undertaking its feasibility study on the sector's ability to regulate public fundraising, while The Wheel and Boardmatch adopted a similar approach in their development of the *Nonprofit Governance Code*, both of which emerged after the Social Partnership era.

Although the third strand of collaboration itself did not necessarily hinge on matters of charity regulation, the sector's involvement in this arena inevitably influenced all stakeholders. The partnership space provided an incubator for nonprofit leaders who, up until this time, had little experience of working together as a sector or engaging with the state on a multilateral consensual basis. It allowed sector representatives to witness and participate in high-level negotiations between the trade unions, business, and the state and again to learn from their partner peers. These experiences changed the attitudes of those involved in terms of both how the parties sought to represent themselves and their capacity to contribute. It awakened the state's realization of the

---

[80] See the Advocacy Initiative website, accessed January 6, 2016, www.advocacyinitiaative.ie.

sector's potential, crystallizing those areas in which the state was happy to involve the sector and those areas in which it was less enamored.

Looking at any one event in isolation might lead one wrongly to assume that failure was the only outcome. It is true that on each occasion outlined the interaction fell short of its initial aims. Comhairle today is a pale imitator of what the NSSC was established to be in the 1970s. The Combat Poverty Agency, despite its valiant efforts, has been reincorporated into the Department of Social Protection. The White Paper's IAG – the closest the sector has come to a vested interest regulatory process – was not successful and left a bad taste in the mouths of all those involved. Social Partnership, while having its highs for those selected to sit in the inner circle, created a greater feeling of mistrust among the broader nonprofit community of elite players looking after themselves and forging their own political connections.

And yet it is arguable that these failed process experiences enabled the nonprofit sector, and particularly the leaders in that sector, to mature and positioned them to take up the core areas of governance and fundraising regulation that currently occupy the self-regulatory space by raising their profiles and making them more credible participants in the regulatory game. The shifting pendulum of power from religious nonprofits' domination of the early twentieth century to the state from the 1970s onward, leading to secular nonprofits' emergence on the policy scene during the 1970s–1980s, right up to the formal entrance of nonprofits in the policymaking sphere in 1990s–2000s, forms the background to today's regulatory context.

To turn then to preliminary conclusions: on the cycle of regulation, where does Ireland currently stand? The recent emergence of nonstatutory regulation in the core areas of fundraising and governance has proved an interesting development. Whereas the initiative for both came from the nonprofit sector, the state financially supported the fundraising project to a large extent. This support has not, however, ensured its successful implementation. If anything, the opposite has occurred: given its high financial dependency on the state, a downturn in financial support hindered an effective high-profile rollout. Moreover, a reverse form of regulatory capture is evident in ICTR's failure to commence the proposed monitoring regime in light of the Department of Justice's request to delay the Monitoring Group's establishment pending the Charities Act's commencement. In contrast, the governance project, developed and financially supported by the sector, has had a higher public profile and managed to engage more nonprofits. Although it faces its own enforcement challenges, the code's rollout has been more effective. It remains to be seen whether without an annual income, the code will be self-sustaining.

The 2016 introduction of the Good Governance Awards for the Not-for-Profit sector may provide useful support in this regard.

The impetus to develop these codes, along with a nonprofit reporting framework for charities, following a twelve-year wait for charity law reform, demonstrates that there are nonprofit leaders who have been prepared to take the initiative when it comes to charity regulation. Many, although not all, have been involved in the earlier state/sector collaborations through Social Partnership, NESF, and the White Paper IAG. It is arguable that their experiences and exposure to political and regulatory decision making enabled these individuals and their organizations to play a larger role in the sector's self-regulation, important in a sector that does not have a recognized representative body.

From a pure statutory-regulation perspective, the Irish government's approach over the centuries has been one conscious of the pitfalls of non-regulation but uncomfortable legislating for strong regulators.[81] The former Commissioners for Charitable Donations and Bequests were never given the powers or resources to act as investigator, making their enforcement powers nugatory. The new CRA will not be an omnipotent presence in this regard either. Unlike many of its common law counterparts, it will require court authorization to exercise many of its powers. Even the newly created Charities Appeal Tribunal will not transform matters, as its jurisdiction is mirrored on the CRA's exercise of power and is thus mainly restricted to reviewing registration or refusal decisions.

The rationale for such a light-touch approach, particularly following recent domestic charity scandals that revealed shocking disregard for public funding,[82] may, to some degree, lie in the state's past overreliance on charities to deliver public services in the areas of health, education, and social welfare. When charitable provision is core rather than supplementary, a finding of lack of probity would undermine the ability to deliver "essential" (rather than charitable) services. In the absence of an alternative state system of delivery, such a finding would not only be damning but also crippling for service provision and have far larger political consequences.

The limited resources available not only for regulatory purposes but also historically for service delivery purposes means that for the foreseeable future, consultation and cooperation remain necessary for success on both fronts. While the Charities Act 2009 will provide the necessary skeleton on which to hang the regulatory framework, the input of stakeholders willing to lead the

[81] Acheson et al., n. 6, 168–69. [82] Breen, *Nonprofit Law Yearbook*, n. 27.

way on governance, reporting, and fundraising standards will be vital to the regime's future sustainability. The emergence of a symbiotic relationship between state and sector would be mutually beneficial. It would not be without its challenges for both the state (in allowing stakeholders' autonomy in areas in which the state is uncomfortable to be criticized) and the nonprofit sector (in learning to charge and sanction its own constituents for both access to and breach of a regulatory regime). The time, however, is ripe for the next wave combining state and sector initiatives to break forth upon Irish shores.

4

Shifting Patterns of State Regulation and NGO Self-Regulation in Sub-Saharan Africa

MARY KAY GUGERTY

4.1 INTRODUCTION

The global growth and reach of the nongovernmental organization (NGO) sector over the last two decades has been accompanied by increasing concerns about NGO transparency and accountability.[1] Governments and donors are increasingly concerned with finding ways to regulate and evaluate the quality of growing NGO activity, but with limited capacity for monitoring and oversight. These capacity challenges are particularly acute in many African countries, which are often characterized by rapidly growing NGO sectors, limited mechanisms of regulatory oversight, weak or newly emergent civil societies, and states that have traditionally been hostile to civil society activity.

The regulatory challenges faced by African NGO sectors mirror broader changes in global governance in which nonstate, nonmarket actors take a larger role in regulatory and rule-making activity previously undertaken by the state.[2] As a result, new forms of self-regulation have emerged as one alternative to traditional state regulation across all sectors, including nonprofits and NGOs.[3] Such self-regulatory regimes consist of institutions in which

[1] Ronelle Burger, "Reconsidering the Case for Enhancing Accountability via Regulation," *Voluntas* 23(1) (2012): 85–108; Alnoor Ebrahim, *NGOs and Organizational Change: Discourse, Reporting and Learning* (Cambridge: Cambridge University Press, 2005); Ruth Grant and Robert Keohane, "Accountability and Abuses of Power in World Politics," *American Political Science Review* 99(1) (2005): 29–43.

[2] David Coen and Mark Thatcher, "The New Governance of Markets and Non-Majoritarian Regulators," *Governance* 18(3) (2005): 329–346; Claire Cutler, Virginia Haufler, and Tony Porter, eds., *Private Authority and International Affairs* (Albany: State University of New York Press, 1999).

[3] Robert Lloyd, *The Role of NGO Self-Regulation in Increasing Stakeholder Accountability* (London: One World Trust, 2005); Robert Lloyd and Lucy de las Casas, "NGO Self-Regulation: Enforcing and Balancing Accountability," *Alliance Extra*, December 1, 2005.

nongovernmental actors set standards and rules of conduct and undertake monitoring and enforcement for the members of the regime.[4] Since these self-regulatory regimes operate without the coercive power of law and provide a mix of public and collective goods, the creation and maintenance of institutions of self-regulation present a collective action dilemma. Self-regulation requires the development of institutional mechanisms that give organizations the incentive to police themselves. Self-regulatory regimes can also pose a potential threat to state power and have often been strongly contested by governments in Africa.[5]

As a result of both collective action challenges and government resistance and repression, self-regulation in Africa has not been easy to institutionalize. This chapter explores the evolution of NGO self-regulation efforts in five countries in sub-Saharan Africa: Kenya, Malawi, Tanzania, Uganda, and Ethiopia. Within each country, the interaction between governments and NGOs sets in motion a series of regulatory waves as governments and NGOs propose and respond to regulatory initiatives. In some cases, the waves of regulatory initiatives never culminate in any institutionalized self-regulatory regimes. In other cases, most notably Ethiopia and Uganda, the interaction culminates in a severe crackdown on NGO activity.

The country cases examined in this chapter suggest that self-regulation in sub-Saharan Africa has taken place in three broad phases. The first took place in the early 1990s, during the initial phase of democratization and a period of immense NGO growth for many countries. This phase is characterized by a high degree of contestation between NGOs and governments over the shape of the regulatory system, and the resultant systems are often quasi-public forms of regulation. The second phase occurred at the turn of the century and in the early 2000s as NGOs became increasingly professionalized and governments sought to consolidate democracies and establish regulatory policy toward the NGO sector. This phase is often characterized by attempts to establish self-regulatory systems that are fully independent of governments and based on NGO norms of professional standards. The third wave of self-regulation is ongoing; arguably, we are even embarking on a fourth phase. In countries where democratic politics and NGO activity are more clearly institutionalized, the third wave is characterized by the development of more sophisticated and professional systems of self-regulation. In others, most notably Ethiopia,

---

[4] Neil Gunningham and Joseph Rees, "Industry Self-Regulation: An Institutional Perspective," *Law and Policy* 19(4) (1997): 363–414.

[5] Mary Kay Gugerty, "The Emergence of NGO Self-Regulation in Africa," *Nonprofit and Voluntary Sector Quarterly* 39(6) (2010): 1087–1112.

the government imposed new regulations that severely limit the activity of NGOs. At the tail of this third wave, however, many African governments evince growing concern with increased advocacy activities and foreign funding of NGOs, and this concern becomes the focus of new regulatory efforts, perhaps mirroring a broader global trend of government crackdown on foreign funding of NGOs.[6]

To explore these waves, this chapter proceeds in three sections. The first lays out the institutional structure of self-regulation and the factors associated with the emergence of regulation as a form of collective action; the second explores the five country case studies to explore how these factors have played out on the ground. The final section looks across the five cases to draw larger conclusions.

4.2 SELF-REGULATION AND COLLECTIVE ACTION

The impetus for NGO regulatory initiatives in Africa is the result of several trends. First, donor funding of NGOs increased dramatically from the 1980s onward; as an example, Organisation for Economic Co-operation and Development (OECD) disbursements to NGOs increased from almost zero to over four billion dollars from 1980 to 2002.[7] This increased availability of funding stimulated rapid growth in the size and influence of the NGO sector in many African countries.[8] As NGOs proliferated, so did well-publicized cases of corruption and misuse of funds that began to threaten the reputation and funding of legitimate organizations.[9] At the same time, NGOs increasingly came into conflict with governments over the terms of their registration and operation.[10] Governments, many of which were in the midst of fundamental political transformations, found themselves struggling to manage their relationships with NGOs. The regulatory frameworks governing the operation of NGOs in most African countries dated back to the colonial period and were ill

---

[6] Kendra E. Dupuy, James Ron, and Aseem Prakash, "Who Survived? Ethiopia's Regulatory Crackdown on Foreign-Funded NGOs," *Review of International Political Economy* 22(2) (2015): 419–456.

[7] Catherine Agg, "Winners or Losers? NGOs in the Current Aid Paradigm," *Development* 49(2) 2006: 15–21.

[8] Julie Hearn, "African NGOs: The New Compradors?," *Development and Change* 38(6) (2007): 1095–1110; Sarah Michael, *Undermining Development: The Absence of Power among Local NGOs in Africa* (Bloomington: Indiana University Press, 2004).

[9] Michael Edwards and David Hulme, *NGOs, States and Governments: Too Close for Comfort?* (New York: St. Martin's Press, 1997).

[10] Julie Fisher, *NonGovernments: NGOs and the Political Development of the Third World* (West Hartford, CT: Kumarian Press, 1998); Michael, n. 8.

suited for oversight of NGO sectors that in many countries were delivering 50 percent or more of basic social services. As a response to problems of both political and administrative control, many governments initiated changes to the regulatory frameworks governing NGOs. Unsurprisingly, such efforts at regulatory reform were highly contested by NGOs, resulting in organized attempts at opposition.

The most common NGO response to regulatory change in many countries was the development of collective, institutionalized codes of conduct for the sector. In some countries, NGOs developed collective self-regulatory institutions that went beyond mere passive codes of conduct and institutionalized some rule-setting powers within the NGO sector. Such codes typically set standards for NGO governance structures, the reporting of financial information, and the conducting of fundraising campaigns. Because such systems are often designed without the coercive power of the state, they pose critical challenges of collective action for participants. The institutionalization of such systems requires collective agreement on the content of standards as well as the development of monitoring and enforcement mechanisms to prevent shirking. The benefits of self-regulation, particularly the benefits of reduced or avoided government regulation, can be shared by all NGOs, but if the costs of undertaking collective action are high, there may be clear incentives for nonparticipation.

At the core of the collective action problem is the challenge of producing collective goods.[11] Pure public goods are characterized by nonrivalry and nonexcludability. With a classic public good, such as clean air or national defense, consumption by one person does not decrease the amount available to others, and no individual can be prevented from enjoying the benefits of the public good. Public goods thus provide a classic rationale for government intervention, since the market is unlikely to provide such goods because producers cannot charge for their provision. Regulation is a public good typically provided by governments; many benefits of regulation – such as regulations that limit pollution emissions – are shared by all, and one person's use does not diminish use by another. Collective or club goods are a type of public good characterized by nonrivalry and nonexcludability among a self-contained group. NGO self-regulation is a collective or club good: since the reputational benefits of self-regulation may accrue to all NGOs, organizations may have incentives to "free ride" and not contribute to its provision.

---

[11] Mancur Olson, *The Logic of Collective Action* (Cambridge, MA: Harvard University Press, 1965).

A long collective action literature suggests that collective action will be more difficult to sustain in larger groups where ties are less dense and norms of trust and reciprocity are less likely to emerge.[12] In this case, as Olson originally noted, participants may require specific inducements, or "selective incentives," to participate in collective action.[13] These incentives are benefits accessed only by members, such as trade discounts, trainings, or privileged access to donors. The literature also suggests that "patrons" who have a large stake in collective action outcomes and are willing to help underwrite costs are another critical factor in the emergence of associational activity.[14] The literature also suggests that such associations are more likely to be successful in their collective action if they are "encompassing" in the sense of being broadly based in an industry or sector.[15] Encompassing associations may be more successful in making demands on the state if the association can discipline and control members.[16]

But perhaps the most pervasive factor associated with the emergence of collective action institutions is the perception of a collective threat.[17] This feature is highly salient in the African context, where historically the activities of NGOs have been viewed with extreme suspicion. NGO/state relationships in many countries in Africa have been characterized by a large amount of distrust, cooptation, and outright repression of NGO operations, which are often viewed by governments as a form of opposition.[18] A key indicator of the orientation of states toward NGOs is the location of NGO registration and oversight functions, which are traditionally housed in strategic security

[12] Robert Axelrod, *The Evolution of Cooperation* (New York: Basic Books, 1984); Russell Hardin, *Collective Action* (Baltimore, MD: Johns Hopkins University Press, 1992); Robert Putnam with Robert Leonardi and Raffaella Y. Nanetti, *Making Democracy Work: Civic Traditions in Modern Italy* (Princeton, NJ: Princeton University Press, 1993).

[13] Olson, n. 11.

[14] David C. King and Jack Walker, "The Provision of Benefits by Interest Groups in the United States," *Journal of Politics* 54(2) (1992): 394–426.

[15] Mancur Olson, *The Rise and Decline of Nations: Economic Growth, Stagflation, and Social Rigidities* (New Haven, CT: Yale University Press, 1982); Eduardo Silva, "Business Elites, the State and Economic Change in Chile," in *Business and the State in Developing Countries*, ed. Sylvia Maxfield and Ben Ross Schneider (Ithaca, NY: Cornell University Press, 1997).

[16] Sylvia Maxfield and Ben Ross Schneider, eds., *Business and the State in Developing Countries* (Ithaca, NY: Cornell University Press, 1997); Jesse Biddle and Milor Vedat, "Economic Governance in Turkey: Bureaucratic Capacity, Policy Networks, and Business Associations," in *Business and the State in Developing Countries*, ed. Sylvia Maxfield and Ben Ross Schneider (Ithaca, NY: Cornell University Press, 1997).

[17] John Mark Hansen, "The Political Economy of Group Membership," *American Political Science Review* 79(1) (1985): 79–96; Maxfield and Schneider, ibid.

[18] Michael Bratton, "Micro-Democracy? The Merger of Farmers Unions in Zimbabwe," *African Studies Review* 37(1) (1989): 9–37.

ministries or in the office of the president so that the state security apparatus can be employed to monitor the activities of organizations.[19]

The collective action lens suggests that the emergence and institutionalization of self-regulation in Africa is mostly likely to occur when NGOs feel threatened by impending government legislation. Even in those cases, however, self-regulation may not emerge without the existence of broad-based NGO umbrella associations and the support of donors who can supply resources (both material and moral) in support of NGO efforts.

4.3 SELF-REGULATION ACROSS FIVE AFRICAN COUNTRIES

This section explores the emergence of self-regulation among NGOs in five countries using a structured comparison across five cases: Kenya, Malawi, Uganda, Tanzania, and Ethiopia. We examine the period from the development of the first system in Kenya in 1990 to the present in order to capture the nature of regulatory waves. In each country, we pay particular attention to the nature of the regulatory threat by the state and the nature of NGO/state interactions, as well as the features associated with the emergence of collective action, including the nature of preexisting NGO associational activity and the role of donor support in the process.

Data collection for the case studies in Uganda, Kenya, and Ethiopia incorporated fieldwork in all three countries that included interviews by the author with fifty-five senior managers and program staff of NGOs, donors, and governments; extensive secondary document review; and the archives of local and international news sources. Data collection for Tanzania and Malawi is based on review of publicly available government and NGO documents, secondary sources, and ten telephone interviews with key informants. Documents reviewed in each case include reviews of available government legislation and national policy frameworks, NGO association evaluations, strategic plans and annual reports, extensive secondary document review including donor assessments, and a comprehensive review of available media reports.

4.3.1 *Early Starters: Kenya and Ethiopia*

4.3.1.1 Kenya

Kenya was the first country in Africa to wrestle with issues of NGO self-regulation. The threat of increased government legislation was a critical

---

[19] Ibid.

driver. In the wake of rapid growth in the nonprofit sector and growing advocacy on the part of some NGOs, the authoritarian government of Daniel arap Moi began to signal its discontent with the current NGO regulatory framework in the late 1980s.[20] In 1989, Moi announced that he was establishing a new directorate to "coordinate" the activities of NGOs. In response, the main national umbrella organization, the Kenya National Council of Social Services (KNCSS), organized a conference on NGO coordination in which NGOs drafted an alternative proposal. The proposal, however, was largely ignored by the government, which subsequently introduced the NGO Coordination Act in Parliament in late 1990. This act was clearly aimed at controlling the activities of NGOs in the country and was pushed through Parliament and rapidly signed into law in early 1991.[21] The act vested large amounts of power in a government-controlled NGO Board that had the sole power to register NGOs. The act also created an ostensibly independent national NGO Council to represent NGOs, but did not endow it with independent power.[22]

NGOs' reaction to the act was highly negative but was constrained by the repressive political environment. At the time, the NGO sector in Kenya consisted of about 400 organizations, about half of which were KNCSS members. Recognizing the weakness of KNCSS, NGOs met and created the "NGO Network" with the sole purpose of discussing the legislation and creating alternative proposals to present to the government.[23] The ten-member standing committee of this Network included a mix of large local and international NGOs.

What followed was a three-year process of contestation and consultation over the promulgation of rules and regulations for implementation of the act. Initially, the government appeared unwilling to consider NGO complaints about the act and its associated regulations, but as the government continued to push through new provisions, NGOs – with strong support from the donor community – grew increasingly bold and coordinated in their actions. Network members lobbied individual government officials and key donors, asking donors to commit to support the efforts of the Network. Donors exhibited increasing willingness to do so, viewing the Network as part of the fledging prodemocracy movement. Donors backed their support with threats to withdraw aid to the government unless it reconsidered its position.[24]

---

[20] Stephen Ndegwa, *The Two Faces of Civil Society: NGOs and Politics in Africa* (West Hartford, CT: Kumarian Press, 1996).

[21] Ibid.

[22] E.A. Adiin-Yaansah, "An Experiment into Self-Regulation in Kenya," Refugee Studies Programme, University of Oxford, March 1997; Ndegwa, n. 20.

[23] Ndegwa, n. 20.   [24] Ibid.

Ultimately, the Kenyan government agreed to delegate some independent powers to the NGO sector. The NGO Council established under the act was given a legal mandate to develop its own governance structures and code of conduct.[25] Development of the NGO code of conduct began at the NGO Council's official inception in 1993 and was codified as Legal Notice no. 306 in 1995. The notice establishes a quasi-judicial regulatory committee charged with the promotion and adherence to the NGO Code of Conduct; all registered NGOs are subject to its jurisdiction.

The initial emergence of self-regulation in Kenya took place in a hostile political environment, just as multiparty democracy was emerging in Kenya. The provisions of the original act were widely viewed as overly repressive, and this helped to mobilize collective action among NGOs, who had an initial organizing platform in the KNCSS. This mobilization was strongly and publicly supported by donors and international NGOs and framed as an issue of democratization.[26] The severity of the threat, combined with the availability of financial and moral support from donors, meant that a coalition of NGOs coalesced quickly around the issue.

The second phase of self-regulation in Kenya spanned the period 1995–2008, a period also characterized by political opening, multiparty elections, and the departure of many civil society leaders into government positions. While the 1991 NGO Act and the codification of the code of conduct in 1995 resolved the initial conflict over the location of regulatory power, the subsequent process of institutionalizing the NGO Council as a self-regulatory body was fraught with challenges. The law was challenging to implement in the absence of a national policy on NGOs, since there was no general framework to reference when the law was unclear on issues. After a two-year process, an NGO Sector Policy was finally agreed on in 2004 and Parliament adopted Sessional Paper No. 1 of 2006 on NGOs, which expanded and clarified the definition of NGOs, recognized the role of the NGO Council and NGO Coordination Board, and called for a new law on NGOs to be drafted. At the same time, however, the NGO Council was suffering from weak and fractured leadership and was unable to act as the coordinating body for the sector.

At the same time as the NGO Sector Policy was developing, Kenya was engaged in the process of constitutional reform. The National Rainbow Coalition (NARC), which ultimately won the 2002 election, had

---

[25] Adiin-Yaansah, n. 22.

[26] Wachira Maina, "Kenya: The State, Donors, and the Politics of Democratization," in *Civil Society and the Aid Industry*, ed. Alison Van Rooy (London: Earthscan Publications, 1998).

constitutional reform as one of the components of the coalition agreement, but postelection fighting over the power of the presidency and other provisions resulted in a constitution that was defeated in a highly contentious national referendum in 2005.[27] The referendum debate fractured the coalition and laid the groundwork for the divisive 2007 election that resulted in several months of violence and bloodshed.[28] The coalition that emerged in the wake of the violence again had constitutional reform as one of its planks. The proposed constitution emerged from a lengthy public consultative process and was supported by the leaders of both components of the coalition. The referendum passed in 2008 with 68 percent of the vote and 70 percent turnout. This constitution included far-reaching forms and enshrined protections for freedom of speech, association, access to information, and the right to assembly.[29]

With a new constitution in place, the NGO sector recognized the need for new legislation and a new institutional framework for self-regulation for the NGO sector. The NGO Council had long been riven by conflict and suffered from weak leadership; as a result, it no longer functioned as a legitimate self-regulatory body. In 2009 NGOs formed a new group to develop a regulatory framework, the CSO Reference Group. The formation of this group marks the beginning of the third phase of self-regulation in Kenya. Unlike previous phases, however, this new effort stemmed from a sense of optimism and opportunity for the civil society sector, rather than in response to repressive regulatory initiatives from government. Through a widespread process of consultation over the course of three years, the CSO Reference Group developed a new bill, the Public Benefits Organisations (PBO) bill.[30] A validation process for the bill was held in ten regions, and more than 1500 civil society leaders provided input.[31] The PBO bill had broad support from the NGO and civil society sector and was passed by Parliament in January 2013.

In spite of these apparently auspicious beginnings, however, the PBO Act has yet to be gazetted by the government, and no date for its initiation has been set.[32] In November 2013, the government introduced thirteen amendments. The CSO Reference Group argued that these amendments signaled

[27] Eric Kramon and Daniel Posner, "Kenya's New Constitution," *Journal of Democracy* 22(2) (2011): 89–103.
[28] Ibid.
[29] International Center for Nonprofit Law (ICNL), *NGO Law Monitor: Kenya*, accessed December 30, 2015, www.icnl.org/research/monitor/kenya.html.
[30] CSO Reference Group, *The Facts on the Proposed Public Benefits Organizations (PBO) Bill* (Nairobi, 2012).
[31] Ibid.   [32] ICNL, n. 29.

an intention to violate constitutional protections of freedom of association, the Sessional Paper on NGOs (2006), and the PBO Act (2013). The amendments included provisions to cap the amount of funding NGOs could receive from external donors at 15 percent of their budget, echoing provisions of Ethiopia's 2009 Proclamation for the Registration and Regulation of Charities and Societies (discussed below), which prohibits those NGOs with more than 10 percent of overseas funding from working on "human rights" issues. In the wake of forceful protest from civil society, international human rights organizations, and aid agencies, the Kenyan government convened a task force in November 2014 to consult with stakeholders regarding these amendments. In October of that same year, however, 957 NGOs were threatened with deregistration, allegedly for financial mismanagement. The NGO sector made vociferous claims that some of these charges were political, and ultimately, the Minister of Devolution reversed the closures. More recently, a number of NGOs have sought orders from the High Court to compel the Cabinet Secretary to commence the PBO Act in its current form.[33]

In the face of a moribund NGO Council, Kenyan NGOs also took the lead in developing a new independent set of standards for NGOs accompanied by a system of certification. With funding from the Aga Khan Foundation, the Kenya Civil Society Competence and Sustainability Programme engaged in consultations across the country. The group developed a set of standards, a code of practice, and an organizational capacity assessment tool. A new organization, Viwango (meaning "standards" in Swahili), was established to carry out voluntary certification of NGOs using the standards, code of practice, and capacity assessment tool. Formed in 2011, Viwango's primary goal is to promote the adoption of minimum quality standards by NGOs in Kenya.[34] Thus at the end of the third wave, Kenya is poised to see the adoption of liberal legislation and the development of an independent, voluntary system of self-regulation.

4.3.1.2 Ethiopia

Regulatory waves in Ethiopia began after Kenya's first wave was complete, but the culmination of the regulatory dance in Ethiopia in 2011 appears to have provided a blueprint for increasingly repressive government regulatory activity in east Africa.

---

[33] Ibid.

[34] Keith Aulick, *Learning Agenda Mini-Case#12, Kenya-Viwango* (2013), accessed January 22, 2016, www.developmentiscapacity.org/sites/default/files/12-Viwengo-Kenya-LA%20Mini%20Case.pdf.

The initial wave of regulatory activity in Ethiopia began in a similar fashion to the other country cases. As the number of NGOs in Ethiopia proliferated throughout the 1990s, government concerns with NGO oversight increased and the government continually instituted increasingly restrictive administrative requirements for NGO registration and operation during the latter part of the decade. As concern over these provisions mounted, NGOs began discussions on the development of a code of conduct for NGOs that might help alleviate some of the regulatory pressure from government.[35] The Christian Relief and Development Agency (CRDA, now the Consortium of Christian Relief and Development Agencies [CCRDA]), the oldest NGO in Ethiopia, provided administrative support for the process, which began in 1998. CRDA was originally formed in 1973 as a relief coordination agency under the Marxist "Derg" regime during a period when NGOs were essentially illegal and remained the largest operational NGO in Ethiopia. Until 2004 CRDA was the only legal umbrella association in the country. The code of conduct was developed by a working group consisting of representatives appointed from CRDA, three NGO networks, and two international NGOs. The code was ratified in 1999 by a national consultative meeting of more than 200 NGOs (at that time a majority of registered NGOs in Ethiopia).[36] While the code was intended to act as a self-regulatory system covering the NGO sector as a whole, it proved challenging to develop the administrative capacity and a new organizational structure to support the code, especially in the absence of a state mandate. Thus, the code remained largely under the auspices of CRDA. CRDA, however, viewed itself as having authority to investigate violations of the code only for its own members.

Starting in 2005, the state's relationships with civil society and NGOs took a turn for the worse. The ruling party, surprised by the strength of the vote for the opposition, began to institute new restrictive policies aimed at curtailing the activities of civil society. In the wake of violence following the 2005 elections, the government accused civil society groups of supporting the violence.[37] Freedom of the press was curtailed, culminating in the Mass Media and Freedom of Information Proclamation law, ratified in 2008.[38] CRDA, which had acted as an election observer during the elections, issued

[35] Jeffrey Clark, *Civil Society, NGOs and Development in Ethiopia: A Snapshot View* (Washington, DC: World Bank, 2000).

[36] Ibid.

[37] Lovise Aalen and Kjetil Tronvoll, "The End of Democracy? Curtailing Political and Civil Rights in Ethiopia," *Review of African Political Economy* 36(120) (2009): 193–207.

[38] Ibid., 200; ICNL, *NGO Law Monitor: Ethiopia*, accessed December 15, 2015, www.icnl.org/research/monitor/ethiopia.html.

a call for an independent investigation into the violence. The government responded by issuing a warning to CRDA, claiming that it needed to make amendments to its mandate to sustain its license.[39]

These crackdowns culminated in the Proclamation to Provide for the Registration and Regulation of Charities and Societies (CSP), issued in 2009. According to Human Rights Watch and Amnesty International, the law violates Ethiopia's own constitution as well as international human rights law.[40] The CSP law divides NGOs into foreign and domestic organizations with "foreign" organizations being those that receive more than 10 percent of their financing from foreign sources. These NGOs were barred from engaging in essentially all human rights and advocacy activities.[41]

In November 2011, the Ethiopian Charities and Societies Agency issued the Guideline on Determining the Administrative and Operational Costs of CSOs, which is applicable to all charities and societies (international and domestic). The guidelines were retroactive to July 2011, involved no consultation with organizations or donors, and limited administrative costs for all charities and societies to 30 percent of their budgets. Some thirty international NGOs received warning letters, informing them that all their costs would be considered as "administrative."[42]

As a result of the 2009 proclamation, a recent study found that most local human rights groups in Ethiopia have disappeared, while survivors either have "rebranded" their work or switched their work from proscribed areas.[43] The proclamation and its aftermath effectively shut down any hope that NGOs could play a role in self-regulation or in the development of NGO policy. As we see below, the Ethiopian strategy may be seen as a model for other leaders. For example, it has been observed that "Uganda's NGO Bill is part of growing authoritarian contagion in the region, with Ethiopia's 2009 Charities and Societies Proclamation serving as the ultimate blueprint. Other leaders in East Africa, and beyond, no doubt observed this strategy with interest, as the United States government in particular failed to mount a serious challenge to this blatant repression."[44] Unlike the years of initial political opening and democratization, donors framed NGO repression as an issue of democratization; in recent years donors and donor governments appear less willing to intervene.

---

[39] Aalen and Tronvoll, n. 37, 201.   [40] Ibid., 202.   [41] ICNL, n. 38.   [42] Ibid.
[43] DuPuy et al., n. 6.
[44] Karen Attiah, "Uganda's NGO Bill: Another Threat to Freedom in East Africa," *Washington Post*, September 11, 2015.

4.3.2 *Uganda*

The development of NGO self-regulation programs in Uganda has had two waves and is perhaps now embarking on a third that follows in Ethiopia's footsteps. The first wave of self-regulation in Uganda began with the two major NGO associations developing codes of conduct for their members. The first association, DENIVA, was founded in 1988 as a support organization for indigenous NGOs. DENIVA's code of conduct, however, had no monitoring or enforcement associated with it. The second association, the NGO Forum, was founded in 1997 to represent both national and international NGOs operating in Uganda. The genesis for its formation was the recognition that the NGO sector had no mechanism for contributing to the policy process in the country. The NGO Forum was registered in May 2000 and launched its code of conduct in 2001. Like the DENIVA code, however, the NGO Forum code of conduct had no provisions for reporting, monitoring, or enforcement. In addition, competition between the two associations for membership and influence weakened the incentives of each association for strict oversight of the code.

The need for a system to promote stronger NGO governance in Uganda was subsequently underscored by two events. First, in 2004 the government reintroduced in Parliament a long-dormant bill to amend the Non-governmental Organizations Registration Act. The provisions of the act gave the government more control over the activities of NGOs and narrowly defined the scope of allowable policy and advocacy activities. The bill was passed by Parliament and forwarded to the president for signature. The reaction among NGOs was swift. Rivalries among networks and associations were laid aside as NGOs formed the Coalition on the NGO Bill (CONOB). The coalition held sector-wide meetings, took out advertisements in the newspaper, and conducted a media campaign against the bill. While President Museveni ultimately did not sign the bill, the threat of the legislation had been enough to galvanize coordinated action.

The second impetus for collective action may have been the suspension of funds to Uganda by the Global Fund to Fight AIDS, Tuberculosis and Malaria on the grounds of corruption and misuse of funds. Subsequent investigations revealed that Global Fund resources administered by the government had been channeled through bogus NGOs linked to members of Parliament, government ministers, and other government officials. The resulting scandal may have provided legitimate NGOs with a strong rationale for developing screening mechanisms that could separate legitimate from illegitimate organizations. Surveys of Ugandan NGOs and the relatively high level of private foreign assistance to NGOs in the country suggest that many organizations may not have purely charitable motivations.[45]

The combination of government threat, public scandal, and a new willingness of previously competitive NGO membership associations to work together also galvanized the support of donors, who saw a window of opportunity for developing a new, national system for NGO governance. With donor support, the two major umbrella organizations collaborated in 2006 on the development of the Quality Assurance Mechanism (QuAM), a certification system that includes detailed and specific standards for NGO behavior and a clear monitoring and enforcement system. To receive certification, NGOs must complete a detailed application and documentation process that is audited by district "quality assurance committees" that act as certification bodies.

The QuAM system had its origins in the perceived weaknesses of the old system. It was clear to NGOs that some form of strong standard setting and accountability was needed. A critical factor in the development of QuAM was the ongoing and consistent support for the process by a major donor, the Danish aid agency DANIDA. In addition, the perceived strength of the regulatory threat gave the NGO Forum and DENIVA incentives to cooperate and to develop a district-level mechanism, even though the districts had been the sites of the most intense competition between the two organizations. Finally, QuAM developers were able to draw on a wide range of existing NGO self-regulation systems worldwide that had not been available to their predecessors in Kenya. QuAM developers hoped that the accreditation system would address the threat of government regulation and the desire of donors to be able to distinguish legitimate NGOs from illegitimate ones.

QuAM was an ambitious initiative, and it struggled to develop a business model and systems to support national- and district-level certification. For the first five years of the program, participation was quite weak and institutionalization hampered by competition between the two main umbrella organizations. By 2015, more than fifty NGOs had sought and received certification at one of the three QuAM levels. QuAM had also been recognized as one of nine partners in a global effort to develop a Global Standard for CSO Accountability.

---

[45] Ronelle Burger and Trudy Owens, "Examining Accountability Mechanisms in Development Projects of Ugandan NGOs: Comparing the Merits of Self-Regulation, Government Regulation and Community Monitoring" (paper presented at International Society for Third-Sector Research Conference, Barcelona, July 9–12, 2008); Marcel Fafchamps and Trudy Owens, "Is International Funding Crowding Out Charitable Contributions in African NGOs?," mimeograph, February 2006.

Just as QuAM was getting its footing, however, the government signaled its intent to narrow the legal space for civil society activity. The president assented to the Public Order Management Bill in 2013, giving police discretionary power to prohibit public meetings and to regulate public discussions of political issues.[46] NGOs were also ordered to reregister with the NGO board. In addition, the proposed Anti-Homosexuality Act 2014 (ultimately nullified in August 2014), posed grave threats to NGOs engaging in any advocacy work for gay rights. The Prohibition of Promotion of Unnatural Sexual Practices bill, introduced in October 2014, is, however, similar in spirit to the Anti-Homosexuality Act. Section 13 of the Anti-Homosexuality Act criminalized any person who "promotes homosexuality," which could be interpreted to include NGOs that advocate for gay rights.[47] The pressure continues. In November 2015, the Ugandan Parliament passed the Non-governmental Organisations (NGO) Bill 2015. Observers speculate that the timing of the bill was not unrelated to elections to be held in February 2016. Section 5 of the bill establishes a National Bureau for NGOs, which is granted broad powers that include the ability to refuse to register an NGO, to issue and/or revoke permits, and to restrict the employment of foreign nationals. NGOs may not engage in activities "prejudicial to the national interest of Uganda," and the bill requires governmental approval of staffing plans and permits the dissolution of NGOs at will.[48] The bill now awaits the president's signature.

NGOs have once more banded together to oppose the bill, with the strongest dissent coming from human rights organizations that may be most affected by the bill's provisions. The Uganda National NGO Forum convened a number of NGOs to prepare a position paper that provides a clause-by-clause rebuttal of the bill's more contentious proposals, including the bill's expressed desire to move forward with mandatory codes of conduct and certification, rather than the voluntary self-regulatory mechanism embodied in QuAM.[49]

4.3.3 *Self-Regulation in Malawi and Tanzania*

Kenya and Uganda have the largest and most institutionalized NGO sectors of the five country cases. Both countries have been able to develop functional systems of self-regulation, although these remain highly contested. In Malawi

---

[46] ICNL, *NGO Monitor: Uganda*, accessed December 30, 2015, www.icnl.org/research/monitor/uganda.html.
[47] Ibid.   [48] Ibid.
[49] Uganda National NGO Forum, "A Position Paper and Clause by Clause Analysis of the NGO Bill 2015," *NGO Forum*, Kampala (2015).

and Tanzania, NGOs have been less able to extract themselves from the reach of the state to develop autonomous systems of self-regulation. The state in both countries has shown a marked preference for mandatory quasi-public regulation, but without a willingness to fund or otherwise institutionalize such systems. As in Kenya and Uganda, mistrust of NGOs on the part of government continues, and elections provide the impetus for repressive regulatory forays.

4.3.3.1 Malawi

In the 1990s the Malawian government began to draft a new act defining a regulatory system for NGOs. The government's stated goal was to develop a regulatory system in which NGO policy was formulated and implemented with NGO participation, similar to the self-regulatory system recently developed in Kenya. The need for a new regulatory system that offered legal protections to NGOs was made clear during the 1999 elections, during which several key civic education NGOs were closed down in the wake of (allegedly politically motivated) accusations of corruption and misuse of funds by donors.[50]

A key NGO player in the consultations over reform was the Council for Nongovernmental Organizations in Malawi (CONGOMA). CONGOMA had been formed in the early 1990s as a relief coordination agency, but by the later part of the decade was the largest NGO umbrella association in the country. During the "consultative" phase of legislative design, CONGOMA facilitated a series of meetings between NGOs and government officials over the content of legislation.

When provisions of the proposed NGO act were made public in late 2000, however, the contents were a surprise to many NGOs, who argued that the legislation included provisions that had not been discussed in the consultative phase. The bill designated CONGOMA as the official coordinating body for NGOs, required all NGOs to join the association, and charged CONGOMA with developing and maintaining a code of conduct for the sector. Some NGOs felt the bill gave the government and CONGOMA excessive powers, and fifteen prominent NGOs issued a public appeal against the bill. CONGOMA's unwillingness to come out against the bill undermined its legitimacy with some NGOs, who felt it could no longer act independently of

---

[50] Heiko Meinhardt and Nandidi Patel, "Malawi's Process of Democratic Transition: An Analysis of Political Developments between 1990 and 2003," Occasional Paper, Konrad Adenauer Foundation (2003), accessed January 22, 2016, www.kas.de/wf/doc/kas_4009-544-2-30.pdf.

government; many NGOs suspected the association was worried about losing the privileges and monopoly status it currently enjoyed.[51]

The NGO act attempted to establish a national self-regulatory system in Malawi. NGOs were required to show proof of membership with CON-GOMA before they could obtain official government registration. Unlike in Kenya, however, the designation of an official coordinating body by government had not been undertaken in full consultation with NGOs. In Kenya, an entirely new body was created as a response to NGO legislation and with widespread NGO participation. In Malawi, the NGO act privileged an existing organization, and the lack of transparency in the process raised doubts among NGOs about its independence. Unlike in Kenya, donors played little role in the development of self-regulation in Malawi. Regulatory reform in Malawi took place after the initial move to democracy, so the issue of NGO regulation was not as clearly framed as an issue of democracy and opposition to an authoritarian regime, as it had been in Kenya and in the early phases in Uganda. In general, the donor community in Malawi has been much less supportive of NGO political activity, and most donors avoided the controversy over CONGOMA completely.[52] Unlike the NGO Council in Kenya, the regulatory power of CONGOMA was not codified in any way, either through legislation or through the development of a concrete administrative structure that could manage the code. Thus, NGOs are required join CONGOMA in principle, but the association has little recourse if NGOs do not comply; it appears that many do not.

Since this process was completed in Malawi, there has been little sustained energy or effort to revisit the NGO regulatory framework until recently. Self-regulation in Malawi was largely dormant during the second regulatory phase. More recently, the government has begun to take a more threatening stance toward NGOs. In spring 2013, the NGO Board threatened to close all NGOs that were not registered under the terms of the 2000 NGO Act by June 30 of that year, although the deadline passed without action on the government's part. In the early months of 2014, the NGO Board again threatened to close unregistered NGOs, even though closure is outside the authority of the board. Many NGO leaders speculated that these threats were undertaken to curtail NGO activity in advance of upcoming elections. In the summer and again in

---

[51] Gilbert Mkamanga and Fanwell Bokosi, *Council for Nongovernmental Organizations in Malawi (CONGOMA) Consultative Appraisal* (Malawi: GilEnterprise Consultants, 2001).

[52] Diane Cammack, "Poor Performing Countries: Malawi, 1980–2002," *Background Paper 3, ODI Study on Poor Performing Countries* (London: Overseas Development Institute Malawi, 2004).

the fall of 2014, the new president announced the government would prioritize a review of the Malawi's NGO Act.

According to members of civil society knowledgeable about the government's plans, the new NGO Act would allow the intelligence service to monitor NGO operations, keeping NGOs under a state of constant surveillance and allowing the president's office to review any request to carry out research in the country.[53] The president, however, claimed the purpose of the new act would be to "improve internal NGO governance," "prevent [NGOs] from being used by politicians," "strengthen the compliance monitoring capacity of the NGO Board," and "ensure more capacity building of NGOs."[54] CONGOMA further undermined its claim to speak for NGOs when the Speaker responded positively toward the prospective legislation, saying that it would improve the NGO/state relations and help prevent NGOs from becoming puppets for politicians.[55] In June 2015, about 320 NGOs in the country, including some led by prominent and vocal activists, were threatened with closure for failing to register with the NGO Board.[56]

4.3.3.2 Tanzania

At roughly the same time as Malawi, Tanzania also embarked on a process designed to produce a new NGO policy framework and regulatory system in 1996. As in Malawi, the process began in a consultative manner with the government seeking out NGO participation. The three major umbrella organizations, the Tanzanian Association of Non-governmental Organizations (TANGO), the Tanzanian Council for Social Development (TACOSODE), and the Association of Non-governmental Organizations of Zanzibar (ANGOZA) were lead actors for NGOs and organized workshops for NGO input on the potential content of a national NGO policy. A series of five draft documents were produced over the course of the next three years, with substantial NGO input at the national and local levels. The participatory and consultative nature of the process was partly a result of the fragmentation of the existing regulatory framework. NGOs in Tanzania had the ability to register with the government in multiple ways (including with a large number of line ministries), and therefore a number of legal frameworks could be

---

[53] ICNL, *NGO Monitor: Malawi*, accessed December 30, 2015, www.icnl.org/research/monitor/malawi.html.
[54] Ibid. [55] Ibid.
[56] Edith Gondwe, "Illegal NGOS under Fire," *Malawi Times*, June 10, 2015, accessed January 22, 2016, www.times.mw/illegal-ngos-under-fire/.

applied to govern registration or operation. Changing the system therefore meant changing the rules of the game for a large number of players.

After several iterations, however, the process broke down when the idea of creating a new apex body for NGOs was proposed. This proposal had strong donor and government support, but NGOs protested. As the fifth draft policy was being developed in 1999, the head of the donor-supported Aid Management and Accountability Program (AMAP) initiated a parallel consultative process on the establishment of an NGO apex body.[57] The key NGO associations and their members threatened to pull out of the policy process altogether, leading to a near breakdown. The fifth draft of the policy was ultimately adopted in 2000. The government, however, continued to develop a new NGO Act, but now without NGO consultation. The final bill was introduced in Parliament in 2002 and retained much of the old restrictive legislation while adding new layers of regulation.[58] NGOs mounted a very public campaign against the bill, but it ultimately passed into law.

The window for negotiating a viable self-regulation system in Tanzania appeared to have closed. Many NGOs and umbrella associations were distrustful of the process and the idea of an apex body with self-regulating powers. The potential for collective action in Tanzania was complicated by the existence of two strong mainland NGO associations, as well as an association representing NGOs on the island of Zanzibar (which has an autonomous legal system). Had the government initially proposed more restrictive legislation, divisions might have been overcome in the quest to oppose it. But the consultative process did nothing to assuage the fears of each association that it might be left out of the final institutional arrangements. Moreover, the government's initiation of a parallel process led to confusion and competition over who might sponsor the code. Finally, donors threw their weight behind the idea of a new apex NGO body, rather than supporting the position of NGO associations, further fragmenting the process.

After the passage of the act, a group of NGOs known as the NGO Act Core Group continued to lobby for amendments to relax the most restrictive of the act's provisions. TANGO was a leader in this effort, along with the Legal and Human Rights Centre (LHRC) and Haki Ardhi (The Land Rights Research and Resources Institute), with support from the international NGO Pact and

---

[57] Cosmas Mogella, *The State and Civil Society Relations in Tanzania: The Case of the National NGOs Policy* (Dar es Salaam: University of Dar es Salaam, 1999).

[58] Emeka Iheme, "Response to Strengthening *Civil Society in the South: Challenges and Constraints – A Case Study of Tanzania*," *International Journal of Not-for-Profit Law* 8(1) (2005), accessed January 22, 2016, www.icnl.org/research/journal/vol8iss1/special_3r.htm.

the International Center for Not-for-Profit Law (ICNL). This group ultimately succeeded in 2005 in getting a number of amendments passed to the NGO Act. These amendments gave legal personality to NGOs, recognizing an NGO as a body corporate capable of owning property, entering into contracts, and to sue or be sued.[59]

Meanwhile, the NGO regulatory and self-regulatory institutional structure in Tanzania has languished. The NGO Act created the National Council of NGOs (NACONGO) and charged it with the responsibility for coordination and self-regulation of NGOs in Tanzania. The council, however, was given no resources for its operation and met only a few times in the first few years of its existence.[60] In 2006, the NGOs Coordination Division was established by the government under the Ministry of Community Development, Gender and Children. Before that, NGO Coordination had been a unit in the vice president's office. The division is split into two sections, with the Registration Section responsible for overseeing NGO registration under the NGO Act, and the NGOs Coordination and Monitoring Section functioning as the registrar and secretariat for the National NGO Coordination Board and charged with working with NACONGO. NACONGO is recognized as the self-regulatory body of NGOs in the country, although it has little institutional structure or resources.[61] Nonetheless, section 27 of the NGO Act charges NACONGO with the responsibility to develop a code of conduct and such other regulations to facilitate self-regulation.

In 2008 NACONGO released its NGO Conduct of Conduct to somewhat mixed reactions from the NGO community.[62] Some felt the code was a creature of the government, rather than NGOs, and others worried that it would be difficult to disseminate and popularize across the country.[63] A 2013 survey by TANGO suggested that knowledge of the code among NGOs remained relatively low.[64]

The situation appeared to be at a stalemate until September 2015, when the Office of the Prime Minister issued a directive under the Non-Governmental

---

[59] Tanzania Association on Non-Governmental Organisations (TANGO), *Reviewing Tanzania's Non Profit Legislative Regime and Need for a New Regulatory Framework* (2013), accessed January 22, 2016, http://eacsof.net/upload/REPORTS/Analysis%20Civic%20Space/TzNGORegimeReport-FinalSept2013.pdf.

[60] Tanzania Commission for AIDS (TACAIDS), "NACONGO," accessed January 22, 2016, www.tacaids.go.tz/index.php?option=com_content&view=article&id=150:nacongo&catid=61&Itemid=107.

[61] Ibid.

[62] Policy Forum Tanzania, "Transparency and Accountability within Civil Society: An Opportunity for Self-Reflection," July 25, 2008.

[63] Ibid.   [64] TANGO, n. 59.

Organisations Act to all civil society organizations to, among others, submit their annual budgetary estimates, lists of activities planned for every quarter, and the regions in which such activities were planned. NGOs found the timing of the provision suspect, seeing a connection between the directive and the upcoming national referendum.[65]

4.4 DISCUSSION

These five country cases highlight the challenges of institutionalizing effective self-regulation regimes among NGOs, as well as how waves of regulatory proposals and responses have shaped the current institutional environment in Africa. Self-regulation was ushered in by Kenya in the early days of democratization, and in recent years NGOs actually took the lead drafting a new NGO law building a new self-regulatory body. In Uganda, initial efforts at self-regulation followed those of Kenya, but, coming later, NGO leaders were able to build on the Kenyan experience and a wider set of global experience to develop a truly independent system of standards and certification. As in Kenya, that self-regulatory system has been strengthened in recent years, but it remains to be seen whether it can survive the government's new efforts at repression. In Tanzania and Malawi, the waves of regulation and self-regulation have been weaker, and this chapter has argued that this is due both to the weak nature of collective action institutions on the ground and to weaker regulatory threats by the state. Ethiopia remains somewhat of an outlier. In spite of reasonably successful efforts to build a self-regulation regime under CRDA, the repressive law passed in 2009 effectively silenced such efforts as NGOs focused largely on survival.

Across the country cases, we see several patterns. First, the level of threat posed by regulatory reform was perceived by NGOs as high in all three countries where the institutionalization of self-regulation took place. In Kenya, government legislation centralized control over registration and sought to control the NGO Board charged with sector oversight. In Ethiopia, the escalating operational requirements for NGOs in the first wave of regulation pushed the only NGO association in the country to develop a system of self-regulation. In Uganda, the rapid passage by Parliament of new legislation in 2004 that gave government stronger powers over deregistration and threatened

---

[65] Bernard Mwinzi, "Jittery Times as Tanzania Tightens in Grip on Civil Society ahead of General Elections," *Daily Nation*, November 13, 2014, accessed January 22, 2016, www.nation .co.ke/lifestyle/DN2/Tanzania-civil-society-General-Elections/-/957860/2521646/-/beqlwkz/-/ index.html.

to curtail political participation galvanized NGOs into collective action. In all three of these countries, the government's initial attempt at reform was relatively hostile and characterized by low levels of engagement with NGOs. All three countries were essentially autocracies at the time of reform, although each was moving toward political liberalization.

Finally, international donors played an important role in all three cases where strong self-regulation emerged. In Kenya, donors provided support to the nascent NGO network opposing the government as part of the democracy movement, and many international NGOs were key actors in the network. Donor countries also placed public pressure on Kenyan government officials by threatening to withdraw aid. In Uganda, donors also supported the emergence of new NGO governance structures, although the support was financial rather than political. Many international agencies and donor countries publicly condemned the NGO legislation passed by the Ugandan Parliament, and the World Bank quietly supported the NGO antilegislation coalition that emerged. DANIDA played an important role by providing ongoing support to the two NGO umbrella organizations for the development of the new accreditation system. In Ethiopia, donor support was again financial rather than political in the first wave. Donors provided ongoing support to CRDA; indeed, many were dependent on CRDA for the identification of local partner agencies. The British NGO ActionAid played a critical role in the development of alternative legislative proposals, and the US organization Pact provided key financial support for the development of the code of conduct. In Ethiopia, as in Uganda and Kenya, donors were the patrons who helped to underwrite the costs of collective action.

In Tanzania and Malawi, donor support was weaker, both politically and financially. In Malawi, NGO reform occurred after the initial political liberalization and was never framed as an issue of democracy. Moreover, donors wavered in their support of the main umbrella association, CONGOMA. In Tanzania, donor support for an alternative plan not supported by most NGO associations actually served to fracture the process. In all three of these countries, the threat to the NGO sector posed by legal reform was initially perceived as less severe than in the other countries. Where donors viewed the threat of government regulation as a threat to democracy, as in Kenya and Uganda, they were more likely to throw their weight behind the collective efforts of NGOs to resist. Where reform emerged more as "politics as usual," as in Malawi and Tanzania, donor support was less forthcoming. In addition, the fragmentation of interests and positions among competing NGO associations may have led donors to resist involvement.

The literature on interest groups and business associations suggests that successful associational collective action emerges in the face of strong threats and broad-based associational representation. The analysis presented here suggests that in the developing country context, donor support also plays a critical role in underwriting collective action and creating a protected space for associational activity. Such donor support may have been more forthcoming in cases of higher threat where donors perceived that democratic reforms were at stake. Where governments took a less hostile attitude toward regulatory reform, donor involvement in the reform process was lower, and NGO associations were more likely to fracture. This was true in Tanzania where multiple associations competed for support, as well as in Malawi where a single association failed to mobilize sufficient support from the sector. Thus in the cases examined here, regulatory threat and donor support appear to be intertwined. Self-regulation regimes emerged largely in countries with relatively hostile governments that pursued policies that were inimical to NGO interests. These threats were severe enough to mobilize support from international donors, particularly when the issue was framed as one of democracy or freedom of association.

The ironic feature of the cases in which self-regulation appears seems to be that a government crackdown is necessary to convince NGOs to put aside their differences and act collectively. More recent events in Ethiopia, however, suggest there is a level of repression beyond which NGOs cannot recover. Uganda's new law approaches this level. In this most recent wave, moreover, donor governments appear less willing to publicly support NGOs. This may be because in a post-9/11 world these governments are seen by Western donors as important allies and bulwarks against terrorism. Moreover, the five cases also suggest that African governments still see NGOs as a threat and a source of opposition. Impending elections appear to result in regulatory crackdowns intended to muffle NGO voices. If Ethiopia provides a dangerous model for government repression of NGOs, Kenya provides a more hopeful model that suggests that as democratic institutions take hold, civil society will be better able to negotiate with the state and take the lead in developing self-regulatory institutions that strengthen the sector.

5

State Regulation and the Emergence of Self-Regulation in the Chinese and Vietnamese Nonprofit and Philanthropic Sectors

MARK SIDEL

5.1 INTRODUCTION

It is beyond dispute that both China and Vietnam are intent on a strong regulatory agenda for their rapidly growing nonprofit and philanthropic sectors. Strong regulation is one aspect of control of civil society groups, and there are a number of reasons for both the intense focus on regulation and its place among the various control mechanisms, formal and informal, available to both the Chinese and Vietnamese states. China and Vietnam utilize diverse means of regulation and other forms of control over the emergence of civil society and its organizations: they seek to channel both nonprofit and philanthropic activity into state-favored paths while allowing the remainder of nonprofit and philanthropic activity to walk paths that are not state disfavored. They differentiate clearly among types of organizations, some being more state favored, others in a more neutral situation; still others are watched carefully; and a fourth category is quasi-banned or formally banned. They seek to prevent nonprofit and philanthropic groups from fomenting contention and competition within party and state apparatuses.

* Research for this chapter was supported by the Indiana University Research Center for Chinese Politics and Business under grants from the Luce and Ford foundations and the University of Wisconsin-Madison. My particular thanks to a number of Chinese and Vietnamese organizations and colleagues for discussions on these themes during multiple visits between 2012 and 2015. This chapter has also benefited from my work as consultant to the International Center for Not-for-Profit Law (ICNL). I also acknowledge with gratitude that I have learned a great deal on these issues through work and research on nonprofit regulation and self-regulation in China with ICNL, the Norwegian Center for Human Rights (NCHR), Gates Foundation, Asia Foundation, Golden Bridges, China Medical Board, and other organizations; and in Vietnam with ICNL, the Research Center for Management and Sustainable Development (MSD) (Hanoi), the LIN Center for Community Development (HCMC), Irish Aid, the United Nations Development Programme (UNDP), NCHR, and other groups. None of those groups is responsible for analysis and conclusions here.

Both broader control and the important subset of control that is regulation have not come easy to either party or state. The content of regulation has been under sharp contention in both countries. Unable to differentiate effectively among organizations and channels of activity at the national level, and understandably wary of national experimentation in such a fraught field, China has turned to local experimentation (in Guangdong and elsewhere) in the nonprofit regulatory sphere – akin to what it has done in economic regulatory reform and in other fields. In both countries, the "control" aspects of regulation remain strong and increasingly differentiated by field, but the transparency and accountability mandates of regulation remain weak. Yet in both countries, earlier and especially in China but now in Vietnam as well, regulatory process seem at times hopelessly unable to keep up with the dual threats of increased contention among powerful state and nonstate actors (including now private philanthropic actors) and the increased complexity of the fields to be regulated. So control remains paramount, while regulation – an increasing important control mechanism, at least in theory – falls further and further behind its goals.

As this volume shows in a number of country and regional contexts, regulatory intervention in the nonprofit arena often comes in waves. This is true even in heavily controlling and channeling oriented states such as China and Vietnam. Such intervention often takes the form of statutory regulation, though it can also involve nonlegal (that is, thuggish) control mechanisms as well, such as extra-legal arrests and detentions of women's rights and labor activists in 2015 or clearly illegal uses of regulatory means. In recent decades – not just in China and Vietnam (more recently) but around the world – regulatory intervention has been accompanied by an array of self-regulatory initiatives as well. Although China and Vietnam are examples of overarching regulator-based control, with strong state regulation to the virtual exclusion of self-regulation, there is now perhaps the very initial emergence of a more nuanced and related development of the two, though state regulation clearly remains in the ascendancy.[1]

---

[1] For an earlier discussion of forms of self-regulation in Asia, including some more general discussion of China, see Mark Sidel, "The Promise and Limits of Collective Action for Nonprofit Self-Regulation: Evidence from Asia," *Nonprofit and Voluntary Sector Quarterly* 39(6) (2009): 1039–1056. For the earliest survey of nonprofit self-regulation efforts in Asia, see Mark Sidel, *Trends in Nonprofit Self-Regulation in the Asia Pacific Region: Initial Data on Initiatives, Experiments and Models in Seventeen Countries* (2003), accessed January 7, 2016, http://asianphilanthropy.org/APPC/APPC-conference-2003/Nonprofit-SelfRegulation-msidel .pdf. On the broader themes, see Alison Dunn and Mark Sidel, "Law Reform and the Regulation of Charities: Some Comparative Thoughts," *Charity Law & Practice Review* 17 (2014–2015): 139–150.

In China and Vietnam, in contrast to some of the other countries discussed in this volume, the party and state have permitted the slow emergence of some entirely nascent self-regulatory or quasi-autonomous sector initiatives that do not threaten state control over the nonprofit sector but help the state control the sector through enforced accountability, data gathering, and other means. In China and Vietnam, the various forms of self-regulation, broadly defined, have facilitated and strengthened state control of the nonprofit sector and have not served as a point of departure – at least not so far – toward more autonomous control of the nonprofit sector's own affairs. In short, in China and Vietnam, self-regulation and sectoral self-development (through data collection, capacity building, and other initiatives) do not currently challenge party and state control but facilitate it. And in some cases in China, particularly the China Foundation Center (CFC) discussed below, some of the quasi-autonomous activities of the nonprofit sector itself are doing a better job than the state in measuring and enhancing sectoral activity.

5.2 THE CHALLENGES OF NONPROFIT REGULATION IN CHINA

The successes, failures, and aims of regulatory practice as part of a control and channeling mechanism are reasonably clear in China. A series of basic documents and the more specific implementing documents under them have provided an initial control- and approval-based framework for formation, registration, governance, oversight, tax status, and other key elements of nonprofits and philanthropic organizations.[2] The fiscal framework for this activity has rapidly become considerably more complex as well, yet still mirrors the political policy of encouraging nonprofit and philanthropic activity that the government favors (particularly in service provision), while serving to discourage, control, and constrain nonprofit activity that the government does not want to see occur.

In the philanthropic framework, the available legal documents and the framework are somewhat sparser. These include the new Charity Law Regulations on the Management of Foundations 2004 (replacing earlier sets of regulations on foundations), as well as the Public Welfare Donations Law 1999 and a range of documents issued over the years that deal with specific

---

[2]   There is of course a wide array of regulatory documents on specific issues and subsectors, including in health – too many to list here, though a more specific discussion is in Mark Sidel, "The Shifting Balance of Philanthropic Policies and Regulation in China," in *Philanthropy for Health in China*, ed. Jennifer Ryan, Lincoln C. Chen, and Tony Saich (Bloomington: Indiana University Press, 2014), 49; the US International Grantmaking China note, accessed January 7, 2016, www.cof.org/content/china.

foundation and other philanthropic issues.[3] These cover a variety of important issues, including regulations on foundation names,[4] on information disclosure by foundations,[5] on annual inspection of foundations,[6] and on audit guidelines for foundations.[7] There are even more specific regulatory documents on particular issues in the philanthropic arena, such as documents on foreign philanthropy[8] or, controversially, on donations of foreign exchange to domestic organizations.[9]

Yet despite all this regulation making, the Chinese framework for legal regulation of both the broader nonprofit sector and the specific philanthropic part of it could not be completed through the promulgation of even more implementing rules and notices. That regulatory framework was now increasingly rickety and out of date and difficult to implement and enforce, particularly in light of inappropriate practices and the occasional charity or philanthropic scandal. And that framework was made either overly general or directly obsolete, by the march of time and particularly by the rapid development of philanthropic and nonprofit organizations around China and by the Chinese government's commitment over the past decade to explore different approaches and reforms in this sector in recent years. This inevitable obsolescence comes from some positive developments, including the growth of the sector and its increasing roles in Chinese society. At the same time, the regulatory structure and the broader legal framework outside nonprofits have been unable to fully respond to emerging problems, such as more instances of fraud or inappropriate practices in the sector. The legal framework for the nonprofit sector has done a considerably better job at

---

3   They govern the basics of the philanthropic sector, at least as envisioned in the early part of the last decade. These include the differentiation of two types of foundations: "public fundraising foundations," generally closer to the government, which are allowed to raise funds from the public (*gongmu jijinhui*), and "non-public fundraising foundations," akin to private foundations in other countries, which receive funds largely from key donors and are generally not permitted to raise funds from the public (*feigongmu jijinhui*).

4   For example, the *Provisions on the Administration of Names of Foundations* (Beijing: Ministry of Civil Affairs, 2004).

5   For example, *Measures for the Information Disclosure of Foundations* (Beijing: Ministry of Civil Affairs, 2006).

6   For example, ibid.

7   In part a response to scandals involving foundations, these are the Ministry of Finance and Ministry of Civil Affairs, *Notice on Strengthening and Perfecting the Audit System of Foundations by Chartered Accountants* (2011).

8   See, for example, *Notice of the General Office of the Ministry of Health on the Provisions on the Administration of the Representative Agencies of Overseas Foundations Whose Businesses Are under the Charge of the Ministry of Health* (March 27, 2008).

9   *Notice of the State Administration of Foreign Exchange on Issues Concerning the Administration of Foreign Exchange Donated to or by Domestic Institutions* (No. 63 [2009]).

facilitating state control of the growth and programmatic directions of the sector than at safeguarding the rights of those who try to form and register organizations or work in them. Recent developments, however, may improve these issues, particularly the enactment of China's first omnibus philanthropy legislation, the Charity Law, in spring 2016.

5.3 THE CHALLENGES OF SELF-REGULATION AND SECTOR SELF-DEVELOPMENT IN CHINA

Into this complex picture of regulation, control, and facilitation in China comes self-regulation.

5.3.1 *The Origins of the Idea of Nonprofit Self-Regulation in China*

The notion of nonprofit self-regulation in China may seem like a contradiction in terms, particularly given the intensive state control of the nonprofit sector, but it is indeed an emerging reality. Self-regulation has a long if slow and fitful developmental history in China, one tied to weaknesses of accountability and transparency. Ideas of nonprofit self-regulation began to percolate in China in the 1990s, but the first detailed proposal came from the leader of the Chinese Nonprofit Organization (NPO) Network, Shang Yusheng, in 2001. Shang's proposed *Standards for NPO Self-Regulation*[10] were tactically visionary for their time in China, if largely impossible to implement. Shang combined self-evident principles of state regulation that the state could not object to ("obey the Constitution and other laws and abide by their own organizational constitutions [bylaws]," "uphold their public benefit mission," "stick to the organization's not-for-profit principle, not pursue self-interest for any individual or family") with goals for a self-regulation process that extended beyond state regulation in careful ways that overlapped with state regulation but clearly exceeded it: "Insist on exchange of information, sharing of resources, and mutual cooperation; Insist on self-autonomy and independence ... ; Follow fair and reasonable sponsorship and evaluation, and not abuse written rules and process under any circumstances ... "[11]

---

[10] For a tribute to Shang Yusheng's early work at the time that the *Declaration of Chinese Private Foundations on Self-Regulation* was being issued and discussed, see 徐永光主题发言:推动中国基金会行业透明的几位代表人物 (Xu Yongguang, Keynote Address, "Representative Figures in Promoting Sectoral Transparency among Chinese Foundations"), (July 8, 2010), accessed January 7, 2016, www.foundationcenter.org.cn/guanli/html/2010-07/1210.html. This early history is also discussed in Sidel, "Promise and Limits," n. 1.

[11] Xu Yongguang, Keynote Address.

This was a long-term strategy for bolstering and improving state regulation, while seeking to set the stage to reach beyond it, very carefully and over much time, to find a somewhat different role for nonprofit self-regulation. Such a long-term strategy has remained a hallmark of Chinese self-regulatory efforts. So too was another aspect of Professor Shang's 2001 initial foray into self-regulation: the attempt to promote self-regulatory initiatives as a way of undertaking organizational self-regulatory entrepreneurship and strengthen the role of umbrella organizations.[12] Building the role and power of umbrella nonprofit organizations as "self-regulatory entrepreneurs" has been as much a goal of self-regulatory initiatives in China and Vietnam as it has been in the United States and other countries.[13]

As a self-regulatory initiative, not much became of Professor Shang's standards. In 2001 in China, there was neither enough activity nor sufficient organizational or sectoral power for even overlapping and mild self-regulatory initiatives to take hold. As a form of organizational entrepreneurism and a thought leadership initiative for an emerging national group of Chinese nonprofits, those initial standards were useful for a time as a basis for discussion and debate. And the principles enunciated echoed clearly with the state's priorities in regulating and controlling the Chinese nonprofit and philanthropic sector.

5.3.2 *The Expansion of Regulation and the Rocky Road for Self-Regulation*

Chinese nonprofit self-regulation languished for another eight years or so, but in the meantime the Chinese state did not languish. The state was undertaking its own waves of regulation, determined to control and channel this burgeoning sector, focus its work on providing social services to China's population, and prevent any part of it from becoming a significant critic or threat to the Chinese Communist Party or the Chinese state. Between 2001 and 2009, the Chinese state undertook extensive regulatory activity on the nonprofit sector, including in the areas of disclosure, accountability, and transparency that were among the few fields even potentially open to self-regulation in China. The state had already monopolized such areas as

---

[12] Little has been written about Professor Shang's initiative in English, though much more in Chinese. I am grateful to him for discussions on these issues in 2007.
[13] For a discussion of this issue (and, in my view, problem) of "self-regulatory entrepreneurs" in the US context, see Mark Sidel, "The Guardians Guarding Themselves: A Comparative Perspective on Nonprofit Self-Regulation," *Chicago-Kent Law Review* 80 (2005): 803–835. This feature is fully on display in Vietnam, as the later part of this chapter shows.

registration, tax treatment, and other key markers of state control.[14] For virtually the full array of social organizations, associations, public non-enterprise units, and foundations, the state promulgated waves of regulation on registration, governance, reporting, disclosure, transparency, accountability, and other areas.

In effect, Chinese state regulation of the nonprofit and philanthropic sector – baseline regulation in the late 1990s and early 2000s, followed by increasingly detailed implementing and other regulatory provisions through the first decade of this century – overwhelmed any inroads or other paths self-regulation might seek to chart, a form of "crowding out" self-regulatory initiatives. For the Chinese state, regulation and control were goals in itself; they were not a "response" to self-regulatory initiatives. For the Chinese nonprofit and philanthropic community, finding its way back to self-regulation in the face of waves of control-based regulatory activity by a highly active state has indeed proven very difficult. Yet two initiatives toward the end of the 2000–2010 decade gave some new life to an expanded notion of self-regulation. One of those was explicitly self-regulatory, while the other might be seen as establishing the foundation for a cautious self-regulatory future.

5.3.3 *The 2009 Reemergence of Self-Regulation in the Chinese Private Foundation Context*

The explicitly self-regulatory initiative was the *Declaration of Chinese Private Foundations on Self-Regulation* (中国非公募基金会自律宣言 (2009年7月)), adopted in July 2009 by the Chinese Private Foundation Forum, a national umbrella association for China's private funders. The Private Foundation Forum initiative and the *Declaration* that emerged from it were, as are many self-regulatory initiatives, motivated by a number of overlapping factors. Certainly, strengthening the quality of practice, transparency, and accountability in the Chinese nonprofit sector was among them. So too was the beginning of a long-term effort to take back from the government some autonomy in the regulation of that transparency and accountability. The *Declaration* called for China's new and rapidly growing private foundations to comply with the law, maintain their public benefit mission, avoid conflicts of interest, give effect to the role of charters (bylaws) and Boards, ensure that their financing should be consistent with mission and values, respect donor wishes, undertake public

---

[14] For a discussion of early disclosure and transparency regulations in the philanthropy arena see, among other sources, Karla Simon, *Civil Society in China* (New York: Oxford University Press, 2013), 252–253.

financial statements and audits, establish monitoring and assessment, establish human resource policies, undertake both competition and partnerships, commit to information disclosure, and submit to supervision and management by state authorities.

The content here is nothing peculiar, innovative, or boundary crossing. Nor was that really the point, since even the general principles enunciated in the *Declaration* were highly useful in the new and somewhat rough and ready world of the Chinese private foundations in 2009. Even more interesting than these attempts to solidify quality practices, however, was the generally implicit attempt, the beginning of a long-term effort, to carve out even a small sphere of regulatory practice that the foundations might share with the state or even, over time, come to "own" as their own.

The other national initiative, less explicitly self-regulatory in nature but also centrally concerned with the long-term autonomy of the foundation sector through autonomous institutions for disclosure and research, was the founding of the CFC, an independent research and data-gathering institution in Beijing. The CFC was a long time in its gestation, and those efforts began several years before the *Declaration*. Yet both foundation practitioners and regulators in Beijing, while lauding the data-driven focus of the CFC, have also noted that it attempted a sort of self-governance carve out as well – an attempt, through building a data-driven institution focused on philanthropic transparency and accountability, to build a separate structure for disclosure, transparency, and research in the foundation context. Its stakeholders were China's private and public foundations, and it worked carefully not to alienate key state regulators such as the Ministry of Civil Affairs.[15]

It was not surprising that these developments occurred in the foundation context. The Chinese foundation sector embodies three characteristics that made this collective action attempt at an initial carve-out of even a small portion of autonomy particularly timely and potentially successful. First, regulation of the rapidly growing Chinese private foundation sector did not keep pace with the growth and diversification of the sector. Regulation remained mired in brief rules issued in 2004,[16] a form of under-regulation that helped give rise to other institutions playing a role in the sector. Disclosure, transparency, and accountability were even less regulated than registration, operations, and reporting to the government, leaving some space – perhaps – for more autonomous self-regulatory activity in those spheres. Periodic scandals in the philanthropic and charitable arena that focused on

---

[15] Interviews in Beijing, November 2012 and August 2013.
[16] Ministry of Civil Affairs, *Regulations on the Management of Foundations* (2004).

overspending or fraudulent receipts[17] only pointed up this problem of under-regulation and insufficient implementation of state regulation.

Second, the Chinese private foundation sector has been dominated by wealthy business people who, while showing clear respect and obedience to central regulatory and political authorities, certainly had more space to experiment with more autonomous self-regulatory governance practices than their domestic NGO and community-based organization counterparts. This combination of under-regulation and economic space set the stage for this initial attempt to carve out the very beginnings of a semi-autonomous area for self-regulation, an initial move in the long path toward some form of self-governance. A third factor, more generic in nature and not necessarily particular to China, is that the foundation sector is often able to provide financing to self-regulatory initiatives more readily than its voluntary sector brethren can to their own self-regulatory initiatives. This has certainly been the case in China, where the only self-funded self-regulatory explorations have been in the foundation sphere.[18]

Faced with these developments and initial moves toward self-governance through the *Declaration* and the formation of the CFC, the state did not sit idly by. In the years that followed the *Declaration*,[19] the state – mostly through central Beijing ministries[20] such as the Ministry of Civil Affairs and Ministry of Finance – stepped in to step up the regulation of foundation disclosure, transparency, and accountability. From 2010 onward, new regulations were promulgated on mandatory disclosure, audits, transparency rules, and other elements of the broad, long-term self-governance agenda initiated by the *Declaration* in 2009. In effect, the state quickly refused to be

---

[17] See, for example, Hannah Beech, "China's Red Cross Is Still Dealing with a 3 Year Old Scandal Involving Sex and Fast Cars," *Time*, August 4, 2014, accessed January 7, 2016, http://time.com/3078429/yunnan-earthquake-red-cross-society-of-china-guo-meimei-sex-scandal/.

[18] The experience in the United States is similar, contrasting the Community Foundations National Standards and National Standards Board, which are funded by the US community foundation sector, and other broader self-regulatory initiatives by Independent Sector, the Panel on the Nonprofit Sector, and others, which have not been easily funded by participants.

[19] Chinese Private Foundation Forum, *Declaration of Chinese Private Foundations on Self-Regulation* (中国非公募基金会自律宣言 (2009年7月)), adopted July 2009.

[20] See, among many other promulgated regulations and documents that could be cited, 民政部关于印发基金会2009年年度检查事项公告的函, accessed January 7, 2016, www.mca.gov.cn/article/zwgk/mzbwg/201002/201005/20100500076882.shtml; a regulatory intensification in 2009–2010, 基金会评估指标 (2011.8 民政部修订), accessed January 7, 2016, www.chinanpo.gov.cn/143606/attachment-143606.html. The rapid attempt to strengthen regulatory responses went down to the provincial level as well. See, for example (Qinghai), 关于对基金会进行2010年年度检查的通知, accessed January 7, 2016, www.qhmgj.gov.cn/Item/Show.asp?m=1&d=1114.

pushed aside, even partly, on these key issues of disclosure, transparency, and accountability.

5.3.4 *Regulation and Self-Regulation in the Chinese Context*

It is not yet fully clear whether the newer wave of foundation regulation in the years following the *Declaration* and the growth of the CFC was merely a response to regulatory gaps and needs and to the reporting of philanthropic and charity scandals, or also a direct response to the implicit, long-term challenge of self-regulation and self-governance. And, as is the case for regulation as well as self-regulation, there are multiple motivations and factors leading to action; it can be very difficult to tease out which are primary in that complex mix.[21] Yet the fact remains that there was an upsurge in government regulation of foundation disclosure, transparency, and accountability after the 2009 *Declaration* and the founding of the CFC. Was that merely a recognition of gaps in that area, gaps that the foundation sector had itself sought to fill? Or was it, as some in Beijing have said, at least in part an attempt by government regulators to maintain a virtual regulatory monopoly on the foundation sector?[22]

Along with a regulatory response to initial self-regulatory impulses came an institutional response as well, one that is perceived by some in Beijing as a response to both disclosure- and transparency-based self-regulatory moves in the *Declaration* and the institutional growth of the CFC. The semi-official China Charity and Donation Information Center was founded in 2006 and gathered steam in 2010 and after. Tied to the Ministry of Civil Affairs, it functioned then and still functions as a form of reporting agency for disclosure, transparency, and accountability for Chinese nonprofits and foundations. In the years that followed, a number of other organizations and initiatives around the Ministry of Civil Affairs also took up the disclosure, transparency, and accountability cause, in part substituting for the *Declaration*'s force and spread. By 2012 and 2013, an entire structure for disclosure and information had arisen under the Ministry, including the national China Charity Information Platform (中国慈善信息平台) on the basis of the earlier and smaller China Charity and Donation Information Center, which still runs these activities.

---

[21] Interviews in Beijing, August 2013.　　[22] Ibid.

5.3.5 *The Future of Regulation and Self-Regulation in China*

If the developments of 2010 and the years after reflect smaller waves of implicitly self-regulatory drafting and institution building interacting with larger and more powerful waves of regulatory initiatives – and not all in China agree on this point, by any means – then the state appears to have had the upper hand from the beginning. We would certainly expect that in China. The *Declaration* remains a training and capacity-building tool in some Chinese foundations, but today in more general terms it is referred to more as a long-term statement of values and goals than as a mechanism toward self-governance. And attention to it seems to have faded.[23] On the other hand, the CFC, while never seeking to assert itself as a separate pole of disclosure and research that might contribute to an explicitly self-governing agenda, has gained institutional strength in the ensuing years. Detailed work by its staff, and a strong link with the Foundation Center in New York, has contributed to that institutional strengthening.

In the meantime, the regulatory situation has grown highly complex. One strand has been identified: the upsurge in disclosure, transparency, and accountability regulation in the years around and after 2010, whether as a response to the *Declaration* or a simultaneous understanding that this area of regulation remained underdeveloped. Other regulatory initiatives have languished, not out of neglect (for legislative and regulatory initiatives may languish in China but they do not do so because they are neglected). Instead, work has proceeded on multiple fronts in terms of regulation of nonprofits and philanthropies at the central level in Beijing, not culminating yet in final action in many of those areas – yet, through that activity, reasserting the power and prerogative of the state rather than the philanthropic and nonprofit sector, as the key regulator of that sector in China.

First, work has continued on the important task of updating the now outdated and overly general foundation, social organization and public non-enterprise institution regulations originally issued in the late 1990s and (for foundations) in 2004. That those revisions have not yet been issued as final documents is owed not to a challenge from self-regulation but to conflicts within the state and between the state and some powerful philanthropic,

---

[23] A 2015 review of the meetings and activities of the China Private Foundation Forum, which had initiated the *Declaration*, had little to say about spread and implementation beyond acknowledging the 2009 announcement of the principles. See *The Seventh China Private Foundation Development Forum* (2015), accessed January 7, 2016, www.cpff.org.cn/newsitem/277132486.

business, and nonprofit interests over specific issues in those sectoral regulations. Added to that – a factor that is sometimes underestimated in exploring
the delays in issuing new laws and regulations on nonprofit and philanthropy
in China – is the constant emergence of new issues that require, in most cases,
years of research and debate to resolve. The treatment of corporate stock
donations – virtually unknown as a significant issue in 2004 when the *Regulations on the Management of Foundations* was issued – is but one example of a
major issue, backed by major government and private actors on various sides,
which slows the updating of sectoral regulation. Other issues have arisen too,
forcing regulators to scramble on shifting ground to regulate charitable trusts,
fundraising, new pressures for tax incentives, and other issues.

Several other factors have slowed the emergence of central regulation even
as regulators have at times sought to blunt self-regulatory urges. An omnibus
Charity Law[24] has been in draft for many years but, until 2015, continued to be
delayed by a combination of interest group politics within the state and from
powerful business, philanthropic, and nonprofit actors, along with – as in the
sectoral regulatory context – the unceasing emergence of new issues that
require significant investment of time, research, and discussion. In 2015, the
National People's Congress, the Chinese national legislature, released a new
draft of the umbrella Charity Law, and it was enacted in the spring of 2016.[25]
Coming to some understanding of how the three main elements of central
regulation should interact – the updating of sectoral regulations on foundations, social organization, and other fields; an omnibus Charity Law; and the
increasing power of a widened variety of central ministries to issue ministry-
based regulations on such issues as tax incentives and other key issues – has
slowed the emergence of a clear regulatory framework.

In that complex arena, though, philanthropy stands as the first part of the
Chinese voluntary sector in which we have seen regulatory and self-regulatory
waves intersect and the response of the state to even the mildest self-regulatory
initiatives. The *Declaration* and the founding of the CFC are two careful and
initial moves toward greater long-term autonomy and self-governance. They
were initial steps in a long path that begins with convening and discussing self-
regulation, and then moves to initial enunciation of principles and the
founding of an information collection, disclosure, and research apparatus,

---

[24] Variously called the 慈善法, 慈善事业法, and the 慈善事业促进法 (Charity Law, Charitable
  Sector Law, and Charitable Sector Promotion Law) in Chinese (and other permutations),
  depending on the reference.
[25] An English translation of the Charity Law of the People's Republic of China is available from
  China Development Brief, accessed August 10, 2016, http://chinadevelopmentbrief.cn/articles/
  the-charity-law-of-the-peoples-republic-of-china/.

with the longer term goal (still many steps away) of carving out a collective action approach toward some aspects of self-governance as a long-term object-ive. In the shorter and medium term, however, they in no way challenge the dominance of the state in controlling the Chinese nonprofit and philan-thropic sector. That process of moving toward some aspects of self-governance will require much negotiation with the Chinese state, and regulatory waves are certain to meet again and again in that process.

5.4 VIETNAM: CARVING OUT A ROLE FOR SELF-REGULATION AND SELF-REGULATORY ORGANIZATIONAL ENTREPRENEURISM

Vietnam, also dominated by a Communist Party and exhibiting some of the same dual motivations of control and encouragement toward the expansion of a voluntary sector, shares a number of regulatory and policy goals with its neighbor to the north when it comes to the voluntary sector and philanthropy. Both Vietnam and China are strong states with strong regulatory- and control-based agendas toward the voluntary sector and philanthropy. Vietnam, like China, seeks to differentiate state-favored organizations and activities through registration, funding, reporting, and other mechanisms, the regulatory differ-entiation of encouragement and discouragement. Vietnam, like China, experiences significant contention and competition within the state on non-profit and philanthropic regulation but seeks – particularly with advocacy organizations – to downplay those internal conflicts when faced with the overall need for differentiated control and encouragement.

Vietnam, like China, strongly favors social services nonprofits and founda-tions and strongly disfavors advocacy groups. Through a combination of regulatory intervention and political policy, the Vietnamese Communist Party and state have pushed groups that might like to focus on advocacy into a more service-oriented agenda through a combination of funding, policy, and regu-latory tools. Vietnam, like China, is relatively weaker on the regulation of disclosure, transparency, and accountability than on other elements of the regulatory agenda such as registration. In Vietnam, as in China, the weakness in regulation of disclosure, transparency, and accountability has created space for a new and mild form of self-regulation to try to step in and begin the process of carving out regulatory differentiation with the state. Currently, however, even the disclosure, transparency, and accountability agenda is dominated by state processes and state regulation, and so nascent self-regulatory impulses remain very weak.

Set amid a strong regulatory environment and a strong state, there was relatively little discussion of nonprofit and philanthropic self-regulation in

Vietnam until about 2013. Domestic umbrella organizations did not form with the scale, scope, and strength that they did, at least to some degree, in China. There was, at least in 2001, no China NPO Network in Vietnam, no Shang Yusheng to propose self-regulation as an expression of values and, perhaps over time, as a counterweight to state regulation. Nor has philanthropy developed in Vietnam with the speed and power that it has in China; neither the strong business community nor the strong philanthropic leadership (in the person of Xu Yongguang[26] and others) has been present in the Vietnamese context in anything like the ways we have noted in China.

For those and other reasons, nonprofit self-regulation did not begin to emerge in Vietnam in any significant way until 2013 and 2014, when a nonprofit umbrella organization called the Research Center for Management and Sustainable Development (MSD), with the support of Irish Aid, issued Vietnam's first self-regulatory principles for the nonprofit sector, the *Code of Practice on Transparency and Accountability for Civil Society Organizations in Vietnam*, and began a national effort to win acceptance of those principles within the Vietnamese voluntary sector.[27]

In China, a lack of transparency and accountability and the power of philanthropic actors set the stage for initial discussion and the initial emergence of self-regulation. In Vietnam, the nascent sprouts of self-regulation have initially emerged from different ground. Nonprofit self-regulation in Vietnam fills an under-regulated gap in transparency and accountability, but its institutional emergence did not come from the growing power of philanthropy, as it did in China – for philanthropy and its backers have very little power in Vietnam. That self-regulatory initiative came largely from an umbrella entrepreneurial group that is seeking to extend its influence within the Vietnamese nonprofit sector and to interact with the state. Multiple motivations characterize virtually every self-regulatory initiative, and that is the case in Vietnam as well. So in addition to the powerful motivating force of organizational entrepreneurism, also at work in Vietnam have been

---

[26] Shawn Shieh, "Profile: Xu Yongguang, founder of Nandu (Narada) Foundation," *NGOs in China Blog*, January 24, 2010, accessed January 7, 2016, http://ngochina.blogspot.com/2010/01/profile-xu-yongguang.html.

[27] MSD, *Code of Practice on Transparency and Accountability for Civil Society Organizations in Vietnam*, accessed January 7, 2016, http://tai.org.vn/tap-code/tap-code-content. I was honored to be asked to assist MSD, with support from Irish Aid, with strategic advice and drafting support for this first nonprofit self-regulatory initiative in Vietnam. My interpretations of the Vietnam experience and comparisons with China are my own and do not represent MSD, Irish Aid, the LIN Center for Community Development (HCMC), UNDP, ICNL, or any other individuals or organizations with whom I have worked on nonprofit self-regulation and regulation in Vietnam.

governmental, media, and public concerns with nonprofit accountability and transparency; some strong donor interest and initial funding; relative state indifference to the self-regulatory initiative (at least for now), since the state continues to dominate nonprofit disclosure, transparency, and accountability in Vietnam; and a certain level of national nonprofit cohesion in a much smaller state than China.

So while philanthropic interests and power were at the root of a key Chinese self-regulatory development, an umbrella nonprofit's self-regulatory entrepreneurism was at the root of Vietnam's development, along with other factors. In a sector with several thousand NGOs and several dozen foundations, the Research Center for MSD's ambition to lead in the Vietnamese nonprofit sector, a key factor in the development of the *Code of Practice on Transparency and Accountability*, is reflected in its other plans. Those include a certification mechanism based on the Code (which they understand they cannot run entirely by themselves) and an expansion of national NGO awards that MSD initiated in 2013.[28]

The initiative that emerged in Vietnam was the *Code of Practice on Transparency and Accountability for Civil Society Organizations in Vietnam*, released by MSD at workshops in Hanoi and Ho Chi Minh City in July and August 2014 after several months of drafting and consultation with an international specialist. The *Code* includes detailed principles and guidelines on accountable and transparent programs, governance, human resource management, financial management, and fundraising and is far more detailed and comprehensive than its initial Chinese analogue issued in 2009. The *Code* addresses the role of a nonprofit's board; conflicts of interest; strategic planning; umbrella organizations and their membership and participation; decision making in organizations; the linkage of programs to mission; involvement of beneficiaries and stakeholders; information disclosure to stakeholders; monitoring and evaluation tools; handling feedback, complaints, and grievances; clear and fair human resource policies; work assignments; assessment of staff performance; staff development; compliance with financial and accounting regulatory standards; audits; resistance to bribery, corruption, and fraud; effective communication and fundraising; the role of funders; fundraising ethics; and interpretation, updating, and implementation of the

---

[28] MSD's commitment to self-regulatory code work as a means of organizational entrepreneurism and filling regulatory and practice gaps in Vietnam was first manifested in the *Code of Practice for Civil Society Organizations Participation in Policy Development*, issued in January 2014 and supported by the United Nations Democracy Fund (UNDEF). This is a considerably less ambitious and more limited foray in code practice, but helped set the stage for the *Code of Practice on Transparency and Accountability for Civil Society Organizations in Vietnam*, ibid.

Code.[29] The *Code*'s organizers, MSD, also plan to establish a detailed certification and recognition process for organizations interested in complying with
the *Code* and to expand an NGO awards process that is already under way, two
other examples of the organization's self-regulatory entrepreneurism.[30] As of
2016, several hundred Vietnamese organizations had signed on to the *Code* or
begun the process of acceding to it, and MSD was hard at work on spreading it
still further.

5.5 SIMILARITIES AND DIFFERENCES IN THE CHINESE AND VIETNAMESE CONTEXTS

The Vietnamese foray into self-regulation was thus quite different in scope
and detail from the slightly earlier Chinese move. Yet they shared one
important feature: each of these initiatives has sought to respond to and fill
some gaps in their powerful state's regulatory agenda, which recognizes that
state regulation is entirely dominant. In China, that regulatory gap filling – in
effect, a long-term attempt to begin to establish a soft form of regulatory
competition with the state – was more in the nature of principles of accountability and transparency (the *Declaration*), accompanied by an institutional
attempt to establish an autonomous disclosure, transparency, and research
body (the CFC). In Vietnam, the *Code* goes further in developing principles
for nonprofit practice, disclosure, transparency, and accountability, in part
taking advantage of the somewhat less detailed Vietnamese regulation of the
sector. The Vietnamese state has outlined regulation for nonprofit formation
and practice, including board governance, finances, and related matters, but
has not regulated as actively as their Chinese counterparts. In different ways,
both are attempts to begin a long-term process of establishing some autonomy
from the state for semi-independent transparency and accountability mechanisms. But in both countries, the state remains dominant, including in the
nascent self-regulatory sphere.

In China, the response to the self-regulatory and disclosure initiatives
around 2010 and after has been to attempt to strengthen state regulation and
structures, in part through the issuance of regulatory documents that mirror
and seek to contain the sphere of self-regulation of transparency and

---

[29] MSD, n. 27. See also Tran Hai Yen, "TAP Code: Code of Practice on Transparency and
Accountability for Civil Society Organizations in Vietnam," (presentation by MSD, July–
August 2014, unpublished).

[30] A brief description of the awards process is provided on the CSO-TAI website, accessed January
7, 2016, http://tai.org.vn/vietnam-ngo-awards-2014/finalists-and-winners/. MSD is also tied to the
Ministry of Civil Affairs through personal ties.

accountability initiated by the 2009 *Declaration*, and the strengthening of state institutional mechanisms, perhaps in part to respond to the rise of a potentially competitive CFC. In Vietnam, the state's response to the emergence of the much more ambitious *Code* has been somewhat more muted, at least in the very earliest stages. Although it has been only a short time since the *Code* was issued for adoption by nonprofit organizations around Vietnam, there is, as yet, no indication that it is directly impacting the state's active nonprofit regulatory agenda. This agenda currently focuses on enacting an omnibus Law on Associations, for the first time, and new regulations on nonprofit practice, governance, and fiscal accountability.

In China, the state is poised to continue with and accelerate its own regulatory initiatives, including both the Charity Law and the revision of the key functional regulations on foundations, social organizations, and public non-enterprise organizations. In addition to specific regulations issued over the past decade, that expanding regulatory agenda includes considerably strengthened provisions on disclosure, transparency, and accountability that have been at the core of the nascent self-regulatory agenda. The state never gave up the accountability agenda and is strengthening its role in it. In that environment, a self-regulatory initiative such as the *Declaration* may not be able to gain strength, while a data-gathering and resource institution for foundations, the CFC, may be able to gradually strengthen its role. In sum, however, the state controls the accountability agenda.

In Vietnam, the powerful Vietnamese state (through the very powerful Ministry of Home Affairs, which issues most nonprofit regulation in Vietnam and is playing a major role in drafting Vietnam's Law on Associations) is highly unlikely to cede disclosure, transparency, and accountability to a self-regulatory code. In fact, the draft of the Law on Associations that emerged in 2015 strengthens disclosure, transparency, and accountability rules. Here too, the state controls the accountability agenda and seems unlikely to cede it, in any significant way, to self-regulation.[31]

At the drafting stage of the *Code of Practice on Transparency and Accountability*, however, the Vietnamese state had little to say. The only state representative who spoke publicly was the Director of the Center for Research on Associations, NGOs and Training in the Institute of State Organizational Science under the Ministry of Home Affairs, who provided a friendly

---

[31] Discussions in Hanoi and Ho Chi Minh City, July and August 2014. For a summary of the draft Law on Associations, see Nguyen Tu Long, "The Bill on Associations," *Vietnam Law and Legal Forum*, accessed January 7, 2016, http://vietnamlawmagazine.vn/the-bill-on-associations-3618.html.

document that called the new *Code* "assistance to the state management of CSOs to be more effective, especially in the financial area," among other more general comments, and called for its acceptance in the Vietnamese NPO community.[32] That, however, is unlikely to be the Vietnamese state's last word on Vietnam's first significant nonprofit self-regulatory initiative. One indirect response has already been identified above – the draft Law on Associations that emerged in 2015 and may be adopted in 2017, which is likely to strengthen disclosure, transparency, and accountability rules and the role of the state in enforcing them. The state may also respond by encouraging the emergence of government or quasi-government entities to monitor that disclosure, transparency, and accountability, in effect setting up official competition for the umbrella self-regulatory initiative.

5.6 SOME BROADER CONSIDERATIONS ON REGULATORY WAVES: THE EXPANSION OF SUBNATIONAL REGULATION AND THE RELATIONSHIP BETWEEN REGULATION AND SELF-REGULATION IN CHINA

A special problem for the analysis of the relationship between regulation and self-regulation, particularly in China, is the gradual expansion of subnational regulation of nonprofit and philanthropic matters. Consistent with national political and legal policy that seeks to encourage, constrain, and mold the development of civil society and philanthropy, local policy and regulatory activity on philanthropy has emerged as an important area of development and experimentation in China. Legal and policy documents on philanthropy, charitable giving, donations, and foundations have now been issued in almost all of China's thirty-two provinces, centrally administered municipalities, and province-level "autonomous regions." In some cases, these subnational regulations have been used to explore new and more innovative approaches to state regulation of the philanthropic sector. Some provinces and municipalities (such as Guangdong, Shenzhen, Shanghai, Jiangsu, and Beijing) have become well known for their progress in this area, including local experimentation with streamlined registration and new forms of nonprofit administration for the central authorities in Beijing to watch and learn from.

---

[32] Quang Thi Ngoc Huyen, "Mot so y kien dong gop hoan thien Bo nguyen tac thuc hanh minh bach va trach nghiem giai trinh cho cac to chuc xa hoi Viet nam" ("Some opinions contributing to the strengthening of the Code of Practice on Transparency and Accountability for Civil Society Organizations in Vietnam"), unpublished paper, July 2014.

A full cataloging of local regulatory and experimental efforts is beyond the scope of this chapter, but they include experiments and innovations in registration and management of social organizations, social contracting for the provision of social services by NPOs, fundraising, charitable donation and charitable transparency rules, supervision and management of local foundations, and management of international NGOs. Some of these localized legal documents go beyond national rules but do not contradict them; some – most famously in Guangdong in southern China – are explicit experiments at the provincial and local level that are being evaluated for national policymaking. They do not yet rise to the level of provincial or other subnational "competition" for philanthropic resources that such subnational regulation has represented for foreign investors interested in arbitraging the differences between local incentives for foreign investment. In short, the local developments in philanthropy and other nongovernmental policymaking and regulation represent some local specificity and, at times, local experimentation with approaches, which may or may not be scaled up for other provinces or cities or national promulgation as Beijing carefully watches their progress in local areas.[33] Some of these initiatives have found their way into the draft Charity Law that is expected to be enacted at the national level in 2016.

Where can self-regulation, and the state's response to self-regulation, fit into this increasingly complex and subnationalized regulatory structure? On the one hand, it is possible that we may begin to see some localized, or branch, self-regulatory initiatives as well, and there have been some indications that this may begin to occur in China.[34] To the degree that begins to occur, it will be useful to look at how regulation and self-regulation interact, and how the state reacts to self-regulatory initiatives, at the provincial level.

At the same time, nonprofit and philanthropic regulation is becoming more centralized in China these days, through both the new national Charity Law and the new Law on Management of Overseas NGOs, and the role of subnational regulation may well decrease. So it may also be that national

---

[33] The role of local regulation on philanthropy and social organizations in policy experimentation and in information provision to national policymakers in Beijing, though it began earlier, is now generally traced most publicly to mid-2009, when the Ministry of Civil Affairs announced a *Cooperative Agreement on Advancing Integrated Reforms in Civil Affairs* with the municipal government of Shenzhen, a major economic area in the southern province of Guangdong and China's original special economic zone. In early 2012, Guangdong also announced, in part as a result of the local regulatory experiments, that the requirement of finding a professional supervisory unit that would sponsor a nonprofit organization's registration would be eliminated in 2012.

[34] Interviews in Beijing, August 2013, August 2014.

self-regulatory initiatives do not necessarily localize, as the state takes a stronger role in nonprofit and philanthropic supervision. As direct government regulation of nonprofits and philanthropy grows stronger in both China and Vietnam, the road to effective self-regulation or autonomous action will be very long indeed.

5.7 SELF-REGULATION AND FREEDOM OF ASSOCIATION: DIFFERENT STATE RESPONSES (TO SAY THE LEAST)

We should also ask how much strong states actually care about, or need to respond to, these sorts of self-regulatory waves, whether those self-regulatory initiatives come from gap filling from emerging and powerful actors (the tycoon-based philanthropic community in China) or from self-regulatory umbrella organizational entrepreneurs in Vietnam. In short, while the state may respond to self-regulatory initiatives, and appears to have responded in both China and Vietnam with a strengthening of its own disclosure, transparency, and accountability mechanisms through the new draft Charity Law in China and the new draft Law on Associations in Vietnam, how much does the state even care about self-regulation?

The initial answers from China and Vietnam may be somewhat different, but may share some characteristics. In China, the state responds with competitive regulation and institutions of its own, but did not challenge the legality or existence of either the *Declaration of Chinese Private Foundations on Self-Regulation* nor the CFC. In that sense, the Chinese state has employed graduated or differentiated control or management (in Chinese, 分类控制, 分类管制) mechanisms and strategies[35] to respond differently to softer self-regulation initiatives (principles and practices, or the emergence of the CFC) than it likely would to a more aggressive freedom-of-association approach to self-regulation, autonomy, and advocacy. Vietnam has similarly carefully differentiated between different types of nonprofits and has allowed many such organizations – including at times some advocacy organizations – to operate, while rigidly controlling the emergence of dissident political activity in group or individual form.

---

[35] On *fenlei guanzhi* and *fenlei kongzhi* strategies, I have learned much from the fine work of Kang Xiaoguang and his colleagues. See, for example, Kang Xiaoguang and Heng Han, "Graduated Control: A Study of State and Society Relations in Contemporary Mainland China" ("Fenlei kongzhi: Dangqian Zhongguo dalu guojia yu shehui guanxi yanjiu"), *Sociological Studies* 6 (2005): 73–89.

While the Chinese and Vietnamese states may respond through their own carefully calibrated waves of re-regulation or re-institutionalization, they will reserve their strongest response to moves that directly challenge state control over the voluntary sector and philanthropy under banners of "freedom of association," "freedom of assembly," or similar calls. In turn, those advocating freedom of association and freedom of assembly will go far beyond self-regulation to more direct confrontation with Chinese and Vietnamese author-ities on these and other rights.[36] In that more difficult and deeper debate, self-regulation itself and regulatory waves may not be the most important issues, for those are really debates over political freedoms and the political system.

[36] See, for example, the calls for freedom of association and freedom of assembly in "China's Carter 08," accessed January 7, 2016, www.nybooks.com/articles/2009/01/15/chinas-charter-08/ (the Chinese version, accessed January 7, 2016, www.cecc.gov/resources/legal-provisions/ charter-08-chinese-and-english-text#body-chinese). These calls, of course, go far beyond self-regulation: "Freedom is at the core of universal human values. Freedom of speech, freedom of the press, freedom of assembly, freedom of association, freedom in where to live, and the freedoms to strike, to demonstrate, and to protest, among others, are the forms that freedom takes. Without freedom, China will always remain far from civilized ideals ... Freedom to Form Groups. The right of citizens to form groups must be guaranteed. The current system for registering nongovernment groups, which requires a group to be 'approved,' should be replaced by a system in which a group simply registers itself." In turn those supra-self-regulatory calls provoke a very different response from the state. See "Liu Xiaobo: Facts," accessed January 7, 2016, www.nobelprize.org/nobel_prizes/peace/laureates/2010/xiaobo-facts.html.

6

The Regulation and Self-Regulation of
Civil Sector Organizations in Israel

NISSAN LIMOR AND NOY BRINDT

6.1 INTRODUCTION

Since the Declaration of Independence of the State of Israel, we have identified regulatory waves in twenty-year cycles that have influenced civil society organizations (CSOs), and in turn affected the emergence of self-regulatory initiatives. In Israel the emphasis has been on statutory regulation, but there have been some steps toward self-regulation, particularly in more recent times. This chapter explores each, and the relationships between them.

The Israeli civil society sector is embedded in the foundation of the State of Israel. The governing institutions of the Jewish community in the pre-state period were CSOs in formal terms. On declaring the independence of the State of Israel in 1948, these CSOs became arms of the newly formed government. The first official government adopted statism as the basis for its public policy in the formative years of the state. CSOs found themselves either as the government's agents or in conflict with the government. Most CSOs harnessed their activities toward government priorities in the process of nation building and laying the essential infrastructure of the new state. These relations characterized the first two decades of the state of Israel, and we identify this period as the first wave of regulation toward Israeli CSOs.

The second wave of regulation started in the mid-1970s, characterized by civil awakening in Israel, including protests against government policy and demands for change. The Labor government of the time failed to read the political and social maps correctly, and in the 1977 election it was replaced by the Likud Party. This was a significant political change, the results of which would be seen in subsequent years in relations with the civil society community.

A third regulatory wave arose in the 1990s, when the government initiated processes to direct and supervise the activity of CSOs. During this wave Israeli

civil society was not fully aware of the regulatory trends and changes under
way. It found itself in the midst of a new legal and regulatory reality that
narrowed its space and subjected it to increasing regulation.

Today, about twenty years after the third wave, in the era of "new public
governance," both government and CSOs find themselves facing a changing
reality. The challenges of contemporary Israeli society have encouraged new
ways of operation and have motivated a more open dialogue and better
cooperation between government and civil society. However, after years of
tension and lack of trust, as well as increased dependence of CSOs on
governmental funds, an appropriate balance in state/CSOs relations has not
yet been achieved. Nonetheless, one can identify signals that imply the
emergence of a new regulatory wave, one that is reshaping current public
policy and regulation regimes toward CSOs, as well as self-regulatory
initiatives.

6.2 ON STATUTORY REGULATION

Various models of regulation have accompanied the modern state – both in
Israel and in other countries – for many years.[1] However, since the 1980s, there
has been a rapid expansion of statutory regulation, and it has spread into
diverse economic and societal spheres, accompanied by the creation of new
forms and different paths of implementation.[2] These processes have been, to a
large extent, a byproduct of the changing role of the state and the adoption of
policies of privatization and commercialization.[3] The post-Fordism approach
regards regulation as a meeting point between public and private interests,
balanced by government.[4] This approach was accelerated through "new
public management," restricting direct involvement of government in the

---

[1] The beginning of statutory regulation in the United States can be seen in 1887, when Congress
established the first modern regulatory agency, the Interstate Commerce Commission:
Stephen G. Breyer, *Regulation and Its Reform* (Cambridge, MA: Harvard University Press,
1982).

[2] David Levi-Faur, "The Global Diffusion of Regulatory Capitalism," *The Annals of the
American Academy* 598(1) (2005): 12–32.

[3] Charles F. Phillips Jr., *The Economics of Regulation* (Homewood, IL: Richard D. Irwin, 1993);
Terenth C. Daintith, "A Regulatory Space Agency?," *Oxford Journal of Legal Studies* 9(4)
(1989): 534–546.

[4] Charlie Dannreuther and Pascal Petit, "Post-Fordism, beyond National Models: The Main
Challenges for Regulation Theory," *Competition & Change* 10(2) (2006): 100–112; Ronen
Palan, "Is the Competition State the New, Post-Fordist, Mode of Regulation? Regulation
Theory from an International Political Economic Perspective," *Competition & Change* 10(2)
(2006): 246–262.

economy.[5] Later, paradigms, models, and tools of regulation taken from the spheres of economics, industry, and finance were reproduced in the public and social arena.[6] If the original goal of regulation was meant to prevent market failures and reduce transaction costs, it soon spread into public administration and then into civil society.

Due to the importance of autonomy and controlling one's own affairs, CSOs in many countries developed voluntary regulation complementary to statutory regulation.[7] The aim of self-regulation was to improve CSO practices and to avoid the need for, or to reduce resort to, statutory regulation by the state.[8]

The structure and conduct of regulation, both statutory and self-regulation, are dependent on culture, geography, fiscal resources, political environment, and time. It is evident in Israel, as elsewhere, that development and application of different models of regulation address the unique characteristics of each country.

6.3 STATUTORY REGULATION AND SELF-REGULATION IN ISRAEL SINCE THE 1990S

Shortly after the change of government in Israel in 1977, the Israeli Association Law was enacted.[9] This legislation established a comprehensive framework for registration, operation, and dissolution of nonprofit organizations, establishing a regulatory authority and accountability and reporting requirements. But the law was enforced partially and in a relaxed manner until the first half of the 1990s.[10]

In the 1990s, changes in public policy affected regulation and regulatory enforcement toward CSOs. The Associations Law was amended in 1996,[11] and

---

[5] Peter Wilenski, "Small Government and Social Equity," *Politics* 18(1) (1983): 7–25; Glenn Withers, ed., *Bigger or Smaller Government?* (Canberra, Australia: Academy of the Social Sciences in Australia, 1983).

[6] Giandomenico Majone, "The Rise of the Regulatory State in Europe," *West European Politics* 17(1) (1994): 77–101.

[7] Kathleen D. Vohs and Roy F. Baumeister, *Handbook of Self-Regulation: Research, Theory, and Applications.* (New York: Guilford, 2004).

[8] Self-regulation can be seen as a subgroup of voluntary regulation.

[9] The law was finally passed in 1980. Up to that time, Israel acted according to the Ottoman Law on Associations of 1909.

[10] "Report no. 36 for the fiscal year 1985," State of Israel Comptroller's (Hebrew, 1986): 686–687; "Report no. 39 for the fiscal year 1989," State of Israel Comptroller's (Hebrew, 1990): 502–506.

[11] This amendment granted the statutory regulator a series of powers he did not have previously, including receiving reports and enhanced supervision. Between 1996 and 2014, a dozen more amendments were added, mainly concerned with increased supervision and regulatory

a series of government decisions expanded regulators' powers and procedures for supervision, control, regulation, and enforcement of publicly funded associations.[12] As a result, the statutory regulator (the State Registrar of Associations) issued numerous directives on the management of organizations (2001, 2005, 2010, 2013); the Tax Authority issued directives on tax benefits for donors (2001);[13] auditing authorities issued accounting standards and reporting directives;[14] the Ministry of Finance issued directives on submission requirements for government grants (1993, 2005, 2013); and other government ministries issued instructions on the contracting out of goods or services to CSOs. This broad range of government policy initiatives and directives attests to the increasing desire for regulatory control of CSO activities, a classic model of "command and control," rather than encouraging autonomy or self-regulation practices.

In 2004, a report by the State Comptroller led the government to appoint a commission to reexamine state support and regulation regarding CSOs.[15] The recommendations that emerged called for greater supervision of CSOs and for strengthening the enforcement powers of government regulators (including the statutory regulator, the Accountant General in the Ministry of Finance, and the tax authorities). Although the Commission's report was brought to the Cabinet, no decision was taken, mainly due to intensive pressure against the recommendations by leaders of the civil society sector.

So the regulatory side was strong and growing. But beginning in 2007 we can also note – in response to the strengthening of state control – the first initiative to adopt civil society self-regulation in Israel, a project called

    powers of the statutory regulator. During this period, we can also identify a policy focusing on transparency, particularly regarding funds from foreign political entities and transparency in salaries. During the same period more than ten bills were tabled, though not passed, in the Knesset restricting the space to be afforded to CSOs.

[12] Uzi Berlinsky and Pnina Sofer enumerate twenty government decisions between 1997 and 2004, and their report specifies a series of multiple government meetings that dealt with reports of the State Comptroller, receipt of reports from the government ministries, amendments and updates to decisions, and the like; see Uzi Berlinsky and Pnina Sofer, *Support for Public Associations and Institutions by the Government* (Jerusalem: Office of the Prime Minister, 2000) (in Hebrew).

[13] In May 2014, the committee appointed by the Minister of Finance (Frisch Commission) submitted its recommendations.

[14] *Auditing Standard No. 69* (1997) of the Institute of Certified Public Accountants in Israel (ICPAI), followed by *Auditing Standard No. 5* (1999) of the Israel Accounting Standards Board (IASB). See also amendment of Standard 36 of the Israel Accounting Standards Board (2014).

[15] The commission for examining state funding to public institutions (Aridor Commission) was appointed in 2004 and submitted its recommendations in May 2006. All the commission's members, except for its chair (a former Minister of Finance), were state employees.

"Naot." Naot was one of several sectoral self-regulatory responses to the statutory regulatory advances of the 1990s, as discussed further below in Section 6.4.

Other responses to the advance of government regulation were brewing as well. In 2003, a committee appointed by the Israeli Center for Third Sector Research at Ben-Gurion University published a report, the *Review Committee of Government Policy towards the Third Sector in Israel*.[16] The following year a further report about the third sector in Israel was published at the invitation of philanthropic foundations.[17] These reports, especially the second, led to changes in civil sector umbrella organizations in Israel.[18] In 2007, due to major legislation changes in the Associations Law that strengthened the powers of the statutory regulator and transparency and reporting requirements, a coalition of CSOs was formed to actively represent CSOs in the legislative process. These activities were a type of voluntary reregulation, through which the sector sought to take responsibility for various issues such as transparency and the duties of the audit committee; in effect, the sector was offering a division of labor with the statutory regulator.

In 2008, another initiative for self-regulation emerged – the "Midot project," discussed further below in Section 6.4 – established by business people and volunteers. This enterprise aimed to engage in the evaluation of organizations and sought to satisfy the demands of donors and philanthropic foundations. In 2009, yet another instrument of voluntary self-regulation emerged – the GuideStar Israel project. This website-based initiative includes data on all registered associations in Israel, espouses transparency, and seeks to assist transparency and accountability.

Meanwhile, a change of government in 2006 opened a new window of opportunity for the regulatory regime to strengthen cooperation between government and CSOs. The new government was aware of the British experience regarding the Compact with the Third Sector (1998), the Accord between the Government of Canada and the Voluntary Sector (2001), and the Irish "Towards 2016" program (2006). In February 2008, following deliberations with the representatives of CSOs, the business sector, and academics,

---

[16] *The Review Committee of Government Policy towards the Third Sector in Israel* (Beer-Sheva: Israeli Center for Third-Sector Research, Ben-Gurion University of the Negev, 2003) (in Hebrew) ("The Galnoor Committee").

[17] Nissan Limor, *The Third Sector in Israel* (Jerusalem: Yad-HaNadiv and the Kahanoff Foundation, 2004) (in Hebrew).

[18] The changes included, inter alia, replacing the leadership, focusing the objectives of the organization, and changing its name from "Volunteer and Nonprofit Sector" to "Civic Leadership."

the government reached a resolution – the first of its type – on relations between government, the business sector, and the civil sector.[19] The Israeli government acknowledged the tri-sectoral concept and the importance of cooperative relations with civil society; CSOs were regarded as an important factor for advancing society and democracy. To promote this policy, the government decided to reform policies toward CSOs in steps related to transparency, regulation, taxation, contracts, and grants.

Following this decision, a roundtable consisting of representatives from the three sectors was established, aimed at implementing the government's decisions and mapping issues that the sectors had to resolve through establishing frameworks for these issues. The problem of regulation was embedded in each framework area, but self-regulation, or cooperation in the division of labor of regulation, was not on the table. Even in a more relaxed policy environment, the government was not ready to give assistance and support to self-regulation in the civil society sector.

6.4 MAIN TRENDS IN STATUTORY REGULATION AND SELF-REGULATION IN ISRAEL

6.4.1 *Statutory Regulation*

Contemporary Israeli public policy toward regulation in general, and toward regulation of CSOs in particular, is characterized by diverse trends and processes, some domestic and some as outcomes of global influences. First, policymakers confront the claim of over-regulation and regulatory burdens in the face of public policy that advocates separation between policy shaping and directing and supervision of service provision.[20] As the state's involvement in the provision of social services has declined, its regulatory role has increased. One of the ramifications of these developments is the emergence

---

[19] Government of Feb. 24, 2008 ("Resolution no. 3190"). See also the government-issued document *The Israeli Government, Civil Society and the Business Community: Partnership, Empowerment and Transparency*, Policy document (Jerusalem: Office of the Prime Minister, February 24, 2008) (in Hebrew), accessed January 14, 2016, www.pmo.gov.il/Secretary/ GovDecisions/2008/Pages/des3190.aspx.

[20] Itzhak Galnoor, David H. Rosenbloom, and Allon Yaroni, "Creating New Public Management Reforms, Lessons from Israel," *Administration & Society* 30(4) (1998): 393–420; Eran Vigoda, "Are You Being Served? The Responsiveness of Public Administration to Citizens' Demands: An Empirical Examination in Israel," *Public Administration* 78(1) (2000): 165–191; Iris Geva-May, "Reinventing Government: The Israeli Exception: The Case of Political Cultures and Public Policy-making," *International Public Management Journal* 2(1) (1999): 112–126.

of service-providing CSOs, which have become a significant economic actor as well as a contributing factor in the fulfillment of public policy.[21]

In this new environment, statutory regulation aimed at CSOs in Israel is influenced by a number of factors. These include mechanisms and models imported from the business world and in particular the public benefit company and the public benefit foundation, new types of civil organizations based on the business company structures.[22] The second is the desire to reshape corporate governance and decision-making mechanisms and to strengthen internal auditing bodies. The motivating factor behind these processes is a response to market and sectoral failures. A third factor in the new statutory regulation of CSOs in Israel is institutional pressure on CSOs, from government and the market, to adopt new management strategies, norms, and standards, resulting in a process of isomorphism.[23]

These developments occurred as criticism of the scope and conduct of statutory regulation of CSOs arose from the State Comptroller, politicians, the government legal advisor, and some public voices. The government was required to respond and did so via two principal arms: the statutory regulator at the Justice Ministry and the Accountant General at the Ministry of Finance. The demands for increased transparency of CSOs were subordinated to uniform regulation of financial and board reporting[24] and through the development of the GuideStar Israel website. As a result of the way CSO regulation has been implemented, statutory regulation has largely captured nonprofit organizations.

[21] Robert Schwartz and Ira Sharkansky, "Collaboration with the 'Third Sector' – Issues of Accountability: Mapping Israeli Versions of This Problematic," *Public Policy and Administration* 15(3) (2000): 92–106; Avishai Benish, "Outsourcing, Discretion, and Administrative Justice: Exploring the Acceptability of Privatized Decision Making," *Law & Policy.* 36(2) (2014): 113–133.

[22] Public benefit companies were added to the Companies Law in Amendment 6 in 2007. Public benefit foundations were added to the Companies Law in 2013 as part of Amendment 23. An additional arrangement based on the model of a commercial company is the draft of the Public Trusts bill, which is in the pre-legislation phase as of 2016.

[23] Paul J. DiMaggio and Walter W. Powell, "The Iron Cage Revisited: Institutional Isomorphism and Collective Rationality in Organizational Fields," *American Sociological Review* 48(2) (1983): 147–160; Sandra Verbruggen, Johan Christiaens, and Koen Milis, "Can Resource Dependence and Coercive Isomorphism Explain Nonprofit Organizations' Compliance with Reporting Standards?," *Nonprofit and Voluntary Sector Quarterly* 40(1) (2011): 5–32.

[24] *Audit Standard 69* of the Institute of Certified Public Accountants in Israel (1997) and *Accounting Standard 5* of the Israeli Accounting Standards Board (1999), which deals entirely with setting standards of accounting and financial reporting suited to the characteristics of civil organizations contrary to those of business corporations.

The result is that statutory regulation focuses on administrative, legal, and accounting matters, while CSOs focus on the professional and qualitative aspects of their work.[25] This kind of regulatory strategy burdens government less, it appears, and seems easier and cheaper for the government. It leads to reduction in costly regulation of the professional aspects of CSOs, which can open the door to self-regulation.

A dominant example of this new form of regulation is the focus on "proper management." This regulatory initiative was based on government decisions in 1998 and 2001 that subjected publicly funded organizations to enhanced scrutiny and procedures developed by the statutory regulator.[26] Under these procedures, designated organizations annually submit a series of organizational, financial, and activity documents to the statutory regulator, which, on examination and approval, may issue a certification of "proper management." Having this certificate is a prerequisite to receiving public funds and participating in government tenders.

The proper management procedure typifies the evolution of CSO statutory regulation in the wave of 1990s. It is not, in fact, a creation of first or secondary legislation, and its constitutional foundation is in doubt. It is also questionable whether the parliament has the power to review it. The development of this procedure is squarely in the hands of the statutory regulator. The regulator enjoys broad discretion without any substantial dependence on external bodies, and with almost no public involvement in the process and particularly no significant involvement by CSOs in setting these rules.

Another key aspect of statutory regulation of Israeli CSOs is the political system's ongoing desire to redefine the boundaries of legitimate civil activities, particularly for organizations engaged in advancing social or political change. One approach to this question of legitimate activities is to increase scrutiny of foreign funding,[27] terrorist financing, and money

---

[25] Michael Power, *The Audit Society*, 2nd ed. (Oxford: Oxford University Press, 1999).

[26] The first edition the Proper Management Rules was published in 2002; since then it was updated in 2005, 2010, and 2013. Each new edition added new rules and widened the scope of the rules, expanding to new areas of operation.

[27] This trend began in the early 2000s, in Israeli parliamentary activity on the question of the legitimacy of foreign funding in Israeli domestic political activity. See, for example, Bill to Prohibit the Receiving of Contributions from Outside of Israel (Legislative Amendments, 2004); Bill on Reporting of Contributions from Outside Israel (Legislative Amendments, 2005); and in 2008, requiring civil organizations to report contributions in excess of NIS20,000 received from a foreign country, commonwealth, international bodies, or any other foreign state entity: Associations Law, Amendment 11 (2008). This reporting requirement has been incorporated into the proper management provisions, discussed above. Other bills to restrict foreign funding were introduced in 2011 and 2013.

laundering.[28] Israel is not the only country where politicians use antiterrorism, anti–money laundering, and foreign influence on public policy as an excuse to supervise, redefine, and even block certain activities of CSOs.[29]

6.4.2 *Self-Regulation Initiatives*

As noted above, there have been several self-regulatory initiatives from the civil society sector over the past two decades.

The first project was Naot, which began as part of civil society sector umbrella activities in 1997 as a response to the restrictive amendments proposed to the Associations Law in 1996 and the new powers granted to the statutory regulator.

Naot was developed and led by the nongovernmental Committee for Standards and Accreditation (CSA), composed of civil society leaders and experts in law, accounting, audit, management, and other relevant fields. The project established a voluntary self-regulation model comprised of two stages: a self-study process followed by external review by independent professionals in different aspects of the organization's operations. Organizations that completed both steps were awarded a stamp of accreditation.[30] Some 257 CSOs entered the process.[31] Most of them introduced major changes as a result of the first phase of self-review. The CSA supported organizations that went through the process, reviewing and commenting on individual self-studies.

The first self-study phase did not require significant budgetary outlay, which was allocated from CSA's annual budget, along with some foundation support. The second phase, the external evaluation, was a larger process and required more funding.

However, despite Naot's potential, the second phase was never implemented, and the project gradually faded. The decline of the project stemmed

---

[28] Bureau of Anti-Money Laundering and Counter Terrorist Financing, *Typologies and Indications of Terror Financing* (Ministry of Justice, 2012); Bureau of Anti-Money Laundering and Counter Terrorist Financing, *Annual Report* (2012), accessed January 11, 2016, http://index.justice.gov.il/Units/HalbantHon/docs/rashut+cover.pdf.

[29] Mark Sidel, *Regulation of the Voluntary Sector: Freedom and Security in an Era of Uncertainty* (London: Routledge Cavendish, 2008).

[30] Nissan Limor and Eli Sharon, *Standards* (Tel Aviv: The Volunteers and Nonprofit Sector, 2000) (in Hebrew). The last update of the standards was published in 2012: Nissan Limor, *Naot – Standards for Proper Management for Nonprofit Organizations* (Tel Aviv: Civic Leadership & BDO, 2012) (in Hebrew).

[31] At that time, only 600 organizations were members in the umbrella organization. The second phase (external evaluation) involved a major operation and needed a multiyear budget.

from a lack of financial resources;[32] rigid rules set by the statutory regulator via the "proper management procedures," which required organizations to obtain the proper management certificate if they sought public funds; and the refusal of the statutory regulator to recognize, support, or give credit to organizations that successfully negotiated the Naot process.

The regulator refused to support the Naot self-regulatory process for several reasons. The first reason was the limited enforcement mechanisms available to the sector's umbrella organization – a reflection of the skepticism of the Israeli Ministry of Justice about the ability of self-regulatory mechanisms to advance the goals of the regulatory regime. Second, the government's privatization policy and shifts in statutory regulation were perceived as inconsistent with this level of self-regulation. Third, the statutory regulator was unwilling to negotiate division of labor with the sector, due to its determination to exercise its regulatory powers. A further reason was the perceived lack of authority to extend any regulatory authority to a nongovernmental body.

The second self-regulatory initiative – Midot – was established in 2008 by venture capital professionals who sought to strengthen evaluation of CSO activities. Midot adopted a donor approach, seeking to assess not only the efficiency and outputs of organizations, but also their impact on beneficiaries and society as a whole. Midot developed a type of social analytical tool and offered CSOs the opportunity to go through a process to use this tool, receive a certificate evaluating their activities, and publish this information on the Internet.

Midot's adoption of business-based approaches, and a sense among some CSOs that these approaches could conflict with CSO values and missions, caused opposition from some groups. Some felt that Midot did not have the right tools to implement the "social efficiency measurement" model; others questioned the very model itself. The statutory regulator's skeptical view toward this self-regulatory project was the same as it was toward Naot.

Despite this opposition, Midot still exists, appealing to a small number of CSOs. This project underwent significant changes in its defined roles and objectives, as well as changes in its analytic tools. But at the end of the day, opposition to Midot, and sparse contributions from business, prevents significant expansion of this self-regulatory initiative.

The third Israeli self-regulatory initiative in recent years is GuideStar Israel, which aims to provide information that advances CSO transparency.[33]

---

[32] As soon as it was clear that the government would not support the Naot initiative and would not extend benefits to organizations that passed the self-study, the foundations reduced their support.

[33] Accessed January 14, 2006, www.guidestar.org.il/.

GuideStar Israel seeks to enable stakeholders and the general public to make better decisions on CSOs, joining organizations, volunteering, and giving.

The need for an instrument and project to enhance CSO transparency was initially raised in the 2004 Limor Report.[34] It took five years to negotiate the project with the government, finally resulting in a government resolution (Resolution No. 3190, 2008), and a five-year contract with the government signed in 2009 (to govern information release and use). Although this initiative came from the civil society sector, it became a joint venture between the government (Ministry of Justice) and the civil sector (the groups Yad Hanadiv and Jewish Distribution Committee-Israel, operated by NPTech, a nonprofit public benefit company). The GuideStar Israel contract with the government was extended until the end of 2016, and the parties are negotiating a further two-year extension.

GuideStar Israel is considered successful in the sense that it provides significant information to the public. There are two basic types of information provided: data that comes from government, and information supplied by CSOs. Organizations seeking wide public donations tend to provide the most data. Today the GuideStar Israel website includes information from the statutory regulator, that is, registration data on each organization, annual financial statements, annual reports, reports on the five highest salaries in the organization, and other information organizations wish to make public. The website has also received information from other government ministries, such as government support data from the Ministry of Finance. The parties to the GuideStar Israel project regard it as a successful partnership; they agreed on its aims and have built a structure that can handle obstacles and conflicts.

These three self-regulatory initiatives differ from each other in important ways. Naot was aimed at combining in-house organizational control of its own processes and evaluation in the first phase, and external examination in the second phase. It has been aimed not at grading the quality of organizational activities but at seeking to ensure that organizations are operating properly according to general standards of best practices.

Midot, on the other hand, seeks to measure the quality and the impact, and grade the organization accordingly. GuideStar Israel aims to provide information about CSOs, letting users draw their own conclusions regarding organizational aims and operations.

The government of Israel has avoided extending any financial support or even public recognition to Naot or Midot, retaining formal regulation and as

---

[34] Limor, n. 17.

much power as possible in the hands of the statutory regulator. The government does support GuideStar Israel by releasing government data on non-profit organizations, of course without expressing any views as to the content or meaning of the data.

There has been little public demand for nonprofit self-regulation in Israel, and public demand has played no significant role in the development of these three initiatives. Even when scandals hit the CSO community, public demands are to government regulators to resolve issues and govern the sector. Opposition from government regulators also blunts any strength in the calls for new self-regulation – the regulators intend to dominate the regulatory field. Co-regulation remains a long-term possibility but has not gained significant momentum thus far.

6.5 THE INFLUENCE OF REGULATION AND SELF-REGULATION ON ISRAELI CSOS

The discussion thus far indicates some of the complexity in the relationship between statutory regulation and self-regulation of CSOs in Israel. Government Resolution No. 3190 of 2008, introduced above, viewed CSOs as having a vital role in advancing government policy. Nonetheless, the broadening scope of CSO activities, as well as their accrued public power, has at times brought about increased tension between them and the government. In the absence of a comprehensive government policy, suitable legislation, and a differentiated regulatory regime, a "one size fits all" regulatory framework has emerged.

Until the 1970s, as discussed earlier, there were strong linkages between CSOs, the government, and political institutions.[35] In the 1980s, Israeli CSOs were more liberated, loosened from tight institutional and political dependency. This unexpected proliferation and newfound autonomy did not necessarily gain sympathy and trust from the government.[36] The new public

---

[35] Shmuel N. Eisenstadt, "Social Conditions for the Development of the Voluntary Organization in Israel," in *The Israeli Social Structure*, ed. Shmuel N. Eisenstadt et al., 2nd ed. (Jerusalem: Academon, 1969): 227–243 (in Hebrew); Yitzhak Galnoor and Dana Blander, *The Political System in Israel* (Tel Aviv: Am Oved, 2013) (in Hebrew); Dan Orowitz and Moshe Lisak, *From Settlement to State: The Jews of Palestine in the Mandate Period as a Political Community* (Tel Aviv: Am Oved, 1977) (in Hebrew).

[36] Limor, n. 17; Michal Bar and Benjamin Gidron, "The Long Journey to the Promised Land: Policy Initiatives towards the Third Sector in Israel," in *Policy Initiatives towards the Third Sector in International Perspective*, ed. Benjamin Gidron and Michal Bar (New York: Springer, 2010), 159–188.

management policy that encouraged privatization of services and administration led to strengthening the statutory regulator, mainly by enhancing supervision of CSOs supplying services funded by the government. This empowerment of the statutory regulator corresponded with Israel's centralized public management culture.[37]

Thus there is a structural conflict between strengthening the statutory regulator and encouraging the development of self-regulatory regimes. At the same time, government officials also reiterate their reservations over the existence of voluntary self-regulation by civil sector organizations. If a need for enforcement should arise, they say, it is the regulator who will have to intervene. They do not entirely reject voluntary and self-regulation, as long as those frameworks do not have the backing provided by government authorization.

The inherent power asymmetry between government and the civil society community, typified by CSOs' resource dependency on public funding,[38] a regulatory regime enforced via "proper management procedures" and other mechanisms, and other contractual provisions regarding the supply of public services have discouraged CSOs from developing self-regulation mechanisms. The reluctance of government to yield regulatory powers to nonstate actors reduces the sector's ability to produce self-regulation. At the end of the day – at least thus far – the lack of public pressure for self-regulation, the absence of resources, government centralization, and the formal power of statutory regulation make it very difficult, if not impossible, for the sector to develop self-regulation in the face of a strong government.

The existence of tight government regulation (some claim over-regulation) motivates Israeli CSOs to invest resources, time, and effort to deal with its directives. Yet where that requires more resources, given regulatory restrictions from the Accountant General of the Ministry of Finance on overhead costs and general expenses, CSOs are forced to seek more resources, and that is very difficult to achieve. Attempts to deal with strict regulation by challenging the regulatory burdens generally meets with a lack of sympathy from government. Other factors weaken the possibility of effective self-regulation as well, such as a lack of understanding of "how the system works," poor experience in working with government, lack of data and knowledge, the inability of Israeli

---

[37] Yitzhak Galnoor et al., "Reform in Government Administration in Israel," in *Public Policy in Israel*, ed. David Nachmias and Gila Menachem (Jerusalem: The Israel Democracy Institute, 1999), 117–157 (in Hebrew).

[38] It is fitting to recall that approximately 80 percent of the organization's resources come from the public domain, primarily from the selling of services, with a small portion, if at all, in the form of government grants.

CSOs to engage energetically in public and political activities and to properly represent the sector, a chronic lack of and competition for resources, and the traditionally poor results of CSO umbrella organizations.[39]

6.6 LOOKING TOWARD THE HORIZON: A NEW WAVE?

As we have outlined, tension, mutual suspicion, mistrust, and asymmetry of power characterize the relations between CSOs and the government in Israel. These relations reflect the controlling regulatory regime and the significant dependency of CSOs on government. In this environment, a division of regulatory labor between government and sector through some effective form of self-regulation is not considered feasible. Despite the new public management principles and a general understanding that a new approach and relationship between government and civil society sector is needed, no viable solutions to that difficult relationship have yet been found.

At the same time, we cannot ignore currents flowing beneath the surface, influencing the government, the general public, the civil society community, and public policy. These currents have the potential to change these sectoral relationships over time, perhaps toward more self-regulation, perhaps toward notions of "co-regulation."[40] We note these trends far beyond Israel, with the potential to shift the relationships between government, the civil society community, business, and the public.[41]

One such sign, or development, was in the Government Resolution of February 2008, which encouraged the role of CSOs in the policy process.[42] The resolution may be a cornerstone in the new design of tri-sectoral relationships in Israel. It does not mention self-regulation per se, but it calls for a rethinking of civil society's involvement in designing public policy. Following

---

[39] Since the publication of the Limor Report, n. 17, the umbrella organization has undergone complex internal processes that included a redefinition of its purpose and goals, several changeovers of management and senior functionaries, and a financial crisis due to the closing of foundations that supported it in the past.

[40] See, for example, the notion of "co-regulation" in Lord Hodgson, *Trusted and Independent: Giving Charity Back to Charities – Review of the Charities Act 2006* (London: Stationery Office, 2012).

[41] Roderick A.W. Rhodes, "The New Governance: Governing without Government," *Political Studies* 44(4) (1996): 652–667; Christie Ford and David Hess, "Corporate Monitorships and New Governance Regulation: In Theory, in Practice, and in Context," *Law & Policy* 33(4) (2011): 509–541; Dafna Barak-Erez, "The Democratic Challenge of Administrative Law," *Tel Aviv University Law Review* 24(2) (2000): 369–412 (in Hebrew).

[42] Bat-Chen Weinheber, *Roundtable Interface, a National Framework for Inter-Sector Discourse – Three-Year Summary* (Jerusalem: Prime Minister Office, 2011), accessed January 11, 2016, www .pmo.gov.il/SiteCollectionDocuments/PMO/mesrad/mediniot/OUTbookletfinal.pdf.

the resolution, a tri-sectoral roundtable was established, which began a dialogue on a series of issues that have included intersectoral relations, volunteerism, philanthropy, taxation, public funding, socially oriented business, and other important topics.

A second sign of changing currents over time is the government's decision to reexamine the overall statutory regulatory regime in Israel, as part of the government's commitments in joining the Organization for Economic Cooperation and Development (OECD).[43] This led to a 2013 government committee on enhancing regulatory efficiency (the Regulatory Committee).[44] In the same year, the Regulatory Committee published a draft government policy paper on frameworks for regulatory impact analysis.[45] That report dealt directly with issues of self-regulation. After examining the advantages and disadvantages of self-regulation models, the committee recommended "[e]ncouraging the implementation of self-regulation or opting for regulatory schemes that are less burdensome than 'command and control' models in suitable cases and circumstances – such that they enable the regulator to focus on issues that require increased government involvement and apply a proportional approach to regulation."[46] The committee pointed out that the good examples of self-regulation are models that are closer to joint regulation.

A third indication of a change in the currents of regulatory policy came from another public committee, the Trajtenberg Committee,[47] appointed by the government following broad social protest in the summer of 2011.[48] One of the central issues that occupied the Trajtenberg Committee was the inherent weakness of government regulation in serving the objectives set for it by public

---

[43] The Israeli Government Resolution No. 4027, enhancement of regulatory efficiency and improvement of government regulation (December 25, 2011). Israel joined the OECD in 2010.

[44] *Report of the Committee for Enhancing Efficiency of Regulatory Mechanisms in Israel* (Jerusalem: Prime Minister Office, 2013), accessed January 11, 2016, http://hazan.kibbutz.org.il/hafrata/doh_veeda_liieol_mngnoni_rgoltzia_-_april_2013.PDF.

[45] *Framework for Regulatory Impact Analysis – Draft for Comments* (Jerusalem: Prime Minister Office, 2013), accessed January 11, 2016, www.pmo.gov.il/policyplanning/mimshal/Documents/hashpaotregulatzya.pdf. This document is based on a document issued by the OECD, *Building an Institutional Framework for Regulatory Impact Analysis (RIA): Guidance for Policy Makers* (OECD, 2008), accessed January 11, 2016, www.oecd.org/gov/regulatory-policy/40984990.pdf.

[46] Committee Report, n. 44, 5, 6, 17–18.

[47] *Report of the Committee for Socioeconomic Change* (Jerusalem: Prime Minister Office, 2011) ("Trajtenberg Committee Report"), accessed January 11, 2016, www.teammanuel2011.org.il/general/fullreport.

[48] Ethan Bronner, "Israelis Feel Tug of Protests, Reviving the Left's Spirits," *New York Times*, August 1, 2011, 4, accessed January 11, 2016, www.nytimes.com/2011/08/01/world/middleeast/01israel.html.

policy. The committee recommended developing a comprehensive regulation doctrine in Israel, authorizing the regulator to relay information to
stakeholders in regulated bodies, involving the public in decision-making
processes, and presenting regulatory actions in a transparent manner to
encourage public review and discussion.[49]

Although the committee's findings did not refer directly to the regulatory
regime for civil society groups,[50] they did indicate the need for a new
approach to regulation, self-regulation, or co-regulation; a rethinking of the
division of labor between the government and other sectors; and involvement
of the public in designing public policy.

The fourth sign of a potential change in the currents of regulation is the
new openness of government toward public participation. In the last few years
the government has asked the public to comment on various issues, as well as
involving representatives from the public in government bodies and
government-appointed public committees.[51] Another example of new openness in receiving public participation is current discussions on enacting a new
Associations Law, which has been an open discourse between the Ministry of
Justice, representatives of CSOs, and academics.[52] This openness has its limits
when it comes to organizational power; for example, although there is wide
representation from individuals, the government has refrained from formal
recognition of the umbrella organization of Israeli CSOs.

A fifth sign of potential changing currents is the "transparency revolution,"[53] a process that has not bypassed Israel. In 2012, Israel joined the Open

---

[49] Trajtenberg Committee Report, n. 47, 164–165.

[50] The members of the Trajtenberg Committee did not include a formal representation from
CSOs. However, the committee appealed to the public and received many responses from the
public, including from CSOs.

[51] See, for example, the recommendation of the public committee that dealt with a tax benefit to
donors (the Frisch Committee, which submitted its recommendations to the Finance
Minister). Among the committee's recommendations is one to add two public representatives
to the Tax Authority's committee that discusses requests of organizations for granting tax
benefits to their contributors. See *Report of the Public Committee for Determining a Public
Institution as Eligible for Article 64 of the Income Tax Law* (Jerusalem: May 2014), section
267, 72.

[52] Thus, for example, the participation of Ministry of Justice officials in a series of discussions held
by the Van Leer Forum for Civil Sector Organizations on principles of legislation for a new
Associations Law.

[53] In 1998, the Israeli Parliament enacted the Freedom of Information Law, which obliged the
government to publish reports and place previously confidential information at the public's
disposal: Zeev Segal, *The Right to Know in the Light of the Freedom of Information Act* (Tel
Aviv: Israel Bar Association, 2000) (in Hebrew).

Government Partnership,[54] with an action plan to promote and strengthen democratic governance principles such as transparency, mandatory reporting, public involvement, and accountability.[55] In the context of CSOs, the Guide-Star Israel project, which delivers extensive information to the general public on associations and companies for the public benefit, is an example of implementation of the legal right to receive information from public authorities. The information is open to the public on the Internet and allows stakeholders to exercise at least some informed decision making via enhanced information. Those demands for information, in the Israeli context, come mainly from donors, government, professional advisors (lawyers, accountants, and others), and the media.[56]

These two political instruments – public participation and the transparency revolution – indicate possible directions for the reform of regulatory regimes in Israel, as well as potential regulatory strategies and mechanisms for future use that differ from the hierarchical regulation of "command and control." This trend has not skipped over CSOs in Israel, where we perceive new a outlook and openness to intersectoral discourse, cooperation, and the use of working tools that have not been available until now. Whether those developments and currents will lead to more self-regulation, or co-regulation, is currently unclear, but the stage is being set for more discussion of reforms and of a regulatory division of labor.

These developments have also affected the Israeli civil society umbrella organization and encouraged the establishment of a coordination forum of associations of directors and a forum for infrastructure organizations. The social protests of the summer of 2011 influenced Israeli CSOs as well, sharpening the discourse over their objectives and roles.[57] Nowadays, Israel's CSO leaders are more alert to the political and social processes happening

---

[54] The Open Government Partnership project, led by the US President and the British Prime Minister, is aimed at advancing reforms for open government. The partnership now comprises sixty-four countries, including Israel; accessed January 11, 2016, www.opengovpartnership.org/.

[55] *Open Government Partnership – Draft Action Plan for 2012* (Prime Minister Office, 2011), accessed January 11, 2016, www.idi.org.il/media/293904/action_plan.pdf. This plan was prepared for the government by the Minister in Charge of Improvement of Government Services.

[56] In recent years, whenever a scandal appeared in the Israeli nonprofit sector, Guidestar-Israel served as an important instrument in providing information about the relevant organization.

[57] Thus, for example, civil society organizations that have focused on fighting governmental corruption make use of social networks in order to enhance public scandals relating to corruption. The ever-increasing use of social communications technology has created an efficient new means of a kind of "enforcement"; Doron Navot and Nissim Cohen, "How Policy Entrepreneurs Reduce Corruption in Israel," *Governance* 28(1) (2015): 61–76; Benjamin Gidron, Nissan Limor, and Ester Zychlinsky, *From "Third Sector" to "Civil Sector": On the*

around them. The sector's leadership senses the need to take an active part in shaping the intersector relationship, to participate in the government's public policy initiatives and initiate their own policy proposals, and to influence the ways in which regulatory mechanisms are developed. The issue of self-regulation comes up repeatedly in discussions and negotiations with the government officials; the sector has published a new version of Noat's best practices;[58] and the sector's umbrella organization has improved its relations with Midot.

6.7 CONCLUSION

In Israel, the regulatory relationships between the government, its statutory agencies, and CSOs are complex. On one hand, government policy seems to promote the independence of CSOs. On the other hand, the rapid expansion of civil society activities in an era of new perspectives on social networks and accrued public influence on social issues has provoked tension between the two sectors: the government and the civil sector.

The complexity of regulating CSOs brought about a policy of "one size fits all" during the third regulatory wave, in the 1990s. As a result, Israeli CSOs labor under a homogenous regulatory regime that does not differentiate between different types of organizations, their activities, and their modes of operation. The main feature of this regime was an increase in the dominance of the statutory regulators. This process fits the Israeli centralized bureaucracy model and does not permit the development of significant "softer" or sectoral regulatory mechanisms; there is no division of labor, in the regulatory sphere, between government and civil society.

That growing regulatory pressure motivated the civil society sector to initiate self-regulation, as this chapter has shown through the discussions of Naot, Midot, and GuideStar Israel, but it did not flourish. The failure of self-regulation to become integrated into the regulatory environment was due to the hard form of state regulation; an asymmetry of power between the statutory regulator and CSOs; the lack of private resources to fund quasi-independent self-regulatory mechanisms or institutions; governmental control over access to resources, data, and information; and poor awareness and understanding of CSOs toward regulatory activities.

Collective Identity of Civil Sector Organizations (Jerusalem: The Van Leer Jerusalem Institute, 2015) (in Hebrew).

[58] Limor, n. 30.

But some of this may be changing. Although Israel has a centralized statutory regime, there are some indications of a new approach to reviewing the overall regulatory policy of the government. The readiness for an open dialogue and the existence of tri-sectoral frameworks on issues of concern to the civilsociety sector are part of the new approach. Civil society has identified a window of opportunity in which to amplify its voice in order to play an active part in shaping public policy and, perhaps, over time, to seek more self-regulatory mechanisms and a new bargain in the regulatory division of labor. The sector's Achilles' heel is its difficulty in shaping its actions; deciding what should be done, when, and how; and developing the resources and mechanisms to act.

It is too early to determine whether a new wave is at the threshold, whether government and civil society will find a new regulatory modus of operation, and whether self-regulation or co-regulation will grow. Time will tell if and how the Israeli discourse between these two sectors will develop, and whether the two sectors together can shape a new division of labor between the statutory regulator and civil society's self-regulation. Israeli society is suffering from major social gaps. One of the keys to reducing these gaps is cooperation between the government and civil society. A better regulatory regime and some division of labor between government and the sector is a cornerstone for fruitful collaboration.

7

Regulation and Self-Regulation in the Mexican Nonprofit Sector

MICHAEL D. LAYTON

7.1 INTRODUCTION

In the second decade of the twenty-first century, the three major sectors of Mexican society are in the midst of a thoroughgoing transformation: from a semi-authoritarian, one-party political system to an electoral democracy;[1] from a government-dominated economy to a (relatively) free, globalized market;[2] and from a third sector dominated by corporatist, clientelistic confederations of labor, business, and *campesinos* to a more independent nonprofit sector.[3] While Mexico's economic opening has proceeded, Mexico's democratic transition has been described as "difficult"[4] and "frustrated"[5] and its democracy as "elusive"[6] and "interrupted."[7] An important element of this incomplete transition to democracy is a historically weak civil society.[8]

---

[1] Roderic Ai Camp, *Politics in Mexico: Democratic Consolidation or Decline?* (New York: Oxford University Press, 2014); Julia Preston and Samuel Dillon, *Opening Mexico: The Making of a Democracy* (New York: Farrar, Straus and Giroux, 2004).

[2] Russell Crandall, Guadalupe Paz, and Riordan Roett, *Mexico's Democracy at Work: Political and Economic Dynamics* (Boulder, CO: Lynne Rienner, 2005).

[3] Jo Tuckman, *Mexico: Democracy Interrupted* (New Haven, CT: Yale University Press, 2012); Camp, n. 1.

[4] Jonathan Fox, "The Difficult Transition from Clientelism to Citizenship: Lessons from Mexico," *World Politics* 46(2) (1994): 151–184.

[5] Alberto J. Olvera, "The Elusive Democracy: Political Parties, Democratic Institutions, and Civil Society in Mexico," *Latin American Research Review* 45(Special Issue) (2010): 79–107.

[6] Alberto J. Olvera, *La democratización frustrada: limitaciones institucionales y colonización política de las instituciones garantes de derechos y de participación ciudadana en México* (Mexico City and Xalapa, Verazcruz: CIESAS and Universidad Veracruzana, 2010).

[7] Tuckman, n. 3.

[8] Michael D. Layton, "Philanthropy and the Third Sector in Mexico: The Enabling Environment and Its Limitations," *Norteamérica Revista Académica* 4(1) (2009): 87–120; Olvera, n. 5.

For most of the two hundred years since independence, the Mexican state has had a contentious relationship with civil society. The legacy of these two centuries is an underdeveloped nonprofit sector and a public that is characterized by low levels of civic engagement, social trust, and confidence in institutions, including nonprofits.[9] This chapter demonstrates that in moments of regime change, when an independent nonprofit sector has been viewed as a threat, the Mexican state has imposed stricter – at times draconian – regulations. In response to these regulatory waves, the sector has historically mounted a vociferous, even at times violent defense. It is only since the 1990s that these struggles have played out in the legislative arena, and only since 2005 that self-regulatory initiatives have come into play.

In Mexico, the embrace of self-regulation arises from three key influences. First, a fundamental element of the democratic transition has been the demand to fight corruption via increased transparency of public actors: nonprofits have taken a leading role in this cultural shift, prompting them to embrace mechanisms of transparency in both their regulation and self-regulation. Second, government-mandated transparency of nonprofits has not had a significant impact on this crisis of public confidence in the sector: the regulatory requirement for transparency has come about as part of the more general cultural shift and in part due to nonprofit advocacy. Third, as nonprofits have increasingly turned to domestic philanthropy as a source of financial support, they have had to address the acute lack of public trust in the sector; this lack of public trust has been a key impediment in soliciting donations.[10]

Self-regulation has been less a proactive effort to forestall greater regulation than a means of achieving increased visibility and transparency of the sector, generating greater public trust, and thereby increasing public support. The impact of these efforts on improving levels of public trust in and support for Mexican nonprofits is, as yet, unproven. The means to strengthen the nonprofit sector must be sought in efforts that include, but go beyond, regulation and self-regulation.

7.2 THE EVOLUTION OF A CONTENTIOUS RELATIONSHIP: FROM INDEPENDENCE THROUGH THE RISE OF THE PRI

Mexico's political history is one of centralized power, from the time of the Aztec empire, the Spanish colony, and the dictatorship of Porfirio Díaz in the

[9] Michael D. Layton and Alejandro Moreno, *Filantropía y sociedad civil en México: análisis de la ENAFI 2005–2008* (Mexico: Porrúa, 2010); Alejandro Moreno and Patricia Mendez, "Attitudes toward Democracy: Mexico in Comparative Perspective," *International Journal of Comparative Sociology* 43(3–5) (2002): 350–367.

[10] Layton and Moreno, n. 9, chapter 2.

late nineteenth century to the emergence of the single-party state in the aftermath of the Mexican Revolution of 1910–1920.[11] In this context, whenever the state has not been able to control the nonprofit sector, be it religious or secular, it has viewed the sector as a rival and threat, and the regulatory framework has reflected that attitude.

This conflict has become particularly acute during times of regime change, including the prelude to independence, the conflict between Liberals and Conservatives in the nineteenth century, the aftermath of the revolution (1910–1920), and the recent democratic transition. Up until the democratic transition, the result of this conflict has been civil war. During the transition, as the state has become more democratic, the struggle is taking place mainly in the public policy arena, although some insurgent movements have remained active.

Throughout Mexico's history, the Catholic Church has played a preeminent role in the provision of charity and poor relief, which at times has brought it into conflict with the state. These tensions are a precursor to the government's relationship to the nonprofit sector today.[12] Throughout the nineteenth century, associations existed largely outside the hierarchies of church and state.[13] The only major aspect of the nonprofit sector to develop during this time was that of traditional charities aimed at the alleviation of poverty through direct services, such as poorhouses, orphanages, and hospitals. Conflict between the Mexican government and the Church peaked during mid-nineteenth century, when the liberal state struggled to legitimize itself in the face of conservative opposition allied with the Church. From 1859 to 1863 the government passed what came to be known as the "Reform Laws," confiscating Church property, secularizing the provision of social welfare, and establishing the first regulatory framework for private, secular charity.[14]

At the end of the nineteenth century, the national government created the first Oversight Board for Private Assistance (Junta de Asistencia Privada [JAP])

[11] Camp, n. 1; Enrique Krauze, *Mexico: Biography of Power* (New York: Harper Perennial, 1998); Richard M. Morse, "Toward a Theory of Spanish American Government," *Journal of the History of Ideas* 15(1) (1954): 71–93.

[12] Silvia Marina Arrom, "Catholic Philanthropy and Civil Society: The Lay Volunteers of St. Vincent de Paul in 19th-Century Mexico," in *Philanthropy and Social Change in Latin America*, ed. Cynthia Sanborn and Felipe Portocarrero (Cambridge, MA: Harvard University Press, 2005).

[13] Carlos A. Forment, *Democracy in Latin America, 1760–1900, vol. 1: Civic Selfhood and Public Life in Mexico and Peru* (Chicago, IL: University of Chicago Press, 2003), especially chapters 5 and 7.

[14] Rodney R. Alvarez, "Social Welfare (Mexico): Before 1867," in *Encyclopedia of Social Welfare History in North America*, ed. John M. Herrick and Paul H. Stuart (Thousand Oaks, CA: Sage, 2005); José María Serna de la Garza, *The Constitution of Mexico: A Contextual Analysis* (Portland, OR: Hart, 2013), 14.

for Mexico City, which was a semi-autonomous organization whose mandate was to regularize and supervise charitable activities delivered by private, nonprofit organizations.[15] The legislation that established the JAP also created a unique legal corporate form, the institution of private assistance, which today includes about 1500 nonprofits, or 5 percent of those on major government registries. Today half of Mexico's states have a JAP or similar organization, and they tend to include traditional charities and some of the largest grantmaking foundations.[16]

7.3 AFTERMATH OF THE REVOLUTION, 1920–1960S

The Mexican Revolution (1910–1920) again pitted progressive elements of society against conservatives aligned with the Church. During the post-revolutionary period, the state imposed a series of onerous restrictions on the Church, and both institutions sought to organize key sectors of society, including workers and *campesinos*, setting them on a collision course.[17] In response, devout Catholics mounted an armed revolt from 1926 to 1928, known as the Cristero Rebellion. During this time a seminary student assassinated the president-elect, Álvaro Obregón, provoking a political crisis that contributed to the formation of the Institutional Revolutionary Party (Partido Revolucionario Institucional [PRI]). The PRI constituted a single-party state that was the longest ruling party in the history of the world, from 1929 to 2000.[18] The preeminent role of the Church in charitable activities was supplanted by the expansive corporatist state of the PRI, which left little room for independent associations aside from the most traditional charities.[19]

From its creation in 1929, the authoritarian, corporatist rule of the PRI systemically suppressed the emergence of an autonomous nonprofit sector, leaving the sector woefully underdeveloped in its ability to participate in the process of democratic consolidation.[20] A particular hallmark of the regime was

---

[15] "Antecedentes históricos," *Junta de Asistencia Privada*, accessed December 17, 2015, /www.jap .org.mx/index.php?option=com_content&view=article&id=15&Itemid=124.

[16] "Directorio," *Coordinación Nacional de Juntas de Asistencia Privada*, accessed December 17, 2015, http://conajap.org/index.php/directorio/instituciones-por-entidad.

[17] Serna de la Garza, n. 14, 185–186; Jean A. Meyer, *The Cristero Rebellion: The Mexican People between Church and State, 1926–1929* (New York: Cambridge University Press, 1976), chapter 2.

[18] Emily Edmonds-Poli and David A. Shirk, *Contemporary Mexican Politics* (Lanham, MD: Rowman and Littlefield, 2012).

[19] Viviane Brachet-Márquez, "Social Welfare (Mexico): Before 1867," in *Encyclopedia of Social Welfare History in North America*, ed. John M. Herrick and Paul H. Stuart (Thousand Oaks, CA: Sage, 2005).

[20] Jonathan Fox and Luis Hernandez, "Mexico's Difficult Democracy: Grassroots Movements, NGOs, and Local Government," *Alternatives: Global, Local, Political* 17(2) (1992): 165–208;

its ability to create popular organizations among workers, *campesinos*, and business people via a corporatist structure that created channels of intermediation and control, thus precluding the emergence of autonomous associations and coopting them when they did emerge.[21] The weakness of associational life in Mexico today is the aftermath of the success of these PRI strategies.[22]

7.4 THE DEMOCRATIC TRANSITION, 1960S–2000

Since the 1960s, a new generation of nonprofits has emerged, focused on issues such as democracy, community development, human rights, and government accountability.[23] At the same time, the nonprofit sector began to advocate for a more propitious regulatory framework, protesting against unfavorable measures and increasingly proposing more favorable legislation.

A series of events beginning in 1968 shook the public's acquiescence to the rule of the PRI, awakened political activism, and revived associational life.[24] These included the violent repression of the student movement of 1968; the debt default and economic crisis of 1982, undermining the PRI's claim of delivering prosperity;[25] the devastating 1985 earthquake, to which the government failed to respond thereby prompting citizens to organize themselves and nonprofits to channel foreign aid;[26] and the electoral fraud of 1988 that resulted in the election of Carlos Salinas of the PRI as president.[27]

Daniel M. Sabet, *Nonprofits and Their Networks: Cleaning the Waters along Mexico's Northern Border* (Tucson: University of Arizona Press, 2008).

[21] Fox, n. 4; Fox and Hernandez, n. 20; Andrew Selee, *Decentralization, Democratization and Informal Power in Mexico* (University Park: Penn State University Press, 2011); Sabet, n. 20.

[22] Clara Jusidman, "Transparencia en las organizaciones de la sociedad civil," in *10 años de transparencia en México*, ed. Federal Institute for Access to Public Information (Mexico: IFAI, 2013); Fox and Hernandez, n. 20.

[23] Gustavo Verduzco, *Organizaciones no lucrativas: vision de su trayectoria en México* (Mexico: Colegio de México, 2003), chapter 3.

[24] Vikram K. Chand, *Mexico's Political Awakening* (South Bend, IN: University of Notre Dame Press, 2001); José Fernández Santillan, *El despertar de la sociedad civil (Con Una Cierta Mirada)* (Mexico City: Océano, 2003).

[25] Rabobank, *Economic Report: The Mexican 1982 Debt Crisis* (The Netherlands: Rabobank, 2013), accessed December 17, 2015, https://economics.rabobank.com/publications/2013/september/the-mexican-1982-debt-crisis/.

[26] Rafael Reygadas Robles Gil, *Abriendo veredas: iniciativas públicas y sociales de las redes de organizaciones civiles* (Mexico City: Convergencia de Organismos Civiles por la Democracia, 1998), 158; Carlos Monsiváis, *"No sin nosotros": Los días del terremoto 1985–2005* (Mexico City: Ediciones Era, 2005).

[27] Stephen D. Morris, *Political Corruption in Mexico: The Impact of Democratization* (Boulder, CO: Lynne Rienner, 2009), chapter 3.

The net result of these events was to create political opportunities for social movements and organizations to coalesce and challenge the hegemony of the PRI.[28] In the process of Mexico's democratic transition, as organizations began to emerge to advocate for free and fair elections and greater governmental accountability, tensions mounted between the organizations and the ruling party. Thus at the end of the twentieth century the regulation of the nonprofit sector took on a newfound importance, both for the state and for the emerging nonprofit sector.

The current cycle of nonprofit regulation began with a fiscal reform package in 1989. Until that time, by virtue of incorporating as a civil association organizations had enjoyed automatic tax-exempt status under Title III of the Income Tax Law as nonprofit legal entities, like unions and housing cooperatives. Their exemption occurred by default rather than through an explicit legal recognition, thus they were in a "fiscal limbo" without an explicit recognition of their public benefit status.[29] At the end of 1989, the Salinas administration put forth its major fiscal reform package, with the overriding goal to increase tax revenue. In the closing days of the legislative session, the treasury secretary proposed reclassifying civil associations as profit-seeking entities under Title II, thereby subjecting them to income tax.[30] Congress concurred, and the reclassification became law.

Following this hostile change in tax law, in 1990 nonprofits began a movement to seek legal reform that not only would undo the initial damage but also would force the federal government to recognize that the activities of associations were of public interest and to provide public funds to nonprofits. The organizations insisted that this financial support should be handled in a transparent manner in order to avoid governmental cooptation and promote fairness, that is, to keep the government honest and preserve the autonomy of the recipient organizations;[31] at this time promoting nonprofit transparency per se and trust in the sector were not considerations.

The leadership of this movement was comprised of three umbrella organizations (Convergencia de Organismos Civiles por la Democracia, Foro de Apoyo Mutuo, and the Mexican Center for Philanthropy), a research center (Fundación Miguel Alemán), and the Ibero-American University. During 1994 the organizers held forums in various states and in the following years

[28] Fox, n. 4; Fox and Hernandez, n. 20; Sabet, n. 20. [29] Reygadas, n. 26, 157.

[30] Reygadas, n. 26; María Teresa Villareal Martínez, "La participación institucionalizada de organizaciones civiles en la construcción de la gobernanza," *Revista Legislativa de Estudios Sociales y de Opinión Pública* 3(5) (2010): 121–154.

[31] Reygadas, n. 26, 197.

repeatedly presented various legislative proposals,[32] but they did not win legislative approval until the first election of an opposition party candidate for president in 2000.

7.5 REFORM AND SCANDAL IN THE FOX ADMINISTRATION, 2000–2006

With the election of the first opposition party candidate to the presidency in 2000, the nonprofit sector had high hopes of transforming its relationship with the federal government. Encouraged by the campaign statements of the presidential candidate, Vicente Fox, on the importance of civil society in the consolidation of Mexican democracy, and bolstered by the convening of roundtable discussions between the incoming administration and the sector in the period between the election and the inauguration, the nonprofit sector redoubled its efforts to achieve a more favorable regulatory framework.[33]

Mexicans suffer a profound lack of trust in their government and their politicians, and this is a legacy of authoritarianism and the birthmark of Mexican democracy.[34] In the wake of Fox's victory, civil society was imbued with a level of moral authority, in contrast to the corruption of the state.[35] The Fox administration enlisted the help of civil society to fight corruption, by informing the public, encouraging public vigilance of governmental action, and promoting ethical behavior within business and nonprofit organizations (NPOs).[36]

The first reform was the Federal Transparency and Access to Governmental Public Information Act 2002. Formulated by academics and NPO leaders, the law created a federal agency to oversee compliance with the law, but more importantly it initiated a shift in public expectations regarding access to information.[37] This shift became a key element both in subsequent government regulation of the nonprofit sector and in self-regulation efforts.

---

[32] Reygadas, n. 26, chapter 3.

[33] Rubén Aguilar Valenzuela, "La sociedad civil y el gobierno en el tiempo de la alternancia," in *El Estado mexicano: herencias y cambios*, ed. Alberto Aziz Nassif and Jorge Alonso (Mexico: CIESAS, 2005).

[34] José Antonio Aguilar Rivera, "El capital social y el Estado: algunas aproximaciones al problema," in *Pensar en México*, ed. Héctor Aguilar Camín et al. (Mexico: Fondo de Cultura Economica, 2006), 102–103.

[35] Fernando Escalante, "México, fin de siglo," in Camin, n. 34; Morris, n. 27, 64.

[36] Morris, n. 27, 102–105.

[37] Morris, n. 27; Federal Institute for Access to Public Information, *10 años de transparencia en México* (Mexico: IFAI, 2013).

The next step in regulatory reform was the Federal Law for the Promotion of Activities Undertaken by CSOs 2003.[38] For its advocates, this was the culmination of a campaign that had begun in 1989 and a consequence of the roundtables that the incoming administration had held in 2000. The most important aspects of the law were its explicit recognition that the activities of civil society organizations are of public interest and the consequent mandate it imposed on the federal government to promote these activities.[39]

Specifically, the law exhorted federal ministries to provide public funds and fiscal incentives for eligible activities and to create opportunities for organizations to participate in the public policy process (Article 6). In order to enjoy these benefits, civil society organizations (CSOs) were required to enroll in a newly created Federal Registry of Civil Society Organizations (Articles 15–25). While the registry does disclose federal funding of CSOs, it does not provide any additional financial information from participating organizations. Nonprofit leaders thus tried to balance two competing goals: first, they wanted disclosure of federal funding to prevent governmental manipulation; second, they wanted to preclude the possibility that the government would use its information against organizations in a repressive manner.[40] At this time nonprofit advocates did not see strengthening public trust in the sector as a priority.

The Promotion Law created two new administrative entities: first, a commission composed of the secretaries of four key ministries (Interior, Social Development, Treasury, and Foreign Affairs), with the mandate "to facilitate coordination of the design, implementation, monitoring and evaluation of the actions and measures to promote the activities" of CSOs (Article 10), and second, a Technical Council, consisting of nine representatives of civil society, four academics, and two federal legislators, which was described as "an honorific body" whose mandate was "to propose, review and make recommendations regarding the administration, management and operation of the Register, and to work with the Commission to conduct a joint annual evaluation of promotional policies and actions" (Article 26). There were high hopes that the creation of the council would represent a major advance in providing an institutional forum for the nonprofit sector to interact with the federal

---

[38] Villareal Martínez, n. 30.

[39] Mónica Tapia-Alvarez and María Isabel Verduzco, *Fortalecimiento de la Ciudadanía Organizada: diagnóstico y reformas para un ambiente propicio en México* (Mexico: Alternativas y Capacidades 2013), 16; Ireri Ablanedo et al., *Defining a Fiscal Agenda for the Development of Civil Society Organizations in Mexico* (Mexico: Incide Social, ITAM, and ICNL, 2007).

[40] Alnoor Ebrahim, "Making Sense of Accountability: Conceptual Perspectives for Northern and Southern Profits," *Nonprofit Management & Leadership*, 14(2) (2003): 191–212.

government and thereby have input into its regulation. As the council did not have decision-making authority, it cannot be considered an example of co-regulation.

Although the council has issued regular evaluations on the implementation of the Promotion Law, it is not seen as an effective and agile interlocutor, and its legitimacy is diminished by the fact that its members are randomly selected and are not truly accountable to their nonprofit constituency. The functioning of both the commission and the council has been undermined by a lack of consistency in the participation of governmental representatives and little or no public funding for their activities.[41]

During the Fox administration, there were two high-profile scandals that affected the public debate over regulation of the nonprofit sector and diminished its previous level of moral authority. The organizations involved were a prolife organization called the National Pro-Life Committee, to which an irregular government allocation was made,[42] and Vamos México, a grantmaking foundation created by Fox's wife, which was mired in controversy for its lack of transparency.[43] The effect of these scandals, particularly the lack of a regulatory response, was to tarnish the image of the nonprofit sector and help set in motion the demand for greater sectoral transparency via both regulation and self-regulation,[44] as described below.

7.6 RECENT REGULATORY DEVELOPMENTS

Despite the mandate of the Promotion Law, the next president proposed the elimination of both tax exemption for nonprofits and the deductibility of charitable donations in the fiscal reform of July 2007.[45] Two months earlier, a group of institutions – Incide Social, AC (an advocacy nonprofit), the Philanthropy and Civil Society Project of the Autonomous Technological

---

[41] Tapia-Alvarez and Verduzco, n. 39.
[42] Helena Hofbauer, "El caso Provida: los alcances del acceso a la información vs. los límites de la rendición de cuentas," in *El poder de la transparencia: nueve derrotas a la opacidad*, ed. Pedro Salazar Ugarte (Mexico: IIJ-UNAM-IFAI, 2007).
[43] Sarah Silver, "First Lady's Foundation That Finds Itself in Shaky Ground," *Financial Times*, June 15, 2004; Sarah Silver, "Mexican First Lady's Foundation Leaves Grey Areas," *Financial Times*, February 24, 2005; Sarah Silver, "Marta Fox's Charity Sees Donations Fall after Exposé," *Financial Times*, May 25, 2005.
[44] Ablanedo et al., n. 39, 57.
[45] Sergio Garcia and Ireri Ablanedo, *Promoción de una agenda fiscal para el desarrollo de las organizaciones de la sociedad civil: sistematización de la experiencia mexicana* (Washington, DC: USAID and ICN, 2008).

Institute of Mexico (a university research effort),[46] the Mexican Center for Philanthropy, or Cemefi (an umbrella organization), and the International Center for Not-for-Profit Law – had presented their own policy proposal, *Definition of a Fiscal Agenda for the Development of Civil Society Organizations in Mexico*.[47] They had spent the preceding two years organizing forums with nonprofit leaders, lawyers, accountants, and government representatives across the country, in order to assess the impact of the fiscal framework on the sector and develop a national consensus on a plan for reform.[48] A remarkably diverse group of approximately sixty organizations and universities endorsed the *Fiscal Agenda* before its publication.

These signatories formed the nucleus of a national coalition that not only opposed the administration's hostile reforms, but also embraced a series of positive measures: expansion of the activities eligible for fiscal incentives, easing onerous registration requirements, and governmental disclosure of the amount donated to tax-exempt nonprofits.[49] The idea that disclosing financial data and undertaking self-regulation could address the lack of public confidence in the sector were also elements of the *Fiscal Agenda* document.[50] Thus key actors in Mexico were simultaneously reacting to a wave of governmental regulation and creating the first wave of nonprofit self-regulation: essentially all the nonprofits who later promoted self-regulatory initiatives played leading roles in this coalition.

This advocacy effort succeeded in convincing the legislature to maintain tax exemption of nonprofits and the deductibility of donations, but the debate in the legislature and in the media revealed a shocking level of distrust in the nonprofit sector and a firm if undocumented belief that charitable fiscal incentives were being abused.[51] Congress took the additional steps of mandating that the Tax Administration Service (SAT) develop a mechanism to ensure the transparency of tax-exempt nonprofits as well as placing a cap on the deductibility of donations of 7 percent of personal income and after-tax profits for businesses.[52]

In 2009 the SAT launched a transparency portal that offered a wealth of information, similar to that found on the Internal Revenue Service Form 990 for charitable organizations in the United States. Unfortunately its limitations soon became apparent, including the difficulty of finding the information on the SAT website, lack of promotion and visibility, and restricted search capabilities. The lack of impact on the part of government-mandated

---

[46] The author of this chapter was the director of this project and coordinator of the coalition.
[47] Ablanedo et al., n. 39.   [48] Garcia and Ablanedo, n. 45.   [49] Ibid., 96–98, appendix 1.
[50] Ablanedo et al., n. 39, 57–58.   [51] Garcia and Ablanedo, n. 45, 23–28.   [52] Ibid., 69.

financial disclosure was a factor in the launch of at least one self-regulatory initiative, Funds in Plain Sight.

In 2013, when the next administration proposed a fiscal reform package, the nonprofit sector was successful in negotiating the inclusion of two key reforms: the recognition of the right of organizations to undertake nonpartisan lobbying, and an expansion of the list of activities eligible for tax exemption.[53] Other damaging proposals were defeated, including one that would have undermined the creation of corporate-sponsored and family foundations. This success in defeating these proposals can be attributed to the increasing sophistication of the nonprofit sector in public policy advocacy, its greater legal expertise, and the development of stronger connections to both the congress and the treasury department.

7.7 SUMMARY OF REGULATORY DEVELOPMENTS

The period from 1989 to 2013 witnessed significant changes in the regulatory framework for the Mexican nonprofit sector. The hostile fiscal reform in 1989 prompted the sector to begin more than a decade of advocacy for the Promotion Law, and fiscal reform proposals have proven to be a key catalyst for activism. The passage of the Promotion Law in 2003, reflecting Mexico's democratic transition, marked an important step forward in the relationship between the sector and the Mexican state; however, both legislators and regulators have had a mixed record in acting in accordance with its mandate, and the administrative bodies it created have fallen short of fulfilling its aspirations.

For the treasury and the tax authorities, the internal institutional imperatives of increasing tax revenue and reducing fraud and abuse have had more weight than what is viewed as the external mandate coming from the Promotion Law. Now both frameworks require financial disclosure from nonprofits, but this enhanced transparency has not resulted in greater public trust in nongovernmental organizations.[54] In 2013 when Mexicans were asked how much trust they had in social or nongovernmental organizations, the most popular response was "none," at 44 percent, followed by "little" at 25 percent,

---

[53] "La Reforma Hacendaria y su impacto en las organizaciones civiles," *Causas Ciudadanas*, September 13, 2013, accessed December 17, 2015, www.causasciudadanas.org/2013/09/la-reforma-hacendaria-y-su-impacto-en.html.

[54] Layton and Moreno, n. 9; Michael D. Layton and Alejandro Moreno, "Key Factors in Individual Philanthropy: National Survey in Philanthropy and Civil Society (ENAFI) 2013" (paper presented at the XIII Third Sector Research Congress, UVM Campus Querétaro, September 9–10, 2013).

"some" at 20 percent, and "a great deal" at 5 percent (even "don't know" at 6 percent came in higher than "a great deal"). Unfortunately these results are all within a few percentage points of those for 2005, and nonprofits suffer the same level of distrust as police and local government, both of which are notorious for their corruption. This distrust reflects a national culture of suspicion,[55] fomented by extensive political corruption[56] and exacerbated by recent scandals in the nonprofit sector.

In the midst of its process of democratic consolidation, the Mexican government has been Janus-faced in its approach toward the nonprofit sector, reflecting the tension between its historically fraught relationship with the sector and the newly emerging values and practices of democratic governance. On the one hand, there has been an impulse on the part of the tax authorities to preclude abuse and tax evasion, to limit tax expenditures, and – at least in the eyes of the nonprofit sector – to exert control over the sector via the Income Tax Law. On the other, there is a broad policy mandate to encourage the activities of nonprofits, as established by a Federal Promotion Law and embraced by the Social Development Ministry. Thus, during the last decade there have been two simultaneous and conflicting crosscurrents of nonprofit regulation emanating from different ministries within the same government. Nonprofits have attempted to use governmental regulation to address a generalized distrust of the sector on the part of the public, but with little success, thus setting the stage for efforts at self-regulation.

7.8 NASCENT SELF-REGULATORY INITIATIVES: A CURE FOR WHAT AILS MEXICO'S NONPROFIT SECTOR?

Increasingly, in Mexico as well as elsewhere, the generation of greater public trust via stronger mechanisms of accountability and transparency has become an important element of recommendations for strengthening the nonprofit sector in terms of greater public support, especially donations.[57] The scandals during the Fox administration and the fiscal reform debate in 2007 accentuated the urgency of these issues for advocates and the importance of the sector putting its own house in order. This movement toward greater disclosure on the part of nonprofits has occurred in two phases: the first two efforts occurred

---

[55] Moreno and Mendez, n. 9.   [56] Morris, n. 27.

[57] Charities Aid Foundation, *Future World Giving: Building Trust in Charitable Giving* (West Malling: CAF, 2014), accessed December 17, 2015, www.cafonline.org/docs/default-source/about-us-publications/future-world-giving1.pdf; Mary Kay Gugerty and Aseem Prakash, eds., *Nonprofit Accountability Clubs: Voluntary Regulation of Nonprofit and Governmental Organizations* (New York: Cambridge University Press, 2010).

in 2005 and were due to the larger shift in Mexico's political culture toward a demand for greater transparency, and the last three were due to a recognition that the governmental disclosure requirements from the Promotion Law of 2003 and the fiscal reform of 2007 had not improved the public perception of the sector.

At the same time, a host of serious challenges confronting the Mexican nonprofit sector have also contributed to the rise of self-regulation. These include weak financial support for the sector, including a heavy dependence on fees for service and limited public and philanthropic support;[58] the withdrawal of international public and private support for the Mexican sector, as it has become a middle-income nation;[59] and lack of trust and the perception of corruption and ineffectiveness in the nonprofit sector.[60] As discussed above, even with greater access to financial data of nonprofits, polling data from 2005 to 2013 show no meaningful change in the level of public (dis)trust in the nonprofit sector.[61]

In addition, the Mexican nonprofit sector is highly fragmented. It lacks a strong, organized representative body that is recognized as being legitimate by its diverse, and at times conflicting, elements. One principal dividing line among Mexican third-sector organizations is between more conservative elements (including traditional charities and some of the largest fundraising efforts) and its more progressive actors (which often take on a more antagonistic role vis-à-vis the government). As one longtime nonprofit advocate recently wrote, "Civil society [is] very weak, very scattered, [and] poorly organized."[62]

The lack of coordinating bodies for the sector has had important implications for self-regulation. It has proven difficult to arrive at a single set of standards for a diverse and divided sector, much less put into place significant

---

[58] Sergio Garcia et al., *Donativos privados 2006. Una aproximación a la contribución ciudadana para las causas sociales* (Mexico: Incide Social/ITAM, 2009); Michael D. Layton, "Focos rojos en las cifras sobre sociedad civil organizada," *Este País: Tendencias y Opiniones* 247 (2011 November): 9–13.

[59] Siân Herbert, "Reassessing Aid to Middle-Income Countries: The Implications of the European Commission's Policy of Differentiation for Developing Countries," *Working Paper* 349 (London: Overseas Development Institute, 2012), accessed December 17, 2015, www.odi .org/sites/odi.org.uk/files/odi-assets/publications-opinion-files/7710.pdf.

[60] Layton and Moreno, n. 9; Michael D. Layton and Alejandro Moreno, "Philanthropy and Social Capital in Mexico," *International Journal of Nonprofit and Voluntary Sector Marketing* 19(3) (2014): 209–219; Mexican Center for Philanthropy et al., *A Snapshot of Civil Society in Mexico: Analytical Report on the CIVICUS Civil Society Index* (2011), accessed December 17, 2015, http://civicus.org/images/stories/csi/csi_phase2/mexico%20acr.pdf.

[61] Layton and Moreno, n. 54.   [62] Jusidman, n. 22, 117.

enforcement mechanisms. No fewer than five nongovernmental, self-regulatory initiatives have emerged over the last decade, all of them emphasizing public disclosure of organizational and financial information and three of them involving some level of certification. Participation in four of the five initiatives is voluntary, and the fifth relies on publicly available data provided by the government. Each of these initiatives is outlined below, in chronological order.

7.8.1 *Pronouncement of CSOs on Internal Transparency and Accountability (2005)*

The first step toward nonprofit self-regulation occurred in 2005, three years after the Access to Public Information Law was passed. A collective of twenty-three nonprofits and one labor union issued the one-page *Pronouncement of Civil Society Organizations on Internal Transparency and Accountability: Congruence between Values and Actions.*[63] Many of these groups were leaders in the field of governmental transparency, both having led the drive to pass the Public Information Law and subsequently using the law to evaluate governmental spending and programs.

The statement emphasized the importance of ethical consistency on the part of organizations and that their transparency would lend greater legitimacy to their standing as public actors. The organizations committed to disclose a wide range of organizational information as well as programmatic reports, tax declarations, and other information on sources of funding, and called on other organizations to follow their example. A year later researchers conducted an independent review of compliance with these voluntary standards and found that while half of the signatories divulged their organizational information, more than 90 percent failed to disclose their financial data.[64]

---

[63] "Pronunciamiento de las organizaciones de la sociedad civil en torno a la transparencia interna y la rendición de cuentas: congruencia entre valores y acciones" (Mexico, 2005), accessed December 17, 2015, http://alternativasycapacidades.org/sites/default/files/adjuntos/ Pronunciamiento%20Transparencia%202005.pdf; Fundar, "Sobre el origen de la transparencia y la rendición de cuentas, así como su fuente legal," *Cultura de la Legalidad: Blog Oficial* (December 6, 2013), accessed December 17, 2015, http://culturadelalegalidad.org.mx/blog/ sobre-el-origen-de-la-transparencia-y-la-rendicion-de-cuentas-asi-como-su-fuente-legal/.

[64] Angel Kuri, Michael Layton, and César Reyes, "Transparencia y rendición de cuentas al interior de las OSC: una evaluación preliminar" (paper presented at the VI Third Sector Research Seminar, Mexico City, September 12–13, 2006).

The effort lacked further institutionalization or follow-up. Perhaps its most lasting impact was that two of the signatories, the Cemefi and Alternativas y Capacidades, subsequently sponsored other self-regulatory initiatives.

7.8.2 *Indicators of Institutionality and Transparency (2005)*

The same year that the *Pronouncement* was issued, one of the participating umbrella organizations, Cemefi, launched a sector-led certification initiative, the Indicators of Accreditation of Institutionality and Transparency.[65] The stated goal for the Indicators was to "increase the transparency and accountability of civil society organizations in order to increase the confidence of donors (corporations, foundations and individuals) and, thus, increase donations and partnerships."[66]

The first eight indicators are basic elements of institutionality, and the last two relate to transparency:

1. Legal incorporation
2. Tax exemption
3. Verifiable telephone and address
4. Three years in operation
5. Three sources of revenue
6. Use of volunteers
7. Distinction between board and paid staff
8. Payment of payroll taxes
9. Publication of an annual programmatic and financial reports
10. Publication of vision, mission, and objectives.[67]

The process of accreditation consists of a self-diagnostic self-assessment or self-evaluation followed by a review of documentation by Cemefi and the determination of a score based on compliance (basic five, medium six to eight, optimum nine to ten). Those that reach the optimum level are recognized at a public ceremony and have permission to publish a special logo on their materials and website. From 2014 to 2016 the number of organizations achieving an optimal level of compliance has held steady at about 700.[68]

---

[65] "Antecedentes," Cemefi, accessed December 17, 2015, www.cemefi.org/programas/indicadores-institucionalidad-y-transparencia/antecedentes.html.

[66] "Indicadores de Institucionalidad y Transparencia," Cemefi, accessed December 17, 2015, www.cemefi.org/programas/indicadores-institucionalidad-y-transparencia.html.

[67] "Los 10 indicadores," Cemefi, accessed December 17, 2015, www.cemefi.org/programas/indicadores-institucionalidad-y-transparencia/los-10-indicadores.html.

[68] "Directorio," Cemefi, accessed December 17, 2015, www.cemefi.org/images/stories/directorios/projet/Directorio-de-Organizaciones-Acreditadas-2015.pdf.

Given the relatively lenient requirements and the lack of sanctions, it is not clear what impact the Indicators have had, as Cemefi does not offer systematic evidence of the benefits to the participants. Consistent with the experience in other countries, it is difficult for an accreditation scheme sponsored by such a membership organization to be effective in enforcing standards of behavior.[69] On the other hand, the initiative may well have helped create a higher level of consciousness about these issues.

7.8.3 *Filantrofilia (2009)*

The next major self-regulatory and accountability initiative was launched in 2009 by a newly created organization that was neither an umbrella organization nor a tax-exempt nonprofit; it might best be described as a self-regulatory entrepreneur.[70] Filantrofilia offers a holistic evaluation that covers five areas: internal governance and strategy, economic sustainability, communications, management and operations, and social return on investment (SROI).[71] In a newspaper interview in 2012, its director described the effort as the pioneer of the SROI methodology in Latin America and stated their intention to rate 2000 organizations in two years.[72]

Although the breadth of the evaluation criteria exceeds that of Cemefi, an assessment of its rigor is impossible as further details of the criteria are not made public. This perhaps reflects the fact that Filantrofilia seems to operate as a for-profit enterprise, thus regarding its methodology as proprietary and its confidentiality as key to its own financial sustainability. (Since 2012 a related nonprofit, Friends of Filantrofilia, has offered scholarships for smaller organizations to participate in the certification process.) The evaluation is done onsite and includes interviews with staff and board, as well as a survey of beneficiaries. The result is a letter grade, similar to bond ratings, from a top score of AA down to F. Two characteristics are unique to this effort among the five initiatives: the calculation of the SROI as a metric of the effectiveness of programs, and the direct facilitation of donations.

---

[69] Dennis Young, "Nonprofit Infrastructure Associations as Reluctant Clubs," in Gugerty and Prakash, n. 57.

[70] Mark Sidel, "Guardians Guarding Themselves: A Comparative Perspective on Nonprofit Self-Regulation," *Chicago-Kent Law Review* 80 (2005): 803–835.

[71] "Metodología," *Filantrofilia*, accessed December 17, 2015, www.filantrofilia.org/metodologia_s4.html.

[72] Karla Rodriguez, "Califica Filantrofilia a 200 empresas," *Reforma*, May 28, 2012, accessed December 17, 2015, www.reforma.com/aplicacioneslibre/articulo/default.aspx?id=66881&md5=84e9cd27648c62f248c66ba6a62c6f02&ta=0dfdbac11765226904c16cb9ad1b2efe&po=4.

Like Cemefi, Filantrofilia charges for its services and gives organizations the right to prohibit the publication of their results: this option of deciding whether or not to publish results is attractive to organizations that are fearful of a poor review, but its consequence in terms of generating public trust is unclear. As of the summer of 2016 there were just over 200 organizations listed on its website: 163 with expired ratings, twenty-three with no public information available, three in process of being rated, and twenty with ratings; oddly enough, Amigos de Filantrofilia was rated F.[73] The website provided an option to donate, but only to the one rated organization. (Ironically, the website provides neither any financial information about Filantrofilia as an institution nor annual reports.) It would seem that the rigor of the evaluation and its financial cost prohibit greater participation. This initiative is a voluntary scheme that is aimed at using membership as an indicator of an organization's performance and trustworthiness.

7.8.4 *"I trust"* (2011)

In 2011, a fourth self-regulatory initiative was launched, called Building Transparent Civil Organizations and nicknamed Confío ("I trust"). A number of elements set this effort apart from the preceding two accreditation processes. Developed in the northern city of Chihuahua rather than Mexico City, Confío has emerged from a partnership between Mexico's strongest community foundation (Chihuahua Business Foundation), its largest private university (Monterrey Technological), and a corporate foundation (Fundación Telefonica). It is an initiative of the state's Center for Strengthening of Civil Society Organizations and is based on a methodology developed by Fundación Lealtad of Spain. Given the origin of its methodology and its membership in the International Committee of Fundraising Organizations (ICFO), Confío has much stronger links to international standards than any of its predecessors.

Like Filantrofilia, Confío provides a rigorous review of an organization's management, governance, and transparency practices, and its report states the organization's compliance with nine principles divided into thirty-six criteria. These principles are:

1. Good governance
2. Clarity of mission

---

[73] "Organizaciones," *Filantrofilia*, accessed December 17, 2015, www.filantrofilia.org/organizaciones_s3.html.

3. Program planning and follow-up
4. Integrity in communication
5. Financial transparency
6. Diversity in funding sources
7. Adequate financial controls
8. Presentation of financial statements and legal compliance
9. Promotion of volunteering.

The evaluation is valid for two years, and then the organization must be reviewed again. Unlike Filantrofilia and Cemefi, Confío offers not only an overall grade but also a detailed report on its website of the evaluated organizations' compliance with each sub-principle. Evaluated organizations can display a seal on their website and promotional materials.

Confío bases its analysis on a review of documentation (like Cemefi), rather than interviews (like Filantrofilia). Unlike the other accreditations, it provides its service free of charge to participating organizations, but it requires that the results be published on Confío's website regardless of the outcome. Organizations may provide written objections to issues raised in their evaluation that are included in the report. The requirement to publish the results of a formal review goes a long way in explaining why, although it has facilitated self-assessments for nearly a thousand organizations in workshops nationwide, only seventy-nine associations are currently listed as "Analyzed CSOs" on Confío's website as of August 2016. Many organizations discover in their self-assessment that they are deficient in terms of financial transparency or governance practices, and fear that publishing their results will diminish rather than enhance their standing with the public.[74] This confirms the typical inverse relationship between the stringency of evaluation criteria and lower rates of participation.

7.8.5 *Funds in Plain Sight (2013)*

The most recently launched initiative is not an accreditation process but is best described as an "information gateway,"[75] along the lines of GuideStar combined with the U.S.-based Foundation Center. It is the only one of these self-regulatory initiatives that relies on information made publicly available by

---

[74] Alberto Hernandez Baqueiro et al., *Transparencia en organizaciones sin fines de lucro: Chihuahua, Distrito Federal, Guadalajara, Monterrey y Puebla* (Mexico: Indesol and Confío, 2012), accessed December 17, 2015, http://confio.org.mx/inicio/wp-content/uploads/2014/03/Transparencia-en-OSFL-2012-Edici%C3%B3n-1.pdf.

[75] Ebrahim, n. 40, 203; Fondos a la Vista, accessed December 17, 2015, www.fondosalavista.mx/.

law. Funds in Plain Sight (FALV) was launched in January 2013 as a partnership between a Mexican nonprofit (Alternativas y Capacidades), a university research project (Project on Philanthropy and Civil Society/ITAM),[76] and the Foundation Center, in addition to a coalition of six founding donors from both the United States and Mexico. The starting point for this effort was the difficulty of accessing and searching the financial data that were made publicly available as a result of the 2007 Income Tax Reform; this effort is therefore the most direct response to a failure of governmental regulation to achieve its stated aim of facilitating access to nonprofit financial data and thereby increasing the possibility of building trust in the nonprofit sector.[77]

The website provides a user-friendly search engine for a database of information on more than 20,000 nonprofits, which includes not only the universe of active tax-exempt nonprofits but also the organizations in the Federal Promotion Law's registry. Thus while the scale of the coverage and the detail on financial data are unparalleled among the self-regulatory efforts, it does not review documentation of governance practices or programs. It is especially important that this website provides detailed information to the public for the first time about grantmaking by Mexico's biggest donor institutions, which are tax-exempt organizations. Unlike the other initiatives, since FALV uses publicly available data, it does not require membership or approval from participating organizations, although organizations do have the opportunity to provide additional information by registering on the site. More than 500 organizations have done so, and they have the right to display a seal on their website and promotional material.

7.8.6 *Analysis of Self-Regulatory Initiatives in Mexico*

This review of self-regulatory initiatives identifies a number of triggers for their creation over the last decade. First, the larger societal trend toward the expectation of greater transparency challenged organizations to be ethically consistent in providing financial information, just as they expected the government to do so. Second, as nonprofits began seeking funding from domestic philanthropy, the lack of public trust in the sector became a major stumbling block. Pragmatically, it was seen as imperative that the sector strengthen its transparency. Third, although the Promotion Law and the fiscal reform both

---

[76] The author is one of the founders of this effort and continues to serve as an advisor.
[77] Michael D. Layton, "Website Aims to Offer Trustworthy Data on Mexico's Civil Sector," *Hispanics in Philanthropy Blog* (2013), accessed December 17, 2015, www.hiponline.org/resources/hip-blog/blog/417.

required financial disclosure by nonprofits, these regulations had not proven sufficient to address the crisis of public confidence in the sector.

It is possible to distinguish two waves of self-regulatory initiatives, the first two projects in 2005 and the subsequent efforts in 2009, 2011, and 2013. What distinguishes the first two efforts in 2005 is their limited nature, the *Pronouncement* in terms of the number of participants and its lack of institutionality, and the Cemefi Indicators in terms of the rudimentary nature of the review. The significant regulatory wave in between the two sets of initiatives was the fiscal reform of 2007, which put in evidence the degree of distrust that policymakers, opinion leaders, and the general public had toward the nonprofit sector. The self-regulatory initiatives in the second wave seemed to aim at addressing that distrust and were much more ambitious, with Filantrofilia and Confío offering a systematic review of operations and accreditation, and Funds in Plain Sight offering detailed financial data on a significant swath of the nonprofit sector. Unfortunately neither of these two accreditation processes has gained much traction, neither among nonprofits nor the public, and distrust of the sector remains pronounced.

Although the two most ambitious accreditation efforts (Filantrofilia and Confío) are of recent origin, all three (including Cemefi's Indicators) have achieved only a limited reach: out of a universe of 40,000 legally incorporated nonprofits, of which there are about 7000 registered tax-exempt charitable organizations,[78] fewer than 800, or less than 2 percent, are currently participating in these efforts. This low participation rate may be attributed to a rather lopsided cost/benefit analysis on the part of organizations: the costs – in terms of time, money, and reputational risk – are immediate and high, while the benefits are uncertain, at best. If any of the four currently operating self-regulatory initiatives are to move the needle and create momentum toward more trust and support for the nonprofit sector, it seems that change will come only gradually and in the long run, unless some combination of tastier carrots and bigger sticks can be devised.

An additional consideration is that access to information technology remains relatively weak in Mexico,[79] and so reliance on the Internet as the means of disseminating information about the sector is a significant limitation:

---

[78] Layton, n. 58.

[79] Beñat Bilbao-Osorio, Soumitra Dutta, and Bruno Lanvin, eds., *The Global Information Technology Report 2014: Rewards and Risks of Big Data* (Geneva: World Economic Forum, 2014), accessed December 17, 2015, www3.weforum.org/docs/WEF_GlobalInformationTechnology_Report_2014.pdf.

online methods of accountability and transparency may not work as well in Mexico as they might elsewhere.

7.9 CONCLUSION

The recent rounds of regulatory reform and the launching of self-regulatory initiatives in Mexico take place against a difficult backdrop. Historically there had been wave after wave of repressive regulations, often followed by armed conflict. As the country progresses through its democratic transition, the government is only slowly shedding the attitudes and behavior of a historically contentious relationship. Punitive fiscal reforms, in 1989 and then in 2007, were met not with armed revolt but with legislative advocacy and with the beginnings of self-regulatory initiatives.

The election of an opposition president in 2000 and subsequent governmental transparency reform, combined with political scandals involving nonprofits, changed the context, undermining the moral authority of the sector and prompting nonprofits to undertake the first wave of self-regulatory initiatives in 2005. The 2007 fiscal reform represented a serious threat to key fiscal incentives and prompted a strenuous and ultimately successful campaign by a broad coalition of nonprofits. Their agenda included the issue of enhanced transparency, and the reform ultimately enacted by the national legislature mandated significant public disclosure of financial data.

It quickly became apparent that this heightened transparency was not adequate to improve the level of public trust and hence public support for the sector. The second, post-2007 wave of self-regulatory initiatives was more ambitious, with two of the three projects offering a detailed process of accreditation well beyond financial transparency, and a third seeking to significantly facilitate access to financial data of a great number of nonprofits.

Thus far, the self-regulatory initiatives that have been launched have not incorporated a critical mass of organizations, perhaps because the direct costs of participation are not offset by immediate, concrete benefits – just an uncertain promise that more disclosure will engender trust and bring in more donations. Unfortunately there is reason to be pessimistic. Based on self-regulation initiatives in Asia, which have a longer track record than Mexico's, Sidel observes that when such mechanisms do not provide access to fiscal incentives or to funding, they are "unlikely to be able to force compliance with norms or to discipline those who violate standards."[80] Somewhat

---

[80] Sidel, n. 70, 804.

similarly in Mexico, after concluding a review of transparency practices of a sample of Mexican organizations, a researcher questioned whether self-regulation can be effective, given the level of distrust in Mexico toward the nonprofit sector.[81]

Given the relatively recent creation of these self-regulatory initiatives, it is too early to assess their impact. This exploration of the interaction of self-regulation and governmental regulation in Mexico thus highlights the challenge of building up an underdeveloped sector in a nation still undergoing its democratic transition, where regulation has only recently and haltingly begun to create a more favorable environment and public skepticism toward both the nonprofit sector and government runs high.

Given this thorny thicket of problems in Mexico, it might be that both regulation and self-regulation, understood as mechanisms of accountability and transparency, will be insufficient to address the crisis of confidence in the sector and the lack of philanthropic support. Beyond these two factors, there are other elements of an enabling environment for civil society that can be points of intervention, including broadening the availability of funding, multiplying opportunities for training and capacity building, and generating a more vibrant civic culture.[82] Given the depth and breadth of challenges confronting Mexico's nonprofits, a multifaceted strategy is the best option for strengthening an underdeveloped sector.

---

[81] Sara Gordon Rapoport, "Transparencia y rendición de cuentas de organizaciones civiles en México," *Revista Mexicana de Sociología* 73(2) (2011): 199–229, 226.

[82] Layton, n. 8.

8

Waves of Nonprofit Regulation and
Self-Regulation in Latin America

Evidence and Trends from Brazil and Ecuador

SUSAN APPE AND MARCELO MARCHESINI DA COSTA

8.1 INTRODUCTION

Since the 1980s, nonprofits in Latin America repositioned themselves, adapting their operations to the context of the emerging structures of democracy. Within the democratic transition, governments have taken regulatory actions toward nonprofits, while the nonprofit sector has adapted and attempted to influence the state's regulatory framework. However, there is a lack of comparative research about the evolution of the regulatory environment for nonprofits in Latin America, which motivates us to survey the current state of regulatory and self-regulatory trends in Brazil and Ecuador, and how those trends interact.

In this chapter, we first present the conceptual framework that guides our analysis, and then discuss the examples of Brazil and Ecuador and our methodology. We narrate the regulatory waves in both countries. We end by discussing regulation and self-regulation in the Brazilian and Ecuadorian contexts, how they interact and intersect, and then suggest avenues for future studies.

8.2 NONPROFIT REGULATION AND ORGANIZATIONAL FRAMEWORKS

Some of the main topics in the literature about regulation of nonprofits are related to the need for and problems associated with regulatory oversight and its alternatives, such as self-regulation.[1] Regulation of the nonprofit sector

---

[1] Angela L. Bies, "Evolution of Nonprofit Self-Regulation in Europe," *Nonprofit and Voluntary Sector Quarterly* 39(6) (2010): 1057–1086; Alnoor Ebrahim, "Accountability in Practice: Mechanisms for NGOs," *World Development* 31(5) (2003): 813–829; Lester M. Salamon and Stephanie L. Geller, *Nonprofit Governance and Accountability*, Listening Post Communiqué No. 4. (Baltimore, MD: The Johns Hopkins Center for Civil Society Studies, 2005), accessed

tends to center on barriers to entry, limitations on engagement in political activity, and restrictions on economic endeavors.[2] One argument for government regulation of the nonprofit sector is based on the assumption that nonprofit organizations are not necessarily always working in the best interests of society, and therefore some kind of supervision is necessary for government and the public to know what nonprofits are doing. Regulation can both incentivize good practices and punish misconduct.[3]

Self-regulation, occurring when an "industry-level (as opposed to a governmental or firm level) organization sets rules and standards (codes of practice) relating to the conduct of firms in the industry,"[4] takes place in the nonprofit context primarily in the development of standards or codes of behavior and performance.[5] However, Ebrahim also observes that self-regulation initiatives "are not simple tools of accountability but are part of a complex accountability process linked to sectoral identity, legitimacy, and normative views on organizational behavior."[6] For example, through self-regulation organizations seek to demonstrate "legitimacy and professionalism" and "stave off excessive government regulation."[7] In this chapter we adopt the understanding of self-regulation as a process of nonprofit legitimacy that influences nonprofit governance, using tools such as codes of conduct, evaluative mechanisms, and formal accreditations or certifications.[8]

Different organizational theories help to explain the emergence of statutory regulation and self-regulation of nonprofits. In institutional theory, regulation is a source of institutional isomorphism that could be coercive, if governmental agencies are exerting the pressure, or normative, if professional norms, such as self-regulation, are driving the process.[9] Institutional entrepreneurship theory accepts the logic of institutional theory, but emphasizes the role of "actors who have an interest in particular institutional arrangements and who

December 24, 2015, http://ccss.jhu.edu/wp-content/uploads/downloads/2011/09/LP_ Communique4_2005.pdf.

2   Elizabeth A. Bloodgood, Joannie Tremblay-Boire, and Aseem Prakash, "National Styles of NGO Regulation," *Nonprofit and Voluntary Sector Quarterly* 43(4) (2014): 716–736.

3   Ronelle Burger, "Reconsidering the Case for Enhancing Accountability via Regulation," *Voluntas* 23(1) (2012): 85–108.

4   Neil Gunningham and Joseph Rees, "Industry Self-Regulation: An Institutional Perspective," *Law & Policy* 19(4) (1997): 364–365.

5   Ebrahim, n. 1.   6   Ibid., 822.   7   Bies, n. 1, 1070.

8   Mark Sidel, "Guardians Guarding Themselves: A Comparative Perspective on Nonprofit Self-Regulation," *Chicago-Kent Law Review* 80 (2005): 803–835.

9   Paul J. DiMaggio and Walter W. Powell, "The Iron Cage Revisited: Institutional Isomorphism and Collective Rationality in Organizational Fields," *American Sociological Review* 48(2) (1983): 147–160.

leverage resources to create new institutions or to transform existing ones."[10] Network theory assumes that organizations are not isolated one from the other but are "embedded in networks of interconnected social relationships that offer opportunities for and constraints on behavior."[11] Finally, resource dependence theory is concerned with how and why decisions are made by organizations.[12] According to resource dependence theory, one key variable for this analysis is the organizational "need for resources, including financial and physical resources as well as information, obtained from the environment."[13]

In illustrating the interplay between regulation and self-regulation in Latin America, we focus on Brazil and Ecuador because in these cases, as in other Latin American countries, nonprofit organizations have a history of playing key roles in development processes.[14] In both Brazil and Ecuador, as elsewhere in Latin America, many nonprofits were closely connected to the Catholic Church, particularly in the first half of the twentieth century. Labor unions emerged in the 1930s, and charitable organizations soon adopted social development objectives.[15] The military regime that came into power in Brazil in 1964 was marked by political repression and market orientation, distinctly inhibiting the growth of the nonprofit sector.[16] Ecuador experienced major change in 1964 in its agrarian reform, followed by its own nationalist military regime in 1972, which also significantly limited nonprofit activity.[17]

---

[10]   Steve Maguire, Cynthia Hardy, and Thomas B. Lawrence, "Institutional Entrepreneurship in Emerging Fields: HIV/AIDS Treatment Advocacy in Canada," *Academy of Management Journal* 47(5) (2004): 657–679.

[11]   Daniel J. Brass et al., "Taking Stock of Networks and Organizations: A Multilevel Perspective," *Academy of Management Journal* 47(6) (2004): 795–817.

[12]   Howard E. Aldrich and Jeffrey Pfeffer, "Environments of Organizations," *Annual Review of Sociology* 2 (1976): 79–105.

[13]   Jeffrey Pfeffer and Gerald R. Salancik, *The External Control of Organizations: A Resource Dependence Approach* (New York: Harper and Row Publishers, 1978), xii.

[14]   Leilah Landim, "The Nonprofit Sector in Brazil," in *The Nonprofit Sector in the Developing World: A Comparative Analysis*, ed. Helmut K. Anheier and Lester M. Salamon (New York: St. Martin's Press, 1998), 53; V. Finn Heinrich, ed., *CIVICUS Global Survey of the State of Civil Society*, vol. 1 (Bloomfield, CT: Kumarian Press, 2007); World Bank, *Civil Society's Role in the Governance Agenda in Ecuador: Assessing Opportunities and Constraints* (Washington, DC: World Bank, 2007).

[15]   Landim, n. 14; World Bank, n. 14.

[16]   Leilah Landim, "Defining the Nonprofit Sector: Brazil," in *Working Papers of the Johns Hopkins Comparative Nonprofit Sector Project*, ed. Helmut K. Anheier and Lester M. Salamon (Baltimore, MD: The Johns Hopkins Institute for Policy Studies, 1993); Natalia Massaco Koga, "Shifts in the Relationship between the State and Civil Society in Brazil's Recent Democracy," PhD thesis, University of Westminster, 2012.

[17]   Heinrich, n. 14.

Our analysis primarily focuses on the situation after re-democratization began in both countries.

Using documentary sources and interviews with key actors from the government and nonprofit sectors in Brazil and Ecuador, we discuss statutory regulation, self-regulation, and their interactions in both countries. Section 8.3 describes the regulatory waves in Brazil, while Section 8.4 presents the Ecuadorian regulatory waves.

8.3 REGULATORY AND SELF-REGULATORY WAVES IN BRAZIL

8.3.1 *Regulation after Re-Democratization and the Creation of Sectoral Identity, 1985–1994*

Nonprofit organizations in Brazil had an important role in the re-democratization process, by articulating common interests[18] and influencing the debates of the new constitution in 1988.[19] In the years following re-democratization, the Brazilian nonprofit sector developed campaigns against corruption, proposed legislation expanding social and political rights, and mobilized public opinion.[20] The concept of the nongovernmental organization (NGO) itself gained relevance, and the Brazilian government reacted to nonprofits' increasing political activities by revoking, in 1993, the "certificate of public utility"[21] conferred to several of these organizations in previous years.[22] This measure did not outlaw nonprofits, but threatened their legitimacy and eliminated some of their tax benefits.

During this period, members of several nonprofit organizations participated in the creation of the Workers' Party, with the belief that this party "would carry their agenda forward if it could just reach national power."[23] This first wave is also marked by the creation of the Brazilian Association of NGOs (Abong) in the early 1990s. Abong's establishment was motivated by an understanding that, in a democracy, nonprofits should also be transparent

---

[18] Koga, n. 16.

[19] Brian Wampler and Leonardo Avritzer, "Participatory Publics: Civil Society and New Institutions in Democratic Brazil," *Comparative Politics* 36(3) (2004): 291–312.

[20] Landim, n. 14.

[21] This certificate was one of the first regulatory pieces addressing the nonprofit sector, dating back to the 1930s. Later it was adopted as a requirement for both tax exemptions and to access government funding; Koga, n. 16.

[22] Landim, n. 14.

[23] Kathryn Hochstetler, "Organized Civil Society in Lula'a Brazil," in *Democratic Brazil Revisited*, ed. Peter R. Kingstone and Timothy J. Power (Pittsburgh, PA: University of Pittsburgh Press, 2008), 33.

about their own work.[24] Abong's first initiatives included a registry of existing nonprofits and the sharing of relevant information. Abong's official goals have included self-regulatory practices, such as exchanges between nonprofits and the consolidation of nonprofits' identity, autonomous from the government, churches, or political parties.[25]

8.3.2 *New Regulatory Intervention and New Sectoral Response, 1995–2002*

During the 1990s, Brazil and many other Latin American countries experienced the influence of neoliberal policies oriented toward liberalization, deregulation, free trade, and privatization of state enterprises.[26] These propositions were especially influential during the two presidential terms of Fernando Henrique Cardoso (1995–2002). One central strategy of the Cardoso administration was the transfer of nonexclusive governmental activities to private for-profit or nonprofit organizations,[27] which was achieved by contracting out or privatizing public goods and services during this second regulatory wave.

The initiatives of Comunidade Solidária, an organization directed by the then First Lady, Ruth Cardoso, led to new state regulation over nonprofits, in the form of the Law of Volunteering in 1998 and the Law of Public Interest Civil Society Organizations (OSCIPs) in 1999. The purpose of these statutes was to contribute to the professionalization of the nonprofit sector and to promote partnerships between the sector and the government.[28] OSCIPs instituted a new certification mechanism for nonprofits, with the intention of allowing faster and less bureaucratic partnerships between these organizations and the government. Application for OSCIPs certification is a voluntary scheme. The process is managed by the Ministry of Justice, which publicizes information about certified nonprofits. These new regulations did not explicitly aim to

[24] Sérgio Haddad, "ONGs, Um Recorte Específico," in *ONGs No Brasil 2002. Perfil E Catálogo Das Associadas À Abong*, ed. Abong (São Paulo: Abong, 2002).

[25] Abong, "Abong Comemora Seus 15 Anos," *Associação Brasileira de ONGs (Abong)*, accessed November 14, 2006, http://abong.org.br/biblioteca.php?id=7721&it=4422; Abong, "Estatuto Social," *Associação Brasileira de ONGs (Abong)*, 2010, http://abong.org.br/quem_somos.php?id=3.

[26] Benjamin Arditi, "Arguments about the Left Turns in Latin America: A Post-Liberal Politics?," *Latin American Research Review* 43(3) (2008): 59–81.

[27] Luiz Carlos Bresser-Pereira, *Texto Para Discussão 9: Administração Pública Gerencial: Estratégia e Estrutura Para Um Novo Estado* (Brasilia: Escola Nacional de Administração Pública (ENAP), 1996).

[28] Carlos Eduardo Guerra Silva, "Gestão, Legislação E Fontes de Recursos No Terceiro Setor Brasileiro: Uma Perspectiva Histórica," *Revista de Administração Pública* 44(6) (2012): 1301–1325.

increase government control over nonprofits, but the new rules did not cancel previous regulation, thereby creating a multiplicity of certificates and procedures for partnerships between nonprofits and government.[29]

The regulatory interventions approved during this period were mostly government initiatives, but some nonprofits were invited to participate in the debates about the new rules. Politically active organizations such as Abong were among the latter, but they remained critical of some of the government's policies.[30] Alleging that the final text of OSCIPs did not reflect civil society's viewpoints and that its benefits were limited, many nonprofit organizations did not adhere to the OSCIPs certification, which was not mandatory.[31] Even in 2014, only 6 percent of existing Brazilian nonprofits obtained the OSCIPs certification.[32] However, new nonprofits created during this period immediately applied for certification, suggesting that their creation was motivated by a goal of establishing partnerships with the government.[33]

This second regulatory wave is particularly characterized by the development of different kinds of nonprofits: politically active nonprofits received strong support from international institutions and foundations,[34] while charities and service providers benefited from the new regulations and opportunities for contracting with the government. This resulted in nonprofits' growth and diversification. Data from nonprofits active in 2014 show that, while only 81,960 nonprofit organizations had been created in Brazil in the period up to 1990, 90,079 new nonprofits were created from 1991 to 2000.[35]

8.3.3 *Renewed Regulatory Pressure and New Forms of Sectoral Response, 2003–2010*

President Lula, from the Workers' Party, was elected in 2002. His administration invited nonprofits to participate in forums, such as councils and conferences,

[29] Ibid.
[30] Elisabeth Jay Friedman and Kathryn Hochstetler, "Assessing the Third Transition in Latin American Democratization: Representational Regimes and Civil Society in Argentina and Brazil," *Comparative Politics* 35(1) (2002): 21–42; Mário Aquino Alves and Natália Massaco Koga, "Brazilian Nonprofit Organizations and the New Legal Framework: An Institutional Perspective," *Revista de Administração Contemporânea* 10(SPE) (2006): 213–34.
[31] Friedman and Hochstetler, ibid.; Alves and Koga, ibid.
[32] Secretaria Geral da Presidência da República, *Mapa Das Organizações Da Sociedade Civil* (Brasilia: SGPR, 2014), accessed December 24, 2015, https://mapaosc.ipea.gov.br/Map.html.
[33] Alves and Koga, n. 30.   [34] Friedman and Hochstetler, n. 30.
[35] IBGE, *As Fundações Privadas e Associações sem Fins Lucrativos no Brasil – 2010* (Rio de Janero: IBGE, 2012), accessed December 24, 2015, ftp://ftp.ibge.gov.br/Fundacoes_Privadas_e_Associacoes/2010/fasfil.pdf.

which discussed and proposed public policies in several areas.[36] Despite recognizing the importance of these initiatives, some nonprofit leaders criticized the dynamics of these forums, in which the government controlled participation and the proposals that would be approved. The government also influenced nonprofits' political activity in these forums through its power to approve contracts and grants. The relative importance of government contracts and grants increased when international foundations reduced funding to Brazilian nonprofits. From the late 1990s onward, as the economic conditions improved and the democratic transition advanced in Brazil, international foundations began focusing their funding priorities on less developed countries.

Media denunciations of nonprofits' misuse of contract funds also began to emerge more frequently in the mid-2000s. Political parties opposed to President Lula's administration pursued these cases, which further damaged the public image of the nonprofit sector. Despite this, an investigative commission created by the legislature did not present any conclusive evidence about any wrongdoing in these government/nonprofit contracts. The most important consequence of this process was, in the words of some nonprofit leaders, a "political criminalization" of nonprofits. In other words, nonprofits became associated with the image of corruption.

The government/nonprofit partnerships that developed during the two terms of President Lula were managed amid a complex state regulatory framework, which included regulations from the 1930s, laws from the 1990s, and several decrees created by the government to regulate nonprofits, particularly in response to allegations about the misuse of resources. Nonprofit leaders referred to this process as a "bureaucratic criminalization," given the complexity of this regulatory environment. At the end of this period no measures had been taken to simplify nonprofits' regulation.[37]

In 2010, at the end of this third regulatory wave, a diverse group of nonprofit organizations, social movements, and foundations created a coalition called the Platform for a New Regulatory Framework for Civil Society Organizations.[38]

---

[36] Secretaria Geral da Presidência da República, *Participação Social No Brasil: Entre Conquistas E Desafios* (Brasilia: SGPR, 2014).

[37] During this period some Brazilian nonprofits became members of international nonprofit networks, such as Abong's participation in the International Forum of National NGO Platforms. These international collaborations became stronger after the first World Social Forums in 2001, organized in Brazil. It is not clear, however, if participation in international networks influenced the behavior of the nonprofit sector in Brazil at large.

[38] Plataforma OSC, *Plataforma por um Novo Marco Regulatório para as Organizações da Sociedade Civil* (Brasilia: Plataforma OSC, 2010), accessed December 24, 2015, http://plataformaosc.org.br/wp-content/uploads/2011/10/Plataforma-principal.pdf.

This initiative emerged during the presidential electoral campaign to encourage more public participation in public policymaking and a better and simpler government regulation of nonprofit organizations. The term "civil society organizations" started to be widely adopted, as a reference to the broad group that participated in the formation of the Platform. The participants in this coalition justified the adoption of this term as a manner of creating unity among different groups and an attempt to regain legitimacy after the political and bureaucratic "criminalization" of the term "NGO" in the previous wave. A stronger nonprofit voice and increased mutual support between nonprofit organizations helped instigate attempts at self-regulation during this period, but the Platform's goals show that nonprofits continued to prioritize the improvement of government regulation over self-regulatory initiatives.

8.3.4 *The Road to a New Regulatory Framework and Diverse Sector Responses, 2011–2014*

Assisted by her commitment to the agenda of the Platform for a New Regulatory Framework for Civil Society Organizations, Dilma Rousseff, a party colleague of Lula, won Brazil's 2010 election. Her rise to power, however, did not lead to the promised new nonprofit statute. Instead, following corruption scandals that resulted in the dismissal of two ministers accused of receiving money and benefits from nonprofits contracted by them, President Rousseff temporarily ceased payments to all federally contracted nonprofits. Adopting an adversarial tone, Platform members reacted with public letters to the government, reinforcing the need for the government to approve a new regulation, in line with nonprofits' suggestions. This scenario raises the question of why, even when the government took harsh measures, the Brazilian nonprofits did not start to explore further self-regulatory options, beyond the public letters. A nonprofit leader who participated in this process explained that:

> [F]or you to think of self-regulation for such a diverse field as is the Platform's field ... it is very difficult. Because these are organizations with huge differences, with different histories, with a diverse social and political density ... We are highly regulated by the state. There is little room left for self-regulation [laughs]. (nonprofit organization leader, personal communication, August 11, 2014)

A scholar who specializes in nonprofit regulation and who participated in the Platform asserted that "[h]ere in Brazil, part is that we don't have a culture of self-regulation; on the contrary, we have a culture of dependence on the state" (nonprofit specialist, personal communication with authors, August 18, 2014).

Another nonprofit leader involved in these negotiations emphasized a further aspect of government/nonprofit relationships in Brazil that contributed to the lack of self-regulatory initiatives:

> The [civil society] organizations end up submitting themselves due to two reasons: first, because they need the state's support. But the second reason is also very important: the organizations believe that the possibilities created by the current state are better than other possibilities previously existing, and that a confrontation with the state could motivate the rise to power of sectors that are much more conservative, sectors much worse. (nonprofit organization leader, personal communication, August 12, 2014)

During this period, an audit was conducted that detected the need for adjustments in a small number of contracts. Thereafter, the Brazilian government normalized the payments for nonprofits in 2012, and finally a working group was instituted in order to discuss the Platform's demands. Several of the Platform's leading nonprofits were invited to participate, and they accepted the invitation. However, after the working group published its final report[39] suggesting a new regulation toward nonprofits, huge street protests occurred in several Brazilian cities in 2013. These protests were initiated in São Paulo against the raises in public transportation fares, but they soon attracted thousands of people unconnected with traditional political parties or social movements. The protests surprised both government and nonprofit leaders. For Platform members, that moment was followed by a more combative open letter to the government, demanding approval of the working group's proposal for new regulation of nonprofit organizations. Nonprofit members have noted in interviews with the authors that the protests made them realize that they were not as closely connected to the Brazilian people as they thought. Similarly, the government understood the need to create new forms of participation and speed up the negotiations for the new regulatory framework of nonprofit organizations. This resulted in the preparation of a draft law based on the working group's final report.

After intense negotiations, Law 13.019 was approved in July 2014.[40] The statute does not institute an entirely new regulatory framework for nonprofit organizations, but it does regulate partnerships between the government and these

---

[39] Secretaria Geral da Presidência da República, *Relatório Final Do Grupo De Trabalho Marco Regulatório Das Organizações Da Sociedade Civil* (Brasilia: SGPR, 2012), accessed January 5, 2016, www.abong.org.br/final/download/OBSERVATORIO.pdf.

[40] Law 13.019 Establishing the Legal Regime of Voluntary Partnerships Involving or Not Financial Resource Transfer between the Public Administration and Civil Society Organizations, accessed July 6, 2015, www.icnl.org/research/library/files/Brazil/brasilia.pdf.

organizations. It introduces two new instruments for partnerships: one dedicated to government projects and the other focused on proposals from nonprofit organizations. Similar to the earlier OSCIPs legislation, the new law aims to facilitate and make less bureaucratic the management of government/nonprofit partnerships, by evaluating them through the results achieved rather than primarily through procedural mechanisms. Among other innovations is a goal to improve transparency to the general public, as both government and nonprofits must make the information related to their contracts available online.

The initial reaction from nonprofits that participated in the Platform for a New Regulatory Framework for Civil Society Organizations regarding this new legislation was one of excitement about the new partnership rules, but also frustration about what was debated in the working group and not approved in the new legislation, such as rules and incentives for private, individual donations to nonprofit organizations. The lack of private donation incentives keeps a large number of nonprofits dependent on the partnerships and resources offered by government. Also missing was the creation of a public fund that would provide stable and reliable government resources to partnerships with nonprofits.

Despite these frustrations, discussions of self-regulation are not a priority among Brazilian nonprofits. The most concrete self-regulatory initiatives are in the level of coordination, sharing information, and defining common agendas. In addition to Abong, which is still an active and influential association of nonprofits, other umbrella organizations have emerged and assumed coordinating roles in Brazil. Their priority, however, continues to be the improvement of government regulation of the nonprofit sector, rather than promotion of more autonomous self-regulation.

8.4 NONPROFIT REGULATORY AND SELF-REGULATORY WAVES IN ECUADOR

8.4.1 *The Initial Growth of Nonprofits, New Social Movements, and Regulation, 1978–1997*

The first regulatory wave in Ecuador is part of Ecuador's democratization period and the rise of neoliberalism. The 1978 Constitution and elections in 1979 marked a key period in the development of civil society and its regulation in Ecuador. Once transition set in, political institutions and political parties were quite weak[41] and the country experienced many bouts of economic

---

[41] Andrés Ortiz Lemos, *La sociedad civil ecuatoriana en el laberinto de la revolución ciudadana* (Quito: FLASCO, 2013).

crisis.[42] Ecuador's nonprofit sector grew during the 1980s[43] due to the open-
ings left by weak political institutions. However, civil society's growth was slow
in comparison to other Latin American countries, at least according to
Ecuadorian scholars.[44]

In the 1980s "new social movements" relating to the environment, women,
and indigenous rights emerged.[45] But civil society did not have clear access to
political power. It was limited in its ability to engage in political activity, not
due so much to regulatory mechanisms but because of what some have called
the "high degree of interpersonal mistrust affecting Ecuadorian society,"[46]
which also affected the nonprofit sector during this period.

8.4.2 *A Constitutional Space for Civil Society, 1998–2007*

The next wave, while not blatantly regulatory by nature, had several implications for government/nonprofit relations and was incited by Ecuador's 1998
Constitution. That 1998 Constitution was the first in the country's history to
explicitly give civil society a space in the public arena,[47] spurred on by
organized civil society, particularly the indigenous movement, which had
been active in demanding political space. The Constitution also decentralized
participation, which motivated a number of innovations at local levels.[48] This
period in Ecuador allowed civil society to enter arenas in which political
society was increasingly losing legitimacy. Indeed, during the 1990s and into
the 2000s, mistrust of public institutions grew and organized civil society
became a key player in the ousting of three presidents between 1998 and
2007 and, at times, a driver of social unrest.[49]

8.4.3 *Re-Regulation and Sectoral Opposition, Self-Regulation,*
and Other Responses, 2008–2014

The emergence of the political figure Rafael Correa marks the most recent wave,
which includes both state regulatory and self-regulatory subwaves. Since 2008,
there have been several initiatives by government to regulate the nonprofit
sector and immediate responses by nonprofit organizations, some of which

---

[42] Carlos A. Cabrera and Edison P. Vallejo, *El Mito al Debate: Las ONGs en Ecuador* (Quito:
Alya-Yala Editing, 1997).

[43] World Bank, n. 14.   [44] Ortiz, n. 41.   [45] Heinrich, n. 14; Ortiz, n. 41; World Bank, n. 14.

[46] Fernando Bustamante, Lucía Durán, and Ana Cristina Andreetti, *Ecuador's Civil Society: An
Efficient Civil Society Going beyond Its Weaknesses* (Fundación Esquel and CIVICUS, 2006), 21,
accessed July 1, 2015, https://www.civicus.org/new/media/CSI_Ecuador_Country_Report.pdf.

[47] World Bank, n. 14.   [48] Ortiz, n. 41.   [49] Heinrich, n. 14.

include self-regulatory initiatives. These entailed three stages of government action and immediate responses from nonprofit organizations from 2008 to 2014.

Before becoming president in 2007, Rafael Correa was named the Minister of Economy and Finance under the Palacio administration in 2005. Correa's discourse as a politician, like many social movements in Ecuador, favored an alternative to the neoliberal logic of development that defined the country in the 1980s and 1990s. Once he became president in January 2007, however, skepticism about his development policies began to grow among civil society and social movements.[50] Social movements and organizations perceived barriers to entry, spurring fears that they were being crowded out by several of Correa's policy initiatives. For example, Correa's Citizens' Revolution was a political and socioeconomic project that revolved around individual rights and a "universal citizen."[51] This was in contrast to a more collective-oriented logic of development supported by organized civil society.[52]

Meanwhile, the new 2008 Constitution incorporated many provisions related to civil society. It recognized nonprofit organizations as a means of expression to strengthen citizenship (Articles 96 and 97), covered key environmental issues, declared rights to nature, and mandated that local communities be consulted about mining and extraction projects on their land.[53] The new Constitution was accompanied by several other shifts in policy and law, such as the creation of the Council for Citizen Participation and Social Control, which seeks to foster citizen empowerment, inclusion, and active transparency.

8.4.3.1 Skirmishing and Nonprofit Response (2008–2009)

After the 2008 Constitution was promulgated, but still early in his administration, President Correa publicly discredited nonprofit organizations in statements and press conferences.[54] He asserted that nonprofit organizations avoided paying taxes, meddled in Ecuadorian political activities, and represented international interests and a neoliberal framework. Increased attention to the sector and its regulation by the executive branch, according to President Correa, sought to curb tax fraud and political action by organizations that disrupted the work of the government.[55]

---

[50] Marc C. Becker, "Indigenous Movements, and the Writing of a New Constitution in Ecuador," *Latin American Perspectives* 38(1) (2011): 47–62.

[51] Ibid., 48. [52] Ibid. [53] Ibid.

[54] "Denuncia Rafael Correa la existencia de unas 50 mil ONG en Ecuador," *La Prensa Latina*, May 30, 2010, accessed November 20, 2010, www.aporrea.org/actualidad/n158261.html.

[55] "Secretaría de Pueblos realizará el Primer Encuentro Nacional de ONG's," *El Ciudadano*, December 1, 2010, accessed December 20, 2010, www.elciudadano.gov.ec/index.php?option=

This government attitude was recognized in new regulation of the nonprofit sector, solidified through the March 2008 Presidential Executive Decree No. 982. The decree sought to establish clear definitions of, and fiscal requirements for, nonprofit organizations and to implement a centralized, national registry of nonprofit organizations.[56] The Decree's Registry of Civil Society Organizations (RUOSC) was a first attempt by the Ecuadorian government to standardize and centralize information on nonprofit organizations and was woven into the process of an organization's legal formation.

Government rhetoric and Decree No. 982 brought about several initiatives. As Decree No. 982 was being rolled out, the government initiated discussion and the drafting of a more comprehensive civil society legal framework, hiring a legal consultant group to elaborate a draft nonprofit law.[57] Nonprofit organizations met to discuss this draft, among themselves and with legal consultant group. A draft law was circulated by the government, on which nonprofit organizations made comments and provided feedback. However, the government abandoned the process for reasons that remain unclear. This left Decree No. 982 as the remaining primary regulatory statute for the nonprofit sector in Ecuador.[58]

Although the process of discussing and drafting a law was first initiated by the government and then abandoned, the discussions that resulted among Ecuadorian nonprofit organizations included mechanisms of self-regulation.[59] In these discussions, the idea of self-regulation as a "process linked to sectoral identity"[60] loomed large. Nonprofits in Ecuador had never before created a space for sector-level conversations. As one nonprofit leader explained:

> I believe that because of . . . the fragmented characteristics of the sector, it has been very difficult in Ecuador to find an element that unified us, an element around which to form a [group of organizations]. (nonprofit organization leader, personal communication, February 10, 2011)

com_content&view=article&id=19187:secretaria-de-pueblos-realizara-el-primer-encuentro-nacional-de-ongs&catid=1:actualidad&Itemid=42ONG.

[56] Executive Decree No.982 (Presidencia de la República del Ecuador, 2008), accessed July 27, 2009, www.sociedadcivil.gov.ec/index.php?option=com_docman&task=cat_view&gid=74& Itemid=153.

[57] Grupo Legal Trade, *Las organizaciones de la sociedad civil en la legislación Ecuatoriana* (Quito: Grupo Legal Trade, 2009).

[58] M.F. Garcés, "Marco normativo para las organizaciones de la sociedad civil," presentation given to the Collective of Civil Society Organizations at Citizen Participation, Quito, September 2010.

[59] Ibid.   [60] Ebrahim, n. 1, 822.

These organizations set out to explore self-regulatory approaches to stave off further restrictive statutory regulation. They discussed a number of formal and informal potential self-regulatory tactics, including outlining the principles and ethics of the sector, creating a formal code of conduct that sets out defined standards, and the possibility of establishing an accreditation system through a third party. A small group of nine Ecuadorian nonprofits explored these options as they released a joint public document, the *Citizens' Contributions to the Regulations of Civil Society Organizations*,[61] which highlighted main concerns about the 2008 Decree No. 982. One nonprofit leader described the concerns about the decree:

> So, what do organizations see? They see that [organizations] are an aspect of regulation. What organizations feel is that the state does not see us as organizations worried for the country, that we want to collaborate, rather [the state] only sees [organizations] as something to regulate. (nonprofit organization leader, personal communication, October 25, 2010)

In the document, organizations began to use language about civil society in Ecuador from the perspective of the organizations themselves. The *Citizen Contributions* document highlights the norms set out in the 2008 Ecuadorian Constitution; in particular, the Constitution's acknowledgment of citizen participation and the construction of a more democratic society. The nine organizations, with consultations from the International Center for Not-for-Profit Law (ICNL), identified several parts of the Decree No. 982 as unconstitutional.[62] There were concerns about too much discretion by ministries, disclosure of the identification of nonprofit organizations' members, and the financial barriers to obtaining legal status.[63]

Along with these critiques, and in reaction to the statutory regulation of Decree No. 982, the nonprofit group identified a need for a sector-level body that would coordinate issues within the sector, manage relations with government, and debate regulatory policy issues. The sector-level body would also discuss further self-regulation mechanisms, as presented below, to respond to statutory regulation.

---

[61] *Aportes Ciudadanos a las Regulaciones de las Organizaciones de la Sociedad Civil del Ecuador* (Quito: September 2009).

[62] International Center for Not-for-Profit Law, *Comentarios respeto al Decreto Presidencial No. 982: Revision de la Leyes Marco de Ecuador Sobre Organizaciones No Gubernamentales* (Washington, DC: ICNL, 2008).

[63] Aportes Ciudadanos, n. 61.

8.4.3.2 Responses to Regulation from a
Collective of Civil Society Organizations, 2010–2013

In late 2010 the government, which hosted a December 2010 'First National Meeting of NGOs,'[64] proposed new draft regulations to help govern the sector. At the late December meeting, the government introduced the Secretariat of People, Social Movements and Citizen Participation and positioned it as the government liaison between the Correa administration and civil society with respect to the proposed reforms to Ecuador's civil society legal framework.[65]

This period brought about a clear response from many in the nonprofit sector. By 2010, a Collective of Civil Society Organizations, as it started to be called, had grown from the nine organizations that had signed the *Citizen Contributions* document in 2009 to a network of about sixty groups. As in the Brazilian case, the use of the term "civil society organization" was deliberately used to rebrand "development NGOs." The Collective participants were uneasy with the new draft regulation, which they saw as virtually the same as Decree No. 982, focusing too heavily on regulatory oversight rather than facilitating the development and strengthening of civil society.

For the first time, the nonprofit organizations requested a sector-specific law, since regulation in Ecuador had traditionally been through executive decrees. The Collective recognized that the issue was about the fundamental right to association that was threatened, and that the regulatory environment was overly restrictive in promoting barriers to entry, limitations on political activity, and restrictions relating to organizations' financial resources. The Collective agreed not to support the proposed regulation and requested co-production of a state regulatory framework for civil society in Ecuador by government and nonprofit organizations.

To further respond to the 2010 proposed government regulatory reform, in early 2011, sixty-seven nonprofit organizations signed a public manifesto that was described by the Collective as a "unified message with multiple voices."[66] As a result of the sector-level conversations about self-regulation, the manifesto proposed four principles for the Collective of Civil Society Organizations. Those included: better understanding of civil society organizations and the

---

[64] Presidencia de la República del Ecuador, *Proyecto de Reglamento de Personas Jurídicas de Derecho Privado con Finalidad Social y Sin Fines de Lucro* (Quito, December 1, 2010).

[65] El Ciudadano, n. 55.

[66] L. Estévez, "Organizaciones de la Sociedad Ecuatoriana Piden a Gobiernos que no Promulgue Reglamento," Press Release (2011); OSC Ecuador, *Manifiesto del Colectivo de Orgnizaciones de la Sociedad Civil (OSC) a la Normativa para su Funcionamiento* (Quito: OSC Ecuador, 2011).

nature of civil society, fostering accountability mechanisms and a culture of transparency, respecting the Ecuadorian Constitution, and developing the state's role in protecting and fostering civil society development.[67]

Nonprofit leaders in the Collective realized that collective accountability was important to the promotion of self-regulatory options and to regain legitimacy for the sector in the eyes of the public and government. In 2011, the Collective released its first report of aggregated descriptive data on civil society, the *Report of Collective Accountability 2010*;[68] a second report, covering 2011, was released in 2012.[69] One nonprofit leader explained:

> We have to show what we are, with who we work, how much of a budget we manage ... look, we are here to be accountable because we believe we are important to society, we are not embarrassed by our work, rather we feel proud of what and who we are. (nonprofit organization leader, personal communication, February 2, 2011)

The *Report of Collective Accountability 2010* included data from thirty-seven organizations and was signed by eleven more organizations in support. The number of organizations participating rose to 102 in the second report in 2011, an increase of 175 percent. Both reports argued that organized civil society is an "important sector" in Ecuador[70] and that civil society is where many of the ideas for citizen well-being are initiated. The reports also provide descriptive data on participating nonprofit organizations, including where organizations are working, thematic areas of work, who the beneficiaries are and how many there are, information about the amount of money organizations manage, and other data. These data previously had not been aggregated nor available to civil society organizations, and even less so to the public or the media.

These two accountability reports further consolidated the Collective but received little attention from the public or government. In addition, as with the draft of the more comprehensive civil society legal framework in 2008, the government once more abandoned the 2010 draft regulation, again for reasons that remained unclear. Decree No. 982 remained the main regulatory framework for nonprofit organizations in Ecuador. After a process of approximately four years, in early 2013, the Collective of Civil Society Organizations was legally formalized into the Ecuadorian Confederation of Civil Society Organizations.

---

[67] OSC Ecuador, ibid.

[68] Collective of Civil Society Organizations of Ecuador, *Informe de Rendición Colectiva de Cuentas 2010* (Quito: Collective of Civil Society Organizations of Ecuador, 2011).

[69] Collective of Civil Society Organizations of Ecuador, *Informe de Rendición Colectiva de Cuentas 2011* (Quito: Collective of Civil Society Organizations of Ecuador, 2012).

[70] Collective of Civil Society Organizations of Ecuador, n. 68.

8.4.3.3 New Government Regulation and the Growing Strength of Sectoral Response, 2013–2014

In 2013, as the Confederation of Civil Society Organizations was being formalized, and after almost five years without regulatory reform, the Ecuadorian presidential office released Executive Decree No. 16.[71] Decree No. 16 replaced Decree No. 982, adding new requirements for legal status; the creation of a new registry for nonprofit organizations, a required part of the legal formation process like the previous registry; and further obligations for international organizations to obtain permission to work in Ecuador.

There was no process of co-production among government and civil society in the development of the new Decree No. 16. In response, the Confederation's analysis of Decree No. 16 asserted that since 2009 nonprofit organizations had proposed working with the state to develop a civil society legal framework that would include both statutory regulatory and self-regulatory mechanisms, such as collective accountability reporting. In addition to joint statements and collective accountability reports, the Confederation considered further self-regulatory approaches. For example, an accreditation scheme through the Confederation was under discussion, but has not gained much traction yet. In addition to conversations among themselves, nonprofit organizational leaders met with public officials in government institutions. Nonprofit leaders attempted to start dialogue, but there was little comprehensive change or progress toward any law and/or broader policy framework toward civil society.

The Confederation of Civil Society Organizations recognized that there were also positive developments included in the new government Decree No. 16, including government funding opportunities for nonprofit organizations, capacity building opportunities, and government assistance to smaller organizations on regulatory requirements. Nonprofits in Ecuador noted that those elements had been advocated by the Collective and now the Confederation.[72] However, the Confederation also highlighted three concerns with this new wave of government regulation: that the new decree threatens civil society's important role in public policy formulation; that it compromises

---

[71] Executive Decree No.13 (Presidencia de la República del Ecuador, 2013), accessed April 4, 2013, www.sociedadcivil.gov.ec/index.php?option=com_docman&task=cat_view&gid=74&Itemid=153Secretaria.

[72] Susan Appe, "Civil Society Organizations Respond to New Regulation in Ecuador: An Interview with Orazio Bellettini Cedeno," *The International Journal of Not-for-Profit Law* 16(2) (2014): 66–71.

voluntary participation in nonprofit organizations since it requires that an organization must accept a request from a citizen who wants to join or be affiliated with an organization; and that government discretion is too broad, particularly in the wide requests government agencies are able to make for information about nonprofit organizations and the discretion government has to close organizations. In some cases, these were similar to the concerns outlined in earlier years about the earlier Decree No. 982. One nonprofit leader, commenting on the discretion allowed for organizational closures, noted:

> An organization can be dissolved for activities that disrupt the "public peace." In practice, what does that mean? If a civil society organization goes to a march in favor of fundamental rights is this cause for dissolution? These causes for dissolution continue to be unconstitutional. (nonprofit organization leader, personal communication, November 11, 2014)

In 2015, the Confederation published a third collective accountability report.[73] With its publication, the role of civil society, its statutory regulation, and further directions for self-regulation initiatives continue to be under debate.

8.5 DISCUSSION AND CONCLUSION

In the case of Brazil, the regulatory debate in the last decade has focused on the partnership between government and the nonprofit sector and the subsequent state regulation of partnership contracts.[74] Ecuadorian nonprofits have experienced several regulatory reforms and have explored self-regulation, both in the abstract during sector-level conversations and through using tools such as joint statements and collective accountability reports as responses to statutory regulation.

Institutional theory helps to explain the political contexts and institutional pressures of these regulatory waves and nonprofit sector responses. The government is a source of institutional pressure that has been more prominent on some occasions than others. For example, during Brazil's Collor de Mello administration in the early 1990s, the Brazilian government used coercive

---

[73] Organizaciones de la Sociedad Civil del Ecuador, *La sociedad civil y la construcción de lo público Tercer Informe De Rendición Colectiva de Cuentas* (Quito: Confederación Ecuatoriana de OSC, 2015), accessed December 12, 2015, www.confederacionecuatorianaosc.org/confederacion/sites/default/files/Tercer-Informe-Rendicion-Colectiva-de-Cuentas.pdf.

[74] The interviews for this research were conducted before the impeachment of President Dilma Rousseff. Significant changes in government–nonprofit sector relations may happen in Brazil without the Workers' Party in the presidency.

pressure to temper nonprofits' political activities, by revoking certificates of public utility. The government also created incentives, such as the promise of easier access to contracts, as President Cardoso did in 1999 with the OSCIPs certificate. These examples indicate that institutional pressures can, in part, characterize regulatory waves and affect the image of the nonprofit sector. This happened in Brazil during the late 1990s, when the Cardoso administration introduced neoliberal policies and the OSCIPs law, leading to a growth and diversification of the nonprofit sector. In Ecuador, with the regulatory components of Decrees No. 982 and 16, the Correa administration established coercive measures that did not allow for growth or diversification of the sector, but rather redefined the legal parameters of nonprofit organizations and their work.

Nonprofits also create institutional pressures, affecting the characteristics of a regulatory wave. In Brazil and Ecuador, institutional entrepreneurs within the nonprofit sector have existed at various points in the waves of regulation and nascent self-regulation. Publications and open letters in Brazil and Ecuador sought to gain legitimacy and garner support across different stakeholders, strategies that have been used by entrepreneurs in other organizational fields.[75] These publications and open letters attempted to give meaning to civil society and the nonprofit sector in each context. In Brazil, institutional entrepreneurs appeared during the first regulatory wave, influencing the Constitution, and during the fourth wave, for the approval of Law 13.019 in 2014. In Ecuador, nine organizations became institutional entrepreneurs in producing the first joint document by nonprofit organizations, which set the stage for self-regulatory initiatives. These strategies during the most recent waves, in both countries, were coupled with nonprofits' efforts to reframe the organizational field of nonprofits by using the descriptor "civil society organizations," as opposed to "NGOs," in an attempt to regain legitimacy and redefine their sector.

Nonprofit organizations in both countries also turned to interorganizational linkages. Network theory posits interorganizational linkages as aiding the exchange of information and mediating conversations, in these cases, among organizations themselves and with government. Networks have the overall objective of opening opportunities to achieve more resources and power. In Brazil, this networking process started in the early 1990s with Abong, but interorganizational linkages grew stronger with the creation of the Platform for a New Regulatory Framework for Civil Society Organizations in 2010.

---

[75] Maguire et al., n. 10.

In Ecuador, sector entrepreneurs were more reactive than in Brazil. This suggests that the context in which institutional entrepreneurs emerge might influence their strategies: a "friendly" relationship with the government, such as Brazil in the 2000s, leads to attempts to introduce reforms across institutions, while a "hostile" environment, such as in Ecuador, leads to attempts to create new institutions. The nonprofit sector in Ecuador went from a void with no sector-level network to nine organizations coming together in 2009. This group then became the Collective of Civil Society Organizations of more than sixty organizations, and then the Confederation of Civil Society Organizations with twenty-six founding members and dozens of affiliates. As was with the redefinition of their identity as civil society organizations, the development of network linkages between nonprofits enabled the sector to strengthen both its public image and its voice.

Given the exchange of information, debate and negotiation with government, and the aim of gaining resources and power, the civil society networks in Brazil and Ecuador have played significant roles. In Brazil, networked nonprofit organizations focused on a framework of partnership with government. In Ecuador, organizations have pursued self-regulatory approaches. Ecuadorian nonprofits started to position themselves as explicitly self-regulatory, pointing to the new collective accountability reports as one way in which nonprofits are creating opportunities to be more accountable to government and the public. Ecuadorian nonprofits have argued that civil society is complementary to government in the provision of services, but not within a framework of direct partnership as is the case in Brazil.

Brazilian nonprofits appear to have become more dependent on government funding. Resources from international cooperation decreased during the 1990s, and this pressured nonprofits to reposition themselves to work in partnership with the government. As a result, nonprofits not only increased their service provision emphasis, but also shifted the kinds of advocacy they pursued. Previously, their advocacy actions were focused on the content of public policies. During the later regulatory waves, however, advocacy became focused on the claims for more and better government partnerships and contracts.

In Ecuador, resource dependency is not so clear. Nonprofit strategy in Ecuador has focused on creating a sector-level body and exploring self-regulatory approaches and was not a result of resource dependencies on government. Institutional pressures have accounted for the pursuit of collective discussion among nonprofit organizations and the exploration of self-regulatory approaches such as joint statements and collective accountability reporting.

It is notable that the debate about government regulation did not produce a debate about self-regulation among Brazilian nonprofits as it did in Ecuador. The perceptions of nonprofit leaders in Brazil have been that government regulation is already so intense that few areas could be self-regulated, and that the range and diversity of civil society organizations raised doubts about if and how self-regulation schemes could be devised or implemented across all organizations.

In Brazil and Ecuador, besides all the strategies and pressures from government and nonprofits, political events have played a major role in the regulatory waves in each country. These Latin American cases indicate that political elements are decisive for the future of government/nonprofit relations. In Brazil, it appears that nonprofits already know and consider the centrality of the political, as the proactive creation of the Platform for a New Regulatory Framework for Civil Society Organizations during the presidential elections of 2010 indicates. In Ecuador, recognition of the centrality of politics in government/nonprofit relations is developing through the Confederation of Civil Society Organizations' charge to establish a dialogue with government and the public. The centrality of political events, however, seems largely limited to national government; our analyses show little reference to local governments affecting nonprofit regulation.

In the Latin American situation, further questions need probing. Across the cases, the use of overarching laws (Brazil) versus executive decrees (Ecuador) to regulate nonprofit organizations should be explored further. How might government's choosing of the regulatory structure be part of the shaping of the organizational field or the "engineering of relations"[76] between government and nonprofit organizations? Or are these merely contextual features of regulation in each country?

We have also identified the role of nonprofit networks in both cases as being important to the development of the nonprofit sector and, in the case of Ecuador, for self-regulatory debate and initiatives. However, further inquiry about the ability of these networks to build relations within government needs attention. In Brazil, politically active nonprofits developed personal and institutional relationships with the Workers' Party, which came to be relevant to their government/nonprofit relations when that party was elected to the presidency. In Ecuador, on the other hand, there is no evidence of such links between the Correa administration and the nonprofit sector. Finally, more research is necessary on how international funding is changing in Brazil,

---

[76] Ortiz, n. 41.

Ecuador, and the Latin American context, and how this affects the civil society sector and regulatory and self-regulatory trends affecting it.

Finally, we turn to an issue that animates this chapter: What kind of regulation do nonprofit organizations want? In Brazil, a segment of the nonprofit sector that has been politically active since re-democratization in the 1980s has significantly increased its contracting with the federal government since 2000. It formed a coalition in 2010 asking for the government to approve a new regulatory framework that is directly situated within the partnership between government and nonprofit organizations. In Ecuador, increased attention to the regulation of nonprofits has been on the agenda of the current administration since 2008. Several regulatory decrees have been proposed and/or enacted, and nonprofit organizations have responded collectively, discussing and beginning to implement new self-regulatory initiatives. The two cases of Brazil and Ecuador indicate that there are few uniform priorities and strategies adopted through the different waves of regulation and that self-regulation is not inevitable. However, in both cases, nonprofits act strategically by taking advantage of political opportunities and interorganizational linkages to advance sector-level goals, including at times self-regulatory strategies of different kinds.

9

Australia

Co-Production, Self-Regulation and Co-Regulation

MYLES MCGREGOR-LOWNDES

9.1 INTRODUCTION

The means by which a society regulates social behavior is shaped by many factors deriving from its history, culture, political system, and economic circumstances.[1] New regulatory measures often arise as conditions allow, as a political response to public pressure often amplified through the public media.[2] We are starting to realize that, within constraints, societies do have choices about the style and nature of regulation. The realization of choice gives rise in participatory democracies to consideration of the most appropriate style and nature of regulation in any particular circumstance. The state and its agencies have traditionally been a central actor with recourse to coercive powers and a mandate to command and control conduct according to due process. However, this overlooks those areas of society with common interests that have, in a variety of ways, regulated their own behavior largely on the edge of the direct sphere of state influence (what we often term self-regulation, or similar). While states have chosen or been forced not to regulate some areas of society directly, states are now cooperating with others to regulate social behaviors, usually reserving a level of overarching control or a threat of it.

Australia appears to be no different from other developed nation states in this regard. It has groups that regulate their own behaviors outside, or overlapping with, state regulation. This includes what is often referred to as the third sector, mostly nonprofit organizations that are not classified as part of the state, or private households, or for-profit business. In Australia, the sector is

---

[1] Robert Baldwin, Martin Cave, and Martin Lodge, *Understanding Regulation: Theory, Strategy, and Practice* (Oxford: Oxford University Press, 2012).

[2] J.W. Kingdon, *Agendas, Alternatives, and Public Policies* (New York: Longman, 1995).

regulated by governments at both federal and state levels, subject to the general law of the nation as the private sector is, as well as by particular laws with respect to entity formation, taxation, and collection of donations from the public. Australian nonprofit organizations are afforded concessions or exemptions from general regulation – usually because they have traditionally been treated differently, general regulation is not applicable or would result in adverse consequences to the achievement of their purposes, or because they provide public benefits and are therefore worthy of subsidy. Public scandal, particularly in relation to fundraising or diversion of assets and income to private uses, is often the impetus for new or revised regulation when the conditions are right. There are a number of identifiable areas where nonprofit communities of interest have set out to regulate their own behaviors.

This chapter examines some recent developments in relation to Australian nonprofit communities seeking to regulate their own collective behaviors. This cannot be done without acknowledging and examining the overlap of mandated government regulation of the sector, along with areas where governments choose to co-regulate with such communities of interest. Scholars have classified this type of regulation as self-regulation where "standards and rules of conduct are set by an industry-level organization, rather than a governmental or firm-level apparatus"[3] or more fully as

> collective action by a significant number of non-state actors to shape their own behavior and that of others in a (sub)sector through the establishment of norms, standards, and credible commitments, supported by mechanisms that induce adherence, which has substantial legitimacy across the sector and with governments, stakeholders, and citizens. The goals of self-regulation may vary from avoiding state regulation to producing fundamental behavioral change in a sector, and the mechanisms can range from relatively non-prescriptive voluntary codes to mandatory accreditation which may, in effect, serve as a license to operate.[4]

Such classifications are a good starting point, but the application of these definitions to recent situations is uncovering myriad arrangements and hybrid entities.[5]

---

[3]   Mary Kay Gugerty, Mark Sidel, and Angela L. Bies, "Introduction to Minisymposium: Nonprofit Self-Regulation," *Nonprofit and Voluntary Sector Quarterly* 39(6) (2010): 1027–1038, 1029, citing Neil Gunningham and Joseph Rees, "Industry Self-Regulation," *Law & Policy* 19(4) (1997): 363–599.

[4]   Susan D. Phillips, "Canadian Leapfrog: From Regulating Charitable Fundraising to Co-Regulating Good Governance," *Voluntas* 23(3) (2012): 808–829, 814.

[5]   Mark Sidel, *Trends in Nonprofit Self-Regulation in the Asia Pacific Region: Initial Data on Initiatives, Experiments and Models in Seventeen Countries*, report prepared for the Asia Pacific Philanthropy Consortium (2003); Mark Sidel, "The Guardians Guarding Themselves:

As Phillips states in relation to Canada,[6] governments driven by fiscal constraints and what has become known as New Public Management (NPM) are seeking to coopt self-regulation to achieve some of their own objectives in relation to regulating social behaviors – "co-regulation."[7] At the same time there is a move toward "co-production," which seeks to involve people in communities more in the design, implementation, and delivery of government services.[8] NPM attempts to harness the power of for-profit markets to bring efficiencies to government outsourcing of community services (often public goods) provision. Traditional market devices of outsourcing via a contest of competitors and giving market power to end users of services are developed within quasi-markets, which must be crafted by the state as they do not naturally arise.

The facilitation and regulation of such markets can be cumbersome and costly for governments to achieve through standard command and control regulatory tools such as prescriptive laws and agency policing, audits, and prosecution. Further, they are likely to collapse under their own bureaucratic weight, negating the cost saving and increased choice and quality anticipated from the market's invisible hand. Shifting these costs to market participants through self-regulatory schemes is attractive, but it is often necessary to have the assurance of overarching control to minimize political risks, thus resulting in co-regulation.

Australia is well down the path of NPM with significant outsourcing of government services, mainly to the nonprofit sector, and governments actively

---

Nonprofit Self-Regulation in Comparative Perspective," *Chicago-Kent Law Review* 80 (2005): 803–835; Mary Kay Gugerty, "The Effectiveness of National NGO Self-Regulation: Theory and Evidence from Africa," *Public Administration and Development* 28(2) (2008): 105–118; Mary Kay Gugerty and Aseem Prakash, eds., *Voluntary Regulation of Nonprofits and NGOs: An Accountability Club Framework* (Cambridge, UK: Cambridge University Press, 2010); Robert O. Bothwell, "Trends in Self-Regulation and Transparency of Nonprofit Organizations in the U.S.," *International Journal of Not-for-Profit Law* 4(1) (2001): 1–6; Shana Warren and Robert Lloyd, *Civil Society Self-Regulation: The Global Picture*, One World Trust Briefing Paper 11 (London: One World Trust, 2009).

[6] Phillips, n. 4, 814.

[7] Neil Gunningham, "The New Collaborative Environmental Governance: The Localization of Regulation," *Journal of Law and Society* 36(1) (2009): 145–166; Cary Coglianese and Evan Mendelson, "Meta-Regulation and Self-Regulation," in *The Oxford Handbook of Regulation*, ed. Robert Baldwin, Martin Cave, and Martin Lodge (Oxford: Oxford University Press, 2010) 1079; John Braithwaite, "Rewards and Regulation," *Journal of Law and Society* 29(1) (2002): 12–26.

[8] Elinor Ostrom, "Crossing the Great Divide: Coproduction, Synergy and Development," *World Development* 24(6) (1996), 1073–1087; Hilary Cottam and Charles Leadbetter, *Health: Co-creating Services, Red Paper 01* (London: Design Council, 2004); HM Government, *Putting People First: A Shared Vision and Commitment to the Transformation of Adult Social Care* (London: HM Government, 2007).

strategizing to create quasi-markets for community services.[9] Attempts by governments and the sector to regulate social behaviors in these newly forming markets has been slow to develop and has required extensive negotiation between the government and nonprofit interests. Most debate has concerned the creation of a national regulator in the form of an independent, but government-funded, agency using modern regulatory tools, which would bring Australia into line with most other Organisation for Economic Co-operation and Development (OECD) jurisdictions. Impetus for this reform came largely from the sector. Unfortunately, no sooner had implementation begun than there was a change of course – a new government driven by one minister's ideological view about regulation and civil society has proposed a larger measure of self-reporting, which is being resisted by much of the nonprofit sector.[10]

This chapter examines the major forces in this context of NPM, the policy debate surrounding a national regulator, and possible future developments as they bear on forms of self-regulation, co-regulation (utilizing and melding both regulation and self-regulation), and co-production (involving people in communities more in the design, implementation, and delivery of government services). The chapter then turns to examine preexisting self-regulatory schemes in various communities of interest in Australia and, in particular, one that is regarded as successful and mature. Finally, some observations are made about the future of self-regulation and the nonprofit sector in Australia.

9.2 THE CONTEXT OF NONPROFIT REGULATION IN AUSTRALIA

A number of contextual issues can help position the occurrence of overt state regulation, self-regulation, and variations of both in relation to nonprofit organizations in Australia. First, Australia's federal system of government has responsibilities for regulation of nonprofit organizations divided constitutionally between Commonwealth and state levels. For the most part, laws are not harmonized between jurisdictions, and most jurisdictions use old, command

[9] Mark Lyons and Bronwen Dalton, "Australia: A Continuing Love Affair with the New Public Management," in *Governance and Regulation in the Third Sector: International Perspectives*, ed. Susan D. Phillips and Steven Rathgeb Smith (New York: Routledge, 2011), 238–259; Linda McGuire and Deirdre O'Neill, "The Report on Government Services: A New Piece in the Accountability Matrix?," in *Strategic Issues for the Not-for-Profit Sector*, ed. Jo Barraket (Sydney: UNSW Press, 2008), 236.

[10] Australian Department of Social Services, *Options Paper: Australia's Charities and Not-for-Profits: Options for Replacement Arrangements Following the Abolition of the Australian Charities and Not-for-Profits Commission* (Canberra: Department of Social Services, 2014), accessed January 4, 2016, www.dss.gov.au/sites/default/files/documents/07_2014/options_paper_-_australian_charities_and_not-for-profits.pdf.

and control regulatory tools that are insufficiently resourced. Second, the NPM agenda is pursued by all governments, driving significant growth, with individual agency contracts being the primary tool of accountability, adding to overlapping and burdensome regulation on the Australian nonprofit sector.

Constitutionally, Australian state governments are given primary power with respect to charitable trusts and community organizations, but the federal (that is, Commonwealth) government can exercise power over much of the field if it wishes, through its powers over corporations and taxation. Faith-based organizations that deliver significant community services but often do not take a corporate form are difficult for the Commonwealth government to regulate other than through grant contracts. Responsibilities for education, health, and community services are shared with state governments, but the Commonwealth usually funds state delivery of these services partially or even fully, consequently retaining a level of control and influence. This gives rise to multiple sources of community services funding, with no central repository of corporate information and with overlapping and inconsistent regulation. For example, state governments enacted fundraising legislation from the time of World War I, and more recently have legislated a legal form for incorporated community associations; these are subject to Commonwealth taxation regulation and often receive contracts to provide outsourced services from both state and Commonwealth agencies. This produces enough complexity in itself but is exacerbated by inconsistent regulatory frameworks that are outdated, not fit for purpose, and inadequately policed.

For example, most fundraising regulations use old-style command and control tools, and state-level authorities in the main do not resource their scrutiny and policing functions adequately. In 2011, only seventeen full-time equivalent staff were engaged in administering fundraising legislation across all the Australian states and territories, including dealing with 204 public complaints. A total of ten prosecutions were reported in 2011. From 2007–2008 to 2010–2011 the total number was forty-seven.[11] The self-regulatory scheme administered by the Australian association of professional fundraisers, which will be discussed below, received and dealt with more complaints.

The case for reforming state and territory fundraising legislation is overwhelming. In Queensland and Western Australia, the legislation has not been reviewed for decades and is not fit for purpose. For example, in Western

---

[11] The Australian Centre for Philanthropy and Nonprofit Studies, *Registered Fundraising Organisations* (Brisbane: ACPNS, 2012), accessed January 4, 2016, https://wiki.qut.edu.au/display/nmlp/Issues+sheets+and+conference+papers.

Australia, some provisions have maximum penalties under A$10[12] and some are taken directly from the (British) Metropolitan Streets Act 1903, which applied to nuisance street collecting from stagecoaches in London.[13] The growth of new technologies and fundraising through the Internet and social media is dealt with briefly in only two jurisdictions.[14]

There has also been a surge in charitable giving in Australia. In 2012–2013, charitable giving amounted to A$8,614 million (8 percent of total sector income and 0.57 percent of GDP) having an 11 percent annual increase since 2000 despite the effects of the global financial crisis.[15] There have been no scandalous tax frauds involving fundraising that might force a regulatory response from the federal government, although there have been scandals in state jurisdictions that have caused enough public concern to require politicians to be seen as fixing the problem.

Against this backdrop of confused state regulation the Australian nonprofit sector is growing rapidly. Sector growth has outpaced the rest of the Australian economy over the last decade. The sector accounts for 3.8 percent of GDP, growing in recent years at an average annual rate of 6 percent, much faster than the Australian economy as a whole.[16] The nonprofit sector has doubled its income in real terms since 2000.[17] Funding received from government has grown strongly, rising from 30 percent of sector income in 1999–2000 to 38 percent in 2012–2013.[18] This growth is being fuelled by an aggressive NPM agenda. All levels of government, no matter what their political color, are contracting out service provision and trying to implement policies to create a market of informed, critical consumers who can choose among providers,

---

[12] Charitable Collections Regulations 1947 (WA), sch. 1, offences under regs. 8(1)–(2), 14(1)–(2).

[13] Street Collections Regulations 1999 (WA), reg. 7(2)(b): collection boxes "must not be fixed to a pole or otherwise designed to be held beyond the reach of the collector." For background, see Peter Luxton, *Charity Fund-Raising and the Public Interest: An Anglo-American Legal Perspective* (Brookfield, VT: Avebury, 1990), 26–36.

[14] Collections for Charities Act 2001 (Tas), s. 3(1); Charitable Collections Act 2003 (ACT), s. 7(2); for consideration of the issues, see Australian Centre for Philanthropy and Nonprofit Studies, *Nonprofit Model Law Project: Issues Sheets and Conference Papers* (Brisbane: ACPNS, 2012), accessed January 4, 2016, https://wiki.qut.edu.au/display/nmlp/Issues+sheets+and+conference +papers.

[15] Productivity Commission, *Contribution of the Not-for-Profit Sector: Research Report* (Melbourne: Productivity Commission, 2010), 77.

[16] Australian Bureau of Statistics, *Australian National Accounts: Non-profit Institutions Satellite Account, 2012–13*, Catalogue No. 5256.0 (Sydney: ABS, 2014), data cube tables 4 and 6, accessed January 4, 2016, www.abs.gov.au/AusStats/ABS@.nsf/MF/5256.0.

[17] M. McGregor-Lowndes, *The Not for Profit Sector in Australia* (ACPNS Current Issues Information Sheet 2014/4), accessed January 4, 2016, http://eprints.qut.edu.au/75397/.

[18] Ibid.

who, in turn, are being encouraged to improve service standards and increase efficiency, transparency, and responsiveness to client demands.[19] This appears to be driven not by concerns with major outsourcing scandals involving nonprofit organizations in the public eye but by the government's belief in improved efficiency and effectiveness through NPM. State and federal government regulation of outsourced services has largely occurred through government agency command and control, using outsourcing contracts that are significantly restrictive and repressive, overtly supervisory, and focused on measuring performance through inputs rather than outputs or outcomes.[20]

In other countries, the NPM agenda has been a trigger to develop nonprofit organizations with the capacity to be suitable participants in an emerging community services market. At the same time, these organizations have had to demonstrate transparency in terms of key financial and governance indicators, so that governments, new "clients" (formerly citizens), and other stakeholders can assess and benchmark the integrity of organizations with which they may deal. The United Kingdom is a classic example, with its Third Way policies and Charity Commissions collecting annual returns, ensuring public benefit outcomes and developing best-practice governance and financial standards through a mixture of legislation and self-regulatory tools.[21] Australia has struggled to follow this path in relation to reconfiguration of state agencies to take on the role of capacity building and quasi-market supervision. The existing institutions that fulfilled some of these roles and the proposed ones will be examined.

---

[19] Lyons and Dalton, n. 9; McGuire and O'Neill, n. 9; Garth Nowland-Foreman, "Purchase of Service Contracting, Voluntary Organizations and Civil Society: Dissecting the Goose That Lays the Golden Eggs?," *American Behavioral Scientist* 42(1) (1998): 108–123; Christopher Hood, "A Public Management for All Seasons?," *Public Administration* 69(1) (1991): 3–19, 5; Patrick Dunleavy, "The Globalization of Public Services Production: Can Government Be 'Best in World'?," *Public Policy and Administration* 9(2) (1994): 36–64, 38; Vic George and Paul Wilding, *Globalisation and Human Welfare* (Basingstoke: Palgrave, 2002).

[20] Amanda McBratney and Myles McGregor-Lowndes, "'Fair' Government Contracts for Community Service Provision: Time to Curb Unfettered Executive Freedom?," *Australian Journal of Administrative Law* 19(1) (2012): 19–33; Myles McGregor-Lowndes and Amanda McBratney, "Government Community Service Contracts: Restraining Abuse of Power," *Public Law Review* 22(4) (2011): 279–297.

[21] Tony Blair, *The Third Way: New Politics for the New Century* (London: Fabian Society, 1998); Martin Powell, "New Labour and the Third Way in the British Welfare State: A New and Distinctive Approach?," *Critical Social Policy* 20(1) (2000): 39–60. This includes not only the Charity Commission for England and Wales, but also the creation of Northern Irish and Scottish institutions along similar lines. See generally Susan D. Phillips and Steven Rathgeb Smith, eds., *Governance and Regulation in the Third Sector: International Perspectives* (New York: Routledge, 2011).

9.3 THE REGULATORY REFORM AGENDA

There has been a two-decade-long discourse about national reform of the nonprofit sector by the federal government, particularly in relation to charities and mostly about legislative reform. Since 1995, several government-sponsored reports have recommended reform, but only minor matters were addressed until 2012.[22] The consultations, government inquiries, draft legislation, public submissions, and evidence transcripts amounted to 15.5 million words on more than 50,000 pages between 1995 and 2011.[23] No stone was left unturned or unconsulted.

The first report in 1995 by the Industry Commission[24] was essentially about the capacity of the nonprofit sector to engage in the forthcoming agenda of significant outsourcing of services to it rather than any forced political response to a public scandal. A change of government to the conservative side saw these recommendations fall away, but this did not slow the pace of the NPM agenda in relation to outsourcing of community services. Greater reliance was placed on micro management of these relationships through individual contractual arrangements with government agencies.[25]

When the Australian Labor Party (ALP) returned to federal government in 2007 there was a growing consensus among ALP politicians, various government agencies, and the sector that there was a need for streamlined state regulation and greater disclosure of community sector performance. The government commissioned the Industry Commission's replacement, the Productivity Commission, to

[22] Ian Sheppard, Robert Fitzgerald, and David Gonski, *Report of the Inquiry into the Definition of Charities and Related Organisations* (Canberra: Treasury, 2001); Industry Commission, *Charitable Organisations in Australia* (Melbourne: Industry Commission, 1995); Australia's Future Tax System Review Panel, *Australia's Future Tax System: Final Report* (Canberra: Attorney-General's Department, 2010), chapter B-3, accessed January 4, 2016, http://taxreview .treasury.gov.au/content/Content.aspx?doc=html/pubs_reports.htm; Senate Standing Committee on Economics, *Disclosure Regimes for Charities and Not-for-Profit Organisations* (Canberra: Parliament of Australia, 2008), accessed January 4, 2016, www.aph.gov.au/ Parliamentary_Business/Committees/Senate/Economics/Completed%20inquiries/2008-10/ charities_08/index.

[23] The Treasury, *Final Report: Scoping Study for a National Not-for-Profit Regulator* (Canberra: Treasury, 2011), 44, accessed January 4, 2016, www.treasury.gov.au/ConsultationsandReviews/ Consultations/2011/Scoping-Study-for-a-National-Not-For-Profit-Regulator. This estimate includes federal government and Council of Australian Governments (COAG) reports and consultations on nonprofit regulation and taxation including the relevant parts of the "Henry Review," that is, Australia's Future Tax System Review Panel, n. 22, 88.

[24] Industry Commission, n. 22.

[25] Mark Considine, "Governance and Competition: The Role of Non-profit Organisations in the Delivery of Public Services," *Australian Journal of Political Science* 38(1) (2003): 63–77.

provide an updated report on the sector, which included a detailed reform agenda. The recommendations included establishing a central regulator and a disclosure register, reform of government contracts for service provision and monitoring, stimuli for philanthropy, social and sector innovation, and improved national data recording and sector capacity.[26] This would have made Australia similar to the three separate jurisdictions in the United Kingdom (England and Wales, Scotland, and Northern Ireland) in relation to an overarching independent government agency that would provide the "market" with basic transparency information about financial performance, governance, benchmarks, and public benefit assurance for tax concession purposes.

The ALP government was reelected on a platform that included nonprofit reforms in the spirit of the major recommendations of the Productivity Commission's report.[27] The initial work to develop such extensive reforms was begun with the appointment of a number of implementation bodies[28] and consultation on specific reforms.[29] The Australian Charities and Not-for-profits Commission (ACNC) was established in December 2012 as an independent statutory body with a mandate to establish a register of charities, enable public access to annual financial statements, oversee governance matters through a mandated minimum standard, promote trust and confidence in the sector, and reduce red tape in respect of charity regulation.[30]

The central register of information fits nicely with the NPM strategies to facilitate regulatory devices to promote markets for community service organizations. The aim to promote public confidence appeared less pressing – a study commissioned by the ACNC about public trust and confidence in the nonprofit sector almost immediately on its creation found that charities ranked third (mean score 6.6) among eleven professions and public institutions (after doctors, mean score 7.1, and police, mean score 7.0).[31] Once the ACNC's role

---

[26] Productivity Commission, n. 15, xli–lii.

[27] Australian Department of Prime Minister and Cabinet, *Record of Election Commitments 2010: Brief to the Prime Minister, the Honourable Julia Gillard MP* (Canberra: Department of Prime Minister and Cabinet, 2010), 8-5.

[28] Treasury, *Budget Measures 2011–12*, Budget Paper No. 2 (Canberra: Treasury, 2011), 37, 322–323.

[29] Treasury, n. 23; Treasury, *Better Targeting of Not-for-Profit Tax Concessions: Consultation Paper* (Canberra: Treasury, 2011), accessed January 4, 2016, www.treasury.gov.au/ConsultationsandReviews/Consultations/2011/Better-Targeting-of-Not-For-Profit-Tax-Concessions; Treasury, Exposure Draft: Public Ancillary Funds Bill (July 14, 2011).

[30] Australian Charities and Not-for-Profits Commission Act 2012 (Cth).

[31] Chantlink, *Public Trust and Confidence in Australian Charities: Research Report* (Melbourne: Australian Charities and Not-for-Profits Commission, 2013), accessed January 4, 2016, www.acnc.gov.au/ACNC/Pblctns/Rpts/PublicTrust/ACNC/Publications/Reports/Trust_con.aspx.

was explained to respondents, their level of trust in charities increased further, to a mean score of 7.0.

Another aim for the ACNC, one that enjoyed political "motherhood" status, was the reduction of nonprofit red tape. However, the regulatory burden lay primarily with paperwork generated by individual service contracts with government (state and federal),[32] as nonprofit organizations were not previously required to file annual returns with the proxy central regulator, the Australian Taxation Office (ATO). Even the Explanatory Memorandum to the ACNC bill indicated that in the short term there was unlikely to be any lessening of red tape.[33] In fact a study commissioned by the ACNC of the red tape burden on charities confirmed that the bulk of it was generated by individual government outsourcing contracts, and ACNC paperwork amounted to less than 1 percent of the burden.[34] The sector mostly saw the ACNC as providing a valuable piece of infrastructure to permit transparency and provide a seal of good housekeeping as well as a voice inside the federal bureaucracy to reduce red tape. The ACNC was well advanced in proposing a Charity Passport[35] – a collection of information (contact details, financial reports, governing rules) – that multiple government agencies recognize as accurate and use for identification and data exchange. Information provided to the ACNC by a charity would not be requested again for grant applications unless the grant was assessed as high risk.

The ACNC was also progressing toward standardization of financial account reporting as recommended by the Productivity Commission.[36] Independent modeling suggests that adopting the National Standard Chart of

[32] Myles McGregor-Lowndes and Christine Ryan, "Reducing the Compliance Burden of Nonprofit Organisations: Cutting Red Tape," *Australian Journal of Public Administration* 68(1) (2009): 21–38; Australian Charities and Not-for-Profits Commission, *Red Tape Reduction Forum Report: Measuring and Reducing Red Tape in the Not-for-Profit Sector* (Melbourne: ACNC, 2014), accessed January 4, 2016, www.acnc.gov.au/ACNC/Report/rtrforumreport.aspx; Australian Institute of Health and Welfare, *Cutting the Red Tape: Preliminary Paper Detailing the Problem of Multiple Entry and Reporting by Service Providers* (Canberra: AIHW, 2006), accessed January 4, 2016, www.aihw.gov.au/publication-detail/?id=6442467913.

[33] Explanatory Memorandum, Australian Charities and Not-for-Profits Commission Bill 2012 (Cth) 3.

[34] Ernst & Young, *Research into Commonwealth Regulatory and Reporting Burdens on the Charity Sector: A Report Prepared for the Australian Charities and Not-for-Profits Commission* (Canberra: Ernst & Young, 2014), accessed January 4, 2016, www.acnc.gov.au/ACNC/Pblctns/Rpts/EY_Report/ACNC/Publications/Reports/EY_report.aspx.

[35] Australian Charities and Not-for-Profits Commission, "Charity Passport," accessed January 4, 2016, www.acnc.gov.au/ACNC/About_ACNC/Redtape_redu/Charity_Passport/ACNC/Edu/Charity_Passport.aspx.

[36] Australian Charities and Not-for-Profits Commission, "Appendix 1: Red Tape Reduction Timeline and Plan," in *ACNC Implementation Report Update* (Melbourne: ACNC, 2013),

Accounts would lead to savings during the next decade of A\$3.1 million per annum in the state of Victoria alone.[37] If completed, these initiatives should improve both the compliance and the administrative costs of grant and service agreements at both national and state levels.

The prime role for this regulation was to further the NPM agenda by creating a facility for market participants to gain information about nonprofit participants and reduce compliance costs of outsourced contracts.

9.4 PROPOSED SELF-REGULATION TO REPLACE ACNC

As noted above, the incoming government in 2013 indicated that it would abolish the ACNC, having vigorously opposed the bills in opposition, and return to the basic regulatory structure prior to the reforms, with the ATO made the gatekeeper for approval of charity status and the Australian Securities and Investments Commission (ASIC) again responsible as corporate regulator for nonprofit organizations that took the legal form of a company. On March 19, 2014, the government tabled the Australian Charities and Not-for-profits Commission (Repeal) (No. 1) Bill 2014 in the House of Representatives. The purpose of this bill is to repeal the Australian Charities and Not-for-profits Commission Act 2012, thereby abolishing the ACNC. The bill will not take effect, however, until the enactment of a later bill, which will provide the details of the arrangements replacing the ACNC. As the government does not control the Upper House, it is not certain that the bill will be passed. After a cabinet reshuffle, the new responsible minister, the Minister for Social Services, indicated that the bill was not a priority for the government.[38]

The previous Minister had suggested that private charity ratings agencies providing third-party certifications, such as those operating in the United States, might be an option worth considering.[39] But this was not pursued since it would rely on primary data from a central tax register of nonprofit organizations, which does not exist in Australia. In July 2014 the Department

accessed January 4, 2016, www.acnc.gov.au/ACNC/Pblctns/Rpts/Imp_up/ACNC/Publications/Imp_Rep/Imp_Up_TOC.aspx.

[37] Strategic Project Partners, *Victorian Standard Chart of Accounts Post-Implementation Review: Report to the Office for the Community Sector* (Melbourne: Victorian Department of Planning and Community Development, 2011), 25.

[38] "Scott Morrison Puts Bill to Abolish Charity Regulator on Backburner," *Sydney Morning Herald*, February 7, 2015.

[39] Helen Rittelmeyer, "Independent Charities, Independent Regulators: The Future of Not-for-Profit Regulation," *Centre for Independent Studies Issue Analysis*, 143 (2014), accessed January 5, 2016, www.cis.org.au/publications/issue-analysis/; Australian Institute of Company Directors, "US Model Has Pros and Cons for Australian NFPs," *The Boardroom Report* 12(3) (2014).

of Social Services released a discussion paper, *Options Paper: Australia's Charities and Not-for-Profits*.[40] Despite being an "options" paper, only one option was discussed:

> the Government proposes that as part of replacement arrangements charities will be required to maintain a publicly accessible website that features the following information:
>
> - Names of responsible persons;
> - Details of all funding received from Government (Commonwealth State and Local); and
> - Financial Reports.
>
> Self-reporting will allow organizations to make more information public if they so choose. This will provide members of the public with insight into how charities are spending public funds and a level of confidence when members of the public consider making donations.[41]

The reason behind this move to self-reporting was expressed as a reduction in unnecessary regulation, with the government being committed:

> to a risk-based, proportionate approach to the oversight of the charitable and not-for-profit institutions that make up Australia's civil society sector. This approach recognises that charities themselves work hard to build the trust of the Australian public and should be accorded with the presumption that they are operating in the interests of those they serve and in accordance with their mission.[42]

The Minister at the time also announced the creation of a National Centre of Excellence that would provide collaborative education, training, and development, moving "the focus from the stick to the carrot" for charities.[43] He elaborated in a speech to the sector that "our governing philosophy is informed by a few humble truths: first that Government is NOT the fount of all wisdom; secondly, that a vibrant, dynamic economy and business community are essential to fund the social services we need, expect and deserve; and thirdly that voluntary mutual co-operation is [a] crucial force to building a responsive and vibrant civil society."[44] The current Minister has not spoken specifically about the proposed Centre and appears to have a more pragmatic view than the former Minister.

---

[40] Australian Department of Social Services, n. 10.   [41] Ibid., 2.   [42] Ibid.

[43] Minister for Social Services, Kevin Andrews, *National Press Club Address*, March 17, 2014.

[44] Ibid.

Clearly there is no crisis of public confidence; the drive for self-reporting flies in the face of majority sector opinion and is ideologically driven by a confused notion of civil society. The individual nature of self-reporting barely constitutes self-regulation for most definitions as it misses industry-level mediation. Whether this provides the conditions for greater sector self-regulation to emerge is yet to be seen, and the sector was underwhelmed by another set of reform proposals.

9.5 SELF-REGULATORY CODES OF CONDUCT

Like most other OECD countries, Australian professional associations and industry bodies use codes of conduct or ethics. A number of codes apply in the nonprofit sector, but the European fundraising self-regulatory initiatives or American charity ratings agencies have not yet taken hold. The most sophisticated code is the Australian Council for International Development (ACFID) *Code of Conduct*.[45] It applies to a numerically small group of Australian charities, which account for more than 80 percent of private international aid in dollar terms. The code governs their conduct in a range of matters including fundraising, transparent financial reporting, ethical principles, and addressing public complaints. These characteristics, together with its integration with government regulation, make it a worthwhile case to consider in detail.

The other significant code is operated by the Fundraising Institute Australia (FIA), which is an association for professional fundraisers.[46] The FIA's *Principles and Standards of Fundraising Practice* include a code of professional ethics and practice, with a public complaints procedure and twelve standards of professional practice in areas such as telemarketing, bequests, and face-to-face solicitations. It was developed in 2005–2006, arising organically from the interests of fundraising professionals seeking to protect the reputation of their profession, rather than from any public scandal or threat of state regulatory initiatives. There are other industry codes applying to particular nonprofit sectors, such as the Association for Data-driven Marketing and Advertising (ADMA) code for direct marketers (including nonprofit fundraisers).[47]

---

[45] Australian Council for International Development, *Code of Conduct* (2015), accessed January 5, 2016, www.acfid.asn.au/code-of-conduct/code-of-conduct; ACFID was previously known as ACFOA, but for simplicity, the term ACFID will be used throughout this chapter.

[46] Fundraising Institute Australia, *Principles and Standards of Fundraising Practice* (2011), accessed January 5, 2016, www.fia.org.au/pages/principles-standards-of-fundraising-practice .html.

[47] Association for Data-Driven Marketing and Advertising, *ADMA Code of Practice* (2015), accessed January 5, 2016, www.adma.com.au/comply/code-of-practice/.

This code has a history in seeking to forestall increased government regulation in response to public complaints about advertising, particularly telemarketing, and privacy concerns.[48]

Some Australian states have also used codes of conduct as a tool in their fundraising regulation. For example in South Australia, a Code of Practice has been mandated by statute since March 1, 2013.[49] It cannot be classified as self-regulation, as it is in fact government regulation, but it was devised with significant input from, and agreement by, interested parties.[50] It arose in response to a government reform paper that in turn was initiated by a number of public scandals involving fundraising abuse.[51] One of the public issues arose from gala fundraising dinners featuring Cherie Blair, wife of the then British Prime Minister, and the alleged lack of return to the charity involved.[52]

In Western Australia, the department responsible for fundraising regulation developed a voluntary code, again with the assistance of interested parties.[53] It does not have legislative force, but nonprofit organizations that adhere to the code and voluntarily lodge their annual returns with the government-appointed reference committee are allowed to include a statement to this effect in their promotional material. It is a classic "club theory" seal of good housekeeping, coveted by nonprofit organizations that seek to raise funds from the public. The stimulus for this arrangement was a public scandal in 1994 involving members of a conservative political party and high commissions for third-party fundraising.[54] In 1996 a voluntary code was developed quickly as an interim measure, while more permanent regulatory reforms were

[48] Rosie Baker, "Australian Advertisers Must Regulate or Be Regulated," *AdNews*, November 5, 2013, accessed January 5, 2016, www.adnews.com.au/adnews/australian-advertisers-must-regulate-or-be-regulated.

[49] Collections for Charitable Purposes Act 1939 (SA), s. 12(2)(b).

[50] FIA Submission, *South Australian Draft Code of Practice: Collections for Charitable Purposes Act 1939* (November 2010); FIA Submission, *Collections for Charitable Purposes Act 1939 – Improving Regulations Issues Paper* (February 2010), accessed January 5, 2016, www.fia.org.au/pages/industry-submission-archives.html.

[51] South Australian Attorney-General's Department, *Code of Practice: Collections for Charitable Purposes Act 1939* (2013), accessed January 5, 2016, www.cbs.sa.gov.au/assets/files/Charities_CodeofPractice_2013.pdf; Government of South Australia, *Improving Regulation – Final Report* (2010), accessed January 5, 2016, www.cbs.sa.gov.au/assets/files/Improving_Regulation_Final_Report.pdf.

[52] Karen Percy, "Questions over Charity Fundraising Techniques," *PM*, ABC Radio National, February 8, 2005, accessed January 5, 2016, www.abc.net.au/pm/content/2005/s1298612.htm.

[53] Western Australia Department of Commerce, *Charities Code of Practice*, accessed January 5, 2016, www.commerce.wa.gov.au/consumer-protection/charities-code-practice.

[54] See address-in-reply to Legislative Assembly, Parliament of Western Australia, Hansard, *Parliamentary Debates* (March 26, 1996, J. McGinty, MLA), accessed January 5, 2016, www.parliament.wa.gov.au/Hansard/hans35.nsf/3e8095c2de81a3b048256c6b002e9930/

deliberated on.[55] One view is that the code performed its political purpose in calming media comment, provides little onerous burden or barriers to fundraising, and is lightly regulated. However, the legislative reforms are still being considered more than a decade and a half later, despite continued pressure from fundraisers and their organizations. Both of these state initiatives were political responses to adverse media publicity when quick responses were demanded by the public.

The ACFID code is arguably the most developed and pure self-regulatory nonprofit code in Australia. It also has mature integration with government regulatory agencies, the ACNC, and AusAID, the government agency supervising overseas aid.[56] Just above US$1.4 billion in Australian private giving goes to developing countries (as of 2013),[57] and much of this is raised from the public. The ACFID code was developed in response to internal members' disquiet about nonmember accountability following the 1984–1985 LiveAid concerts, and public responses to major humanitarian crises at the time.[58] The first draft code was approved in 1986 and adopted in 1987, but was revised and made mandatory for all ACFID members in 1989.

In 1995 serious accountability issues were raised in the popular media, about a non-ACFID member's international aid program, which caught the attention of the responsible federal government Minister. At the same time, the Industry Commission was completing its final report on regulation of

f5d3b4cebcbea31a482578f600177949?OpenDocument; Ministerial Statement, "Charitable Collections Advisory Committee," Hansard, *Parliamentary Debates* (May 1, 1996, C. Edwardes, MLA, Minister for Fair Trading), accessed January 5, 2016, www.parliament.wa .gov.au/Hansard/hans35.nsf/NFS/979b69fc31aac433482578f60017ab06?OpenDocument; and Ministerial Statement, "Charitable Collections Advisory Committee, Fundraising Industry Discussion Paper," Hansard, *Parliamentary Debates* (June 26, 1996, C. Edwardes, MLA, Minister for Fair Trading), accessed January 5, 2016, www.parliament.wa.gov.au/Hansard/ hans35.nsf/NFS/36096abba9deed13482578f6001de57e?OpenDocument.

[55] See response to question on notice regarding monitoring of charities, Legislative Assembly, Parliament of Western Australia, Hansard, *Parliamentary Debates* (August 19, 1997, D. Shave, MLA), accessed January 5, 2016, www.parliament.wa.gov.au/Hansard/hans35.nsf/NFS/ bdd16of6c89f805d482565fb002c7b5f?OpenDocument.

[56] Until October 31, 2013, the Australian Agency for International Development (AusAID) was the Australian government agency responsible for managing Australia's international aid and development program. The objective of the aid program was to assist developing countries to reduce poverty and achieve sustainable development, in line with Australia's national priorities. This is now administered through the Department of Foreign Affairs and Trade.

[57] OECD Development Assistance Committee, *OECD Development Co-Operation Peer Review: Australia 2013* (Paris: OECD, 2013), 52.

[58] Australian Council for International Development, *ACFID Code of Conduct – Historical Contexts*, accessed January 5, 2016, https://acfid.asn.au/sites/site.acfid/files/resource_document/ Code-of-Conduct-History-summary.pdf.

the charitable sector, which would be handed down a few months later.[59] The Commission was tasked by the government to examine the regulation of the sector, not in response to any defaults or public scandals, but to pursue an agenda on contracting out of government services. The Commission's task was a clear sign of the impending NPM strategies that were to be adopted by all governments in Australia.[60] As implementing any recommendations by the Industry Commission would require extensive consultation, led by a Minister in another portfolio, the Minister decided to establish a process for appointing an advisory committee to make recommendations on interim codes of practice and reporting, relating to accountability of international aid programs. These interim measures would fall away once the general regulation of the whole sector had been established by the government.

An advisory committee was formed, and it recommended that ACFID develop an industry self-regulatory scheme. On receiving the report three months later, the Minister immediately accepted the recommendations and announced:

> This will be the first time that a Code of Conduct covering ethical principles, operational arrangements and detailed financial reporting standards has been developed for this sector. It will represent a major step forward in self-regulation and will build on the clear commitment of NGO's [*sic*] to greater public accountability.[61]

By the time of this announcement the Industry Commission had published its final report, which recommended a register of charities, harmonization of state fundraising laws, and creation of a nonprofit accounting standard and taxation changes.[62] The recommendations were opposed by the sector for a number of reasons, including a change to the Fringe Benefits Tax impacting on salaries, but ultimately they were not implemented because of a change of federal government in 1996. The incoming Conservative government agreed to the code concept after significant lobbying by the sector, led by ACFID.

[59] Industry Commission, n. 22.

[60] Maryann Zarnegar Deloffre, "NGO Accountability Clubs in the Humanitarian Sector: Social Dimensions of Club Emergence and Design," in *Voluntary Regulation of NGOs and Nonprofits: An Accountability Club Framework*, ed. Mary Kay Gugerty and Aseem Prakash (Cambridge: Cambridge University Press, 2010), 169–200, 178; Maryon MacDonald, "Accountability, Anthropology and the European Commission," in *Audit Cultures: Anthropological Studies in Accountability, Ethics and the Academy*, ed. Marilyn Strathen (London: Routledge, 2000), 106–132.

[61] G. Bilney MP, "Code of Conduct for NGOs," *Media Release*, MDC 73, August 31, 1995.

[62] Industry Commission, n. 22, Recommendation 24.

At the same time the international development sector was preoccupied with calls for greater accountability with respect to several international aid–related crises, particularly that in Rwanda, which resulted in a Joint Evaluation Report of that crisis.[63] This led to several large-scale projects to develop transnational codes, such as Sphere and COMPAS Qualité, which resulted in loose self-regulatory codes. These were mainly technical reference tools and aspirational statements, driven by differing ideological perspectives and with weak enforcement and reporting.[64] No doubt these international discussions of self-regulation played a part in the umbrella body and the sector in Australia pushing for a national self-regulatory scheme. In the end, the sector persuaded the incoming Minister to act, but he declined to launch the final Code of Conduct, possibly because it was seen as a legacy of the previous government. Instead, the Governor-General did the honors.[65]

ACFID adopted the Code of Conduct as mandatory for its members, and AusAid made it mandatory for all those wishing to access its government funding from June 30, 1997. Nonmembers could pay a fee to subscribe to the code but did not enjoy other benefits of ACFID membership. A Code Committee was established under the auspices of ACFID, but was independent from it. The committee has an independent chair, an independent donors' representative, accounting experts, and representatives from the sector. It was specifically tasked with hearing public complaints under the code[66] and examining member organizations' public financial reports annually for compliance with it.

Self-regulatory schemes are often faced with a "club" dilemma – having low standards or weak enforcement as a way to maximize or retain members in order for the association to survive.[67] Having and maintaining high standards requires far greater resources and thus usually higher membership fees and more enforcement action, particularly public enforcement. This can drive members to seek less expensive alternatives, such as other, possibly less onerous codes or other reputational assurances for donors and stakeholders.[68]

The ACFID Code Committee has been active in hearing complaints and making the results public and has conducted thorough annual examinations of both the financial and narrative reporting aspects of annual reports. This

---

[63] Deloffre, n. 60, 170.   [64] Ibid., 194.

[65] The Governor-General is the Queen's representative in Australia and seen as above politics.

[66] In the first decade, nine complaints were investigated and one review was undertaken.

[67] Mary Kay Gugerty and Aseem Prakash, "Voluntary Regulation of NGOs and Nonprofits: An Introduction to the Club Framework," in Gugerty and Prakash, n. 5, 3–38, 20.

[68] Ibid.; Ronelle Burger, "Reconsidering the Case for Enhancing Accountability via Regulation," *Voluntas* 23(1) (2012): 85–108, 94.

has kept its brand strong, but the challenge of costs remains, particularly for small organizations. The government allocated some funding to ACFID, through an AusAid general grant, to support the operation of the code when it began, and this has continued. AusAid can contribute nearly half of ACFID's income from year to year, through fees for performing service contracts. ACFID has been mindful of the challenges of a peak organization accepting funds from government and has been careful to maintain its governance standards and independence. It appears to have managed this well enough, while also keeping costs in check.

Over its first decade, the committee developed the code extensively, adding guides on child safety and protection, gender equity, aid with religious and political "strings," improved financial reporting, and an annual self-assessment of the nonfinancial standards by member organizations' governing bodies. The code now sets out more than fifty principles and 150 obligations in three areas of accountability:

- *Program principles*, including obligations for effectiveness in aid and development activities, human rights, and working with partner agencies
- *Public engagement*, including obligations on member organizations to be ethical and transparent in marketing, fundraising, and reporting
- *Organization*, including obligations for governance, management, financial controls, treatment of staff and volunteers, complaints handling processes, and compliance with legal requirements.[69]

Major revisions in 2010 (effective from 2012)[70] paid particular attention to the code's integration with existing international codes and other regulation common for such bodies.[71]

Compliance with the code is a prerequisite for AusAID's accreditation for some government funding, which is a front-end risk-assessment mechanism designed to ensure that funded organizations have the capacity to carry out sustainable development activities. Such an arrangement has the potential to be a significant driver for membership of the code and adherence to its provisions. However, throughout the life of the code only about half of its

---

[69] ACFID *Code*, n. 45; ACFID, *Code of Conduct Good Practice Toolkit*, accessed January 5, 2016, www.acfid.asn.au/code-of-conduct/implementation-guidance/introduction-to-code-and-guidance.

[70] The author of this chapter was chair of the ACFID Code committee during part of this period.

[71] For example, the Active Learning Network for Accountability and Performance in Humanitarian Action (ALNAP), Humanitarian Accountability Partnership (HAP), People in Aid, and the Sphere Project.

signatories have been in receipt of such funding, and for various reasons many members would not seek funding under the particular scheme.

The ACNC has acknowledged that the ACFID code meets the minimum governance standards of the ACNC regulations.[72] In fact, the code goes substantially further than the ACNC governance standards. The ACNC governance standards are devised to provide assurance that registered entities (charities) meet community expectations about the efficient use of their resources, for example, public monies, volunteer time, and donations, and minimize the risk of mismanagement and misappropriation. The standards are set under the authority of the ACNC Act;[73] all registered charities must comply with them, and the ACNC has a range of powers that it can exercise in the event of noncompliance.

The effectiveness of the ACFID code was amply demonstrated in 2005 after the Asian tsunami. Some A$300 million flowed into the coffers of aid agencies almost overnight because of the significant public interest in the natural disaster. It was recognized by the Code Committee as well as development agencies that this significant public response could have a downside if there was a perception that public generosity was abused. The code was amended quickly, to require agencies responding to the tsunami disaster to include more detailed financial and descriptive information regarding their application of funds for this cause, separate from their normal activities. It also required them to specify what would happen to donations that were surplus to tsunami needs, and ACFID prepared regular global reports for donors. This was particularly successful in communicating with the Australian public and preventing ill-informed media stories about misplaced aid donations. It would have been difficult for a government to achieve preventative measures in a timely fashion with such light touch action, which illustrates one of the benefits of self-regulation.

What has contributed to the apparent success of the ACFID code? A number of features may explain its creation, longevity, and sustained credibility with its stakeholders. The code has been incorporated into the regulation of a small section of specialist nonprofit organizations in Australia, which allows it to be focused on a specific area and cover the field in this niche part of the sector. This is a considerably easier task than trying to develop and maintain a code for the entire nonprofit field.

---

[72] Australian Charities and Not-for-Profits Commission Regulation 2013 (Cth); ACNC, ACNC *Governance Standards: ACFID Code of Conduct*, accessed January 5, 2016, www.acnc.gov.au/ ACNC/FTS/ACFID_code.aspx.

[73] Australian Charities and Not-for-Profits Commission Act 2012 (Cth), s. 45-10 (excludes those charities that are Basic Religious Charities).

Moreover, the code is recognized by the federal government department that supervises overseas aid, both as an important co-regulatory tool and in relation to its funding. This illustrates what Sidel identifies as an emerging trend in Asia, in a motivation to pursue effective self-regulation by making it a gateway to government funding, which also acts as a market mechanism to exclude "competitive or unproductive actors."[74] This style of arrangement is unusual in Australia, as government is cautious in promoting a single umbrella organization over others, but there appears to be no opposition to the situation. There are benefits in terms of cost savings for the department (Foreign Affairs and Trade) in having an external body to carry out close vetting work of aid organizations, and the code goes much further than might have been achieved by government regulation, in terms of prescriptive measures. The scrutiny of annual financial reports by committee staff and independent accounting experts is certainly as thorough as other nonprofit regulatory regimes in Australia, if not more so.

While the code appears to favor one umbrella body over other organizations, the government may be prepared to tolerate the situation because it is not strictly a monopoly – the code requires all members of ACFID to adhere to it, but nonmembers can adhere to it (and derive associated benefits) for a fee. While this is comforting for the government, it does cause potential problems for ACFID as identified in a report in relation to legal sanctions, done on behalf of the Panel on the Nonprofit Sector.[75] An organization can make a voluntary code legally binding on its members, with sanctions for noncompliance, through the contractual power of its corporate constitution, but to make it binding on nonmembers requires a separate relationship such as a private contract.[76] This requires nonmembers to agree to changes of the code through a negotiated contract every time there is an amendment. This is administratively challenging and is more likely to be legally challenged.

In 2014, ACFID moved to require full membership to gain access to code branding, and most associate members became full members. Surprisingly, there were no objections by government to this arrangement despite its anticompetitive features. Both government and ACFID appear to be satisfied with

---

[74] Mark Sidel, "The Promise and Limits of Collective Action for Nonprofit Self-Regulation: Evidence from Asia," *Nonprofit and Voluntary Sector Quarterly* 39(6) (2010): 1039–1056, 1040.

[75] National Center on Philanthropy and the Law, *Study on Models of Self-Regulation in the Nonprofit Sector* (New York: NCPL, 2005), accessed January 5, 2016, www1.law.nyu.edu/ncpl/resources/rp_report.html.

[76] *Hickman v. Kent or Romney Marsh Sheep Breeders Association* [1915] 1 Ch 881; *Bailey v. NSW Medical Defence Union Ltd* (1995) 184 CLR 339; *NSW Medical Defence Union Ltd v. Crawford* (1995) 13 ACLR 1695.

the arrangements, despite tensions arising from issues about funding administration of the code. It has also allowed the self-regulatory measures to develop
and mature over time. The ACNC's acceptance that adherence to the code
meets its minimum governance standards is also recognition of its status by
another regulator, and reduces the regulatory overlap. The other main regulator, the ATO, has little if anything to do with the code.

The code began out of a concern by ACFID members regarding a particular matter, but once a public scandal required government response, there was
a framework that could be resorted to. The code was developed at a period
when other nonprofit reform proposals were competing for attention, and a
change of government meant altered priorities, but through good lobbying by
ACFID, it managed to weather the changes, survive, and grow. It is ironic that
this "temporary" fix has proved more permanent than reforms to charity sector
regulation that took nearly two decades to arrive and are now being
dismantled.

Some clues to this resilience may lie in the code being developed carefully
to provide a means for members to demonstrate accountability to their donors
as well as to the public, while also serving government's interests. The Code
Committee is seen as independent, with volunteer consumer representatives
as well as accounting and legal experts. The committee has not shirked the
difficult task of dealing with organizations that have fallen short of the code's
requirements and making this public. The ability of the code's members to
manage the enormous inflow of donations in response to the Asian tsunami
and use the code effectively to maintain accountability and transparency is
testament to its worth, not only to ACFID members and the government but
to the Australian community.

9.6 CONCLUSION

Australia has, until recently, stood apart from other OECD states in relation to
the regulation of its nonprofit sector, particularly its charities and community
service organizations. The absence of a national regulator with a public
database of organizations' annual financial statements, governance details,
and assurance of public benefit for taxation concession qualifications was
almost unique. The journey to the creation of an independent, dedicated
national regulator of charities was a drawn-out affair that took almost two
decades of stakeholder debate. In all this debate there was little regard given to
the option of self-regulation. The stated reasons for establishing a national
regulator were to ensure public trust and confidence in charities in order to
maintain and bolster private philanthropy, and also to reduce the burden of

government administrative red tape. However, as discussed, neither of these reasons is particularly compelling, and the real motivating force was the NPM agenda's need for a central regulatory infrastructure.

The growing preoccupation with outsourcing and the need for information to support consumer choice in quasi-markets required a central repository of corporate information. Without that public source of information, government agencies have sought to regulate the conduct of nonprofit organizations using private contracts, to provide some assurance of their capacity to deliver services and their adherence to the terms and quality standards of the service provision. This has involved much administrative red tape that could be reduced significantly by a central repository of information.

Both sides of the political spectrum have supported the NPM agenda, but only one side has thought it necessary to provide institutional mechanisms for state regulatory infrastructure, in the form of a national regulator providing a central repository of financial and governance data, which can be benchmarked and demonstrate public benefit in relation to fiscal concessions. Creating such a national regulator is difficult in Australia because of the constitutional division of responsibilities for nonprofit organizations, and state jurisdictions are reluctant to cooperate with federal bodies or concede their constitutional powers.

Classic self-regulation in Australia has been in relation to raising funds from the public. The association for professional fundraisers has a code of conduct that grew organically and is active in guiding its members and providing best practice guides. Public scandals in two states have resulted in codes of conduct being developed via quite different routes: one began as a convenient temporary political solution that has persisted, and the other is a hybrid code with the force of legislation. Both appear equally effective, being a product of the unique political circumstances of the time and a regulatory tool requiring minimal operational financing. The ACFID code is an example of a sophisticated self-regulatory system that has kept developing in order to be relevant to its stakeholders. While it began as a temporary political response in reaction to a public scandal, through strong lobbying it has weathered an early change of government, managed to integrate itself into government funding gateways, secured a government subsidy for its administrative costs, and built a solid brand reputation with its stakeholders. Its success is due partly to the tight community of interest and lack of competing codes. Its members' appreciation of its worth in preventing rogue operators has also contributed to success, minimizing the risks of public scandal and managing those risks if they arise. It is also useful to government, with an element of co-regulation.

At the federal level, legislative reform or preserving the status quo appears to depend on party ideology. There has been no recent national public scandal that has demanded the federal government of either persuasion to address such issues, and state scandals are quickly dismissed as being state issues. To serve as a federal trigger, a public scandal would have to cross state boundaries and be squarely within federal constitutional powers, such as fundraising involving misuse of Internet technologies.

It is too early to predict the future course of events for the ACNC and self-regulation of the charity sector. The current government has always indicated it would pass legislation to abolish the ACNC and its infrastructure, which will likely mean a return to little or no direct regulation by the ATO for tax concession fidelity and some type of Internet-based self-reporting by charitable organizations. The source of this commitment to a mild form of co-regulation appears to be idiosyncratically ideological. The government has also promised to reduce the burden of red tape accompanying contract administration in community service outsourcing, but without a central data repository to inform the market. Any future change of government may begin a fascinating policy debate about establishing an "ACNC mark 2." However, once the egg has been scrambled, future governments may choose to let the situation rest, unless there are more compelling reform drivers. The next developments will be interesting indeed.

10

The Relationships between State and Nonstate Interventions in Charitable Solicitation Law in the United States

PUTNAM BARBER AND MEGAN M. FARWELL

10.1 INTRODUCTION: STATE AND NONSTATE INTERVENTIONS IN CHARITABLE SOLICITATION LAW IN THE UNITED STATES

Since the first decades of the twentieth century, American state governments have been regulating solicitation of funds for charitable purposes, while nongovernmental organizations have also sought to bring order to the process. This chapter traces the evolution from command and control through regulation to consumer protection, involving both state regulation and self-regulation. It describes how some states extended their registration and reporting requirements – first to direct limits on fundraising fees, then to requiring point-of-solicitation disclosure, and most recently to online posting of information derived from the reports received by the regulators. We also discuss the development of strategies by nonstate actors (often called watchdogs) to prevent abusive fundraising and other misdeeds through their own investigations and by use of official data. The past century of developments in the United States coincides with the transformation of fundraising from activities largely controlled by local elites and local governments to an enterprise relying fully on new forms of communication and sophisticated data processing.

By 1963, when the patterns that are the focus of this chapter began to appear, nineteen American states had enacted statutes providing for some form of governmental oversight of fundraising. Today, forty-seven states and

* The authors thank William Suhs Cleveland; Fran Huehls, Philanthropic Studies Librarian at Indiana University–Purdue University Indianapolis; Cindy Lott; Valerie Lynch; James Sheehan; Robert Tigner; the Reference Librarians at the Gallagher Law Library, University of Washington; participants in the panel on "Regulatory Waves" at the International Society for Third Sector Research (ISTR) conference in Muenster, Germany (July 2014); and the volume editors for advice and encouragement during the preparation of this chapter.

the District of Columbia authorize oversight of charitable solicitations in their statutes.[1] In regulatory terms, states commonly require soliciting organizations to provide details about themselves and their financial affairs to a state charities office before and while seeking charitable contributions from residents of the state. The details of the required registration and reporting – what sorts of organizations or transactions are regulated and what information must be included in the registration documents and periodic reports – vary greatly.

The uses state officials make of the information provided by fundseekers have changed over time in important ways. Before World War II, requiring reports of planned and completed fundraising campaigns was an adjunct of the role of states as guardians of the public interest in preventing "excessive" costs or appeals for "unnecessary" causes. In the years immediately after the war, state officials increasingly regulated directly the solicitation behavior of commercial fundraisers and the charitable organizations themselves. Beginning in the 1970s, the emphasis shifted to supplying information to the public about the costs of commercial fundraising and, more generally, the fundraising activities of charitable organizations. The development of quasi-regulatory action by nonstate actors coincides and is consistent with the increased emphasis on supply of information to the public and transparency.

In addition to state regulation, nonstate interventions have also played a role in charitable solicitation regulation in the United States. They come in a number of forms, including advisory action by groups of officials, watchdog ratings and publicity, media treatment of fundraising excesses, online services that transmit donations to organizations meeting the operators' criteria, and other private sector activities.

Over the course of a century, one trend has been clear: government agencies and community-based organizations have progressively lost the power to limit solicitations addressed to donors and to guide charitable contributions. This loss of regulatory power has its roots in legal development and in the development of technology, as this chapter shows. In the twenty-first century, the use of the Internet to collect and distribute information about fundraising practices and charitable organizations' financial affairs has become a dominant characteristic of both governmental and nongovernmental regulatory activities. In fact, provision of information has become more and more widely the standard form for state and nonstate intervention in the activities of fundseeking charitable organizations and commercial fundraisers.

---

[1]   Hereafter in this chapter the District of Columbia is included as a "state."

10.2 THE KEY FEATURES OF STATE REGULATORY
INTERVENTION IN HISTORICAL PERSPECTIVE

Beginning in the second decade of the twentieth century, many US states and municipalities adopted rules to license, control, or narrowly restrict solicitations for charitable purposes. Early examples of this approach to controlling solicitations were often grounded in an attempt to distinguish between strictly local and more widespread solicitations. Often, the policy goal of the earliest regulations, in states such as Kansas and Iowa, was quite transparent: to erect barriers in the path of fundraisers from external jurisdictions.

To cite one example, in 1911 the Board of Control in Kansas was granted unlimited discretion to approve or deny permission for charitable organizations "to solicit in more than one county within the state of Kansas funds" for their operations.[2] Laws like this Kansas Act were typical of the early twentieth-century approach to the problem. They provided for the collection of information to support government officials in overseeing solicitations and limiting fundraising campaigns to those that had affirmative approval, usually those from local institutions. No state charities official today has anything close to that sort of authority to intervene directly in the conduct of charitable appeals, and regulatory efforts by local governments are much less common today.

This tension between local and outside fundraisers, as reflected in the Kansas statute, grew to a fever pitch during World War II. The successes of the March of Dimes, beginning in 1938, and of fundraising for war-related causes led to rapid growth in the number of campaigns seeking public support. The longstanding local traditions that focused on a familiar list of local organizations (often known collectively as Community Chests and Councils – predecessors of the United Way network), now had to co-exist with increasingly visible national campaigns, particularly those that appealed for support for war-related causes or for addressing life-threatening illnesses such as cancer and heart disease.[3]

A central argument in this contest between locally managed fundraising and the national campaigns was the claim made by local groups, and reflected in state legislation, that national fundraising efforts often incurred unacceptably high costs. In the years immediately after World War II, the statutory grounds for identifying disallowed solicitations shifted from the location of the

---

[2] Kansas Senate Bill No. 295 1911, s. 1.
[3] Scott M. Cutlip, *Fund Raising in the United States: Its Role in American Philanthropy* (New Brunswick, NJ: Rutgers University Press, 1965); United Way of America, *People and Events: A History of the United Way* (Alexandria, VA: United Way of America, 1977).

benefiting organization to more directly limiting fundraising costs. Virginia in 1948,[4] and then Connecticut[5] and Pennsylvania[6] in 1963, specified either a maximum allowable fee that could be paid to a commercial fundraising firm or a minimum proportion that must be delivered to the charitable organization from any fundraising on its behalf. These limits usually provided a distinct advantage for local over national causes, since the former relied almost entirely on volunteer-based efforts while national fundraising usually required paid staff.

This regulatory and political concern with the cost of fundraising was frequently discussed during the postwar years as a form of charity fraud, itself a broader concern in the postwar era. The Council of State Governments (CSG) reported in 1954 that a "number of states, increasingly concerned by 'charity rackets,' have enacted legislation directed against fraudulent practices and improper operations by certain charitable organizations, promoters and solicitors." Its published legislative recommendations for that year urged that states adopt legislation: (1) preventing unauthorized use of celebrities' names in solicitations, (2) requiring informational filings from charitable organizations, and (3) requiring registration by professional fundraisers and solicitors.[7] In the years that followed, a number of states followed and then expanded these recommendations to include reporting on the results of fundraising activities.

In addition to fundraising costs and charity fraud, concern about diversion of support intended for charitable purposes into various abuses – exorbitant compensation, excessive payments to fundraisers and other contractors, or extravagant expenditures on facilities, travel, and other "overhead" – is a long-running issue for nonprofit and fundraising regulators. A direct approach, such as Virginia's, Connecticut's, and Pennsylvania's limits on the proportion of solicitors' receipts that the solicitors could retain as fees or for expenses – generally ranging from 10 to 50 percent – flourished in the 1970s and 1980s. In a slightly different approach focusing on the same issue, states such as Illinois[8] and Georgia[9] required a minimum percentage that must be spent on the charitable purpose, in effect limiting solicitor fees to the remaining amount. Arkansas[10] and Oklahoma[11] did both, setting an upper limit on fees and a minimum on the amounts to be spent by the charitable organization.

---

[4] Acts of 1948, chapter 403.   [5] Public Act Number 551, 1963.
[6] Solicitation of Charitable Funds Act 1963, chapter 337.
[7] Council of State Governments, *Suggested State Legislation Program for 1955, as Approved by the Drafting Committee of the Council of State Governments* (Chicago, IL: Council of State Governments, 1954).
[8] Illinois House Bill 690 1963, §9(c).   [9] Georgia House Bill 397 1980.
[10] Arkansas Act 400 1979.   [11] Oklahoma Statute 18–552 1980, chapter 364.

These strategies were immediately challenged and rapidly prohibited by decisions of various courts – so rapidly, in fact, that it is impossible to determine whether they would have had positive effects on the behavior of fundseekers. In 1980, the US Supreme Court decided the first of three critical cases concerning the regulation of fundraising: *Village of Schaumburg, Petitioner, v. Citizens for a Better Environment et al.*[12] The Court held that Schaumburg's cost-of-fundraising limitations were unconstitutional because they limited the nonprofit organization's ability to raise the funds necessary to exercise its First Amendment right to advance its mission and programs. The Supreme Court reinforced this ruling in its 1984 decision in *Secretary of State of Maryland v. J. H. Munson Co.*,[13] holding that permitting regulators to allow higher costs of fundraising (based on special circumstances) did not sufficiently mitigate the harm to a charitable organization's First Amendment rights.

Another state regulatory approach that was tried beginning in the early 1970s – requiring disclosure of the cost of the solicitation itself at the moment the request was made – was called "point-of-solicitation" disclosure in legal and policy discussions at the time. As the number of states regulating solicitations grew and the Supreme Court set limits on what their regulations could require, the National Association of Attorneys General (NAAG) appointed a drafting committee to develop a "model act" on charitable solicitations with the goals of strengthening the regulation of solicitations and standardizing the regulatory environment for multistate fundraising. The NAAG committee adopted (at §6(e)) the requirement for point-of-solicitation disclosures in its *Model Act Concerning the Solicitation of Funds for Charitable Purposes.*[14]

Meanwhile, states continued to experiment with enacting various regulatory approaches to requiring disclosure of costs of fundraising (or other ratios) at the point of solicitation. For state officials, the attraction of point-of-solicitation disclosure of fundraising costs in this context was not just that it would make fundraising difficult, if not impossible, for high-cost firms, in some regulators' view a worthy goal in itself. Such a disclosure would also substitute the judgment of a prospective donor for administrative review of organizations' financial activities, thus reducing administrative burdens in regulators' offices. As the number of professionally managed (commercial)

---

[12] *Village of Schaumburg, Petitioner, v. Citizens for a Better Environment et al.* 444 U.S. 620 (1980).
[13] *Secretary of State of Maryland v. J. H. Munson Co.* 467 U.S. 947 (1984).
[14] National Association of Attorneys General, *A Model Act Concerning the Solicitation of Funds for Charitable Purposes* (1986), accessed June 6, 2014, www.nasconet.org/wp-content/uploads/2011/05/Model-Law-for-charitable-solicitations.pdf.

fundraising campaigns grew, the challenge for the regulator of reviewing the details of each registration statement or report grew as well. If donors who learned the facts would reject costly campaigns, there would be less need for the state to exercise such oversight and control.

In its third major fundraising opinion, *Riley v. The National Federation of the Blind*,[15] issued by the Supreme Court in 1988, the Court declared point-of-solicitation disclosure (as embodied in North Carolina statutes[16]) unconstitutional because the disclosure requirement violated the charitable organization's freedom of speech: "A speaker's rights are not lost merely because compensation is received," said the Court, reaffirming the *Schaumburg* and *Munson* decisions.[17] Such disclosure requirements, by then a part of fifteen states' laws, have since been repealed in all but two states; in the states in which they remain formally in effect (Connecticut and Oregon), neither mentions the rules in their online instructions for charitable solicitors.[18]

The expectation of greater accountability and transparency from nonprofit organizations, in particular those soliciting contributions from the public, has become more widespread over time. The trend in regulation has been toward more, and more detailed, disclosure of the activities and finances of both charitable organizations and commercial fundraisers. On the legislative front, many of the acts adopted since the beginning of the 1980s have clarified definitions in order to foreclose claims of exemption by commercial fundraisers or have specified more fully the financial reporting that registered organizations and firms must supply.

10.3 THE KEY FEATURES OF NONSTATE INTERVENTION: HISTORY AND CURRENT PRACTICE

While concerns about fundraising – especially by "out-of-town strangers" soliciting for unfamiliar organizations – can be traced back well into the nineteenth century, the dramatic increase in solicitations during World War I gave new urgency to the issue. World War I fundraising sparked additional

---

[15] *Riley v. The National Federation of the Blind* 487 U.S. 781(1988).

[16] North Carolina Session Laws 1985, chapter 497.

[17] *Riley*, n. 15. These decisions are discussed in detail in Ellen Harris et al., "Fundraising into the 1990s: State Regulation of Charitable Solicitation after *Riley*," *University of San Francisco Law Review*, 24(4) (1989): 571–652.

[18] Connecticut General Assembly, "Chapter 419d: Solicitation of Charitable Funds Act," accessed December 28, 2015, www.ct.gov/dcp/cwp/view.asp?a=1654&q=441268; Oregon Legislature, "Chapter 128 – Trusts; Charitable Activities," accessed December 28, 2015, www.oregonlegislature.gov/bills_laws/lawsstatutes/2013ors128.html.

nonstate intervention as well as the state regulatory interventions discussed above. There were new calls from nonstate actors for limitations on the number of appeals based in both pity and patriotism. There were also calls for better information about the actual work being done, of necessity, under difficult conditions in faraway places. Overlapping campaigns to provide support for soldiers, sailors, and their families were of most direct concern to the War Department, but the proliferation of appeals of all sorts troubled nonstate actors as well, including community leaders and larger, well-established organizations such as the Red Cross, the Young Men's Christian Association (YMCA), and the Knights of Columbus. An initial nonstate solution was explored when the Council of National Defense invested the newly formed National Investigation Bureau of War Charities with the authority to review and comment on any and all appeals for public support for war-related charitable works.[19]

In 1919 the National Investigation Bureau of War Charities was renamed the National Information Bureau (NIB), which remained an active organization, under a progression of names, until the 2000s, when it merged with the Philanthropic Advisory Service of the Council of Better Business Bureaus to become a division of the BBB known as the Wise Giving Alliance. The NIB investigated the validity of charitable appeals, published standards for financial administration and governance of charitable organizations, and participated throughout its history in studies, task forces, and blue-ribbon panels concerned with solicitations. Its work was based on the view that "control by state law or municipal ordinance is difficult" and "judicious publicity" directed at unsavory practices could go a long way toward protecting donors.[20]

Another nonstate innovation can also be traced to the era of World War I: the concept of nonstate charitable "federations" as a means of limiting and coordinating fundraising campaigns. Community leaders in Cleveland, Ohio, refined this idea into the first enduring example in the first decades of the twentieth century. It was strongly supported by both the Chamber of Commerce and Cleveland's Mayor Newton Baker, later President Wilson's Secretary of War. As Secretary, Baker pressured the major national organizations with war-related missions and appeals to work together to seek public support rather than running separate (often perceived as competing) campaigns.[21] This effort was only partially successful; the rivalries and jealousies continued

[19] Cutlip, n. 3, 141–142, 229–232.
[20] Ann L. New, *Service for Givers: The Story of the National Information Bureau, Inc.* (New York: National Information Bureau, 1983).
[21] Cutlip, n. 3, 68–73, 141–142.

behind a façade of cooperation. Nonetheless, the idea of federation was firmly established as a promising solution to the problem of unfettered, overlapping, competing, and (in many observers' opinion) wasteful campaigns. To federate or not became one of the enduring controversies and sources of friction for fundraising organizations and communities throughout the interwar years.

Commercial fundraising as a distinctive activity began as the staff leaders of both independent and federated campaigns during World War I moved on to develop private consulting and solicitations management firms in the postwar years. Despite, or perhaps because of, the successes of these firms, they were often portrayed as illegitimately profiting by diverting funds intended to serve charitable ends – "mulcted" was the pejorative verb used by a New York legislative committee in support of its successful 1954 proposal to require registration and reporting of all solicitors operating in the state.[22] In that same year, the Association of Direct Fund-raising Counsel, which included the major commercial fundraising firms as members, opened its first headquarters in New York City with a full-time executive director drawn from the industry and charged with its advancement.[23]

Attempts to implement federated fundraising continued after World War II, enthusiastically promoted by some and just as enthusiastically denounced by others. Support for the idea frequently came from local business and community leaders who found themselves on the receiving end of increasing numbers of solicitations. In 1959, *Syracuse Herald-Journal* editor Alexander F. (Casey) Jones charged: "We're being duped. The health foundation racket has expanded to the point where there are 50 such organizations for ills of every part of the body... Here in Syracuse, our announced policy is that this community does not owe any health foundation one thin dime ..."[24]

Opposition was centered on charitable organizations that solicited funds for prevention and relief of disease, international antipoverty efforts, and other causes that did not rely on local institutions to meet their goals. The leaders of those organizations, with various degrees of indignation, resisted the idea that their work should be weighed in the same terms as that of community service organizations with a visible local presence. In particular, they opposed the idea that there should be one annual nationwide "health" appeal that raised funds to be allocated among all the disease-related organizations.[25] As Basil

---

[22] Council of State Governments, n. 8, 14.   [23] Cutlip, n. 3, 343.

[24] "The Fund-Raising Muddle," *Newsweek*, June 15, 1959, 31–33.

[25] Cutlip, n. 3; United Way of America, n. 3; Eleanor L. Brilliant, *The United Way: Dilemmas of Organized Charity* (New York: Columbia University Press, 1990); Putnam Barber, "Regulation of U.S. Charitable Solicitations since 1954," *Voluntas*, 23(3) (2012): 737–762.

O'Connor, president of the March of Dimes, wrote in a 1947 paper called "Do We Want a Health Trust?":

> These well-meaning individuals are suggesting that we uniform our vast army of health supporters in the grey clothes of centralization, that we merge all our health agencies supported by public contributions into one super-colossal, all-inclusive, totalitarian-type health trust which would conduct one fund-raising campaign, once a year, and divide up the "take" among all the good causes ...[26]

A great deal of nonstate activity related to fundraising (or, more generally, the financing of large-scale charitable organizations) took place in the decade of the 1960s. Concerned that the "strife which centered on 'federated' versus 'independent' fund-raising campaigns was fast becoming intolerable," the Rockefeller Foundation financed a study of the work of national health and welfare organizations that came to two broad conclusions: there should be a permanent facility for improving coordination and cooperation among such organizations, and "the development of standardized accounting for voluntary agencies" should be encouraged.[27]

Neither recommendation was fully implemented, but nonstate self-regulatory activity would continue to take steps forward. In the early 1960s the National Health Council (NHC, an association of national nonprofit organizations active in health-related activities) and the National Social Welfare Assembly, again with support from the Rockefeller Foundation, developed and published *Standards of Accounting and Financial Reporting for Voluntary Health and Social Welfare Organizations*, known to professionals by the color of its covers as "the Black Book."[28]

NHC also initiated a campaign to be carried out by local chapters and affiliates across the country aimed at preventing adoption of licensing laws that, as we have seen, often preferenced local over national fundraising efforts.

---

[26] Basil O'Conner, "Do We Want a Health Trust?" (1947), annotated draft of speech in authors' files, 3.

[27] Robert H. Hamlin, *Voluntary Health and Welfare Organizations in the United States: An Exploratory Study by an Ad Hoc Citizens Committee* (New York: The Schoolmasters' Press, 1961), ii, 35.

[28] National Health Council, Inc., and National Social Welfare Assembly, Inc., *Standards of Accounting and Financial Reporting for Voluntary Health and Social Welfare Organizations* (New York: National Health Council, 1964). The American Institute of Certified Public Accountants required a different treatment of fundraising costs in its guidance for the preparations of nonprofit financial statements, a divide many – including Bruce Hopkins, author of *Charity under Siege: Government Regulation of Fund-Raising* (New York: John Wiley & Sons, 1980) – saw as deeply unfortunate.

In 1965, NHC published the first of several editions of its *Viewpoints* to present "guidelines, standards or principles that should be incorporated in state or local regulatory legislation."[29] The NHC Committee on Regulatory Legislation worked through the 1960s and 1970s to develop draft language that would help states adopt consistent statutes embodying its "criteria for regulatory law." In the issues of *Viewpoints* (1965, 1971, and 1976), the NHC offered "Examples of Provisions of State Legislation" drawn from the work of earlier ad hoc committees and existing statutes so that voluntary agencies would be prepared to "make constructive criticism for sound legislation" as states considered new laws.[30]

During these decades, the practices of fundseeking organizations also changed. The rapid development of techniques for direct mail and telemarketing approaches to donors following World War II allowed national charities to bypass local campaigning and instead directly address wide populations of prospective donors. During the 1970s, the annual fundraising campaign addressed to all federal employees was opened to a broad range of qualifying organizations, after a series of court challenges to its focus on supporting members of local United Ways.[31] Toward the end of the century, United Ways across the country gradually shifted from raising funds (primarily through workplace giving) to support a limited number of "member agencies" toward an approach known as "donor choice," which permitted a wider range of contributors to designate virtually any recognized charity to be the recipient of their gifts.

Other nonstate innovations have played very important roles in reshaping the fundraising landscape. The Wise Giving Alliance of the Council of Better Business Bureaus, building on the work begun decades earlier by the NIB, distributes ratings of national fundseeking charitable organizations on a published list of standards that include governance practices and financial performance.[32] Since the 1990s, Guidestar has published online copies of charitable organizations' reports to the Internal Revenue Service (IRS) – the

[29] National Health Council, *Viewpoints on State and Local Legislation Regulating Solicitation of Funds from the Public* (New York: National Health Council, 1965), ix.

[30] National Health Council, *Viewpoints: State Legislation Regulating Solicitation of Funds from the Public* (New York: National Health Council, 1976), xi. This proposal and statutes on the topic already adopted by several states are discussed in a contribution to the Filer Commission's extensive research reports. They can be found in Gabriel G. Rudney, ed., *Research Papers Sponsored by the Commission on Private Philanthropy and Public Needs* (Washington, DC: US Treasury, 1974), vol. 5, 2705–2780.

[31] Brilliant, n. 25, 118–129.

[32] Better Business Bureau Wise Giving Alliance, *Wise Giving Guide* (2013), accessed July 5, 2014, www.bbb.org/us/Storage/113/Documents/wise-giving-guide-2013.pdf.

Form 990 – under an agreement with the IRS. Charity Navigator uses the financial data in Form 990 to create online ratings for larger charitable nonprofit organizations.

During the 1980s, as outlined above, several states adopted legislation requiring point-of-solicitation disclosure of the cost of fundraising or commercial solicitors' fees. This requirement was included, for example, in the NAAG Model Act discussed above, published in 1986.[33] These new standards sparked resistance from fundraisers and from their professional associations.

While generally endorsing most of the Model Act's terms, and particularly the idea of standardizing state-level regulation of solicitations, the private sector advisory group on the Model Act, in a "consensus view," resisted point-of-solicitation disclosure on the grounds that the costs of fundraising should be discussed with a prospective donor only when the donor raised the question.[34] In addition, Harvard law professor Adam Yarmolinsky prepared a seven-page memorandum to the NAAG Model Act Committee arguing that point-of-solicitation disclosure of fundraising fees would, in any case, likely be found unconstitutional.[35] As he predicted, the US Supreme Court ruled in the 1988 *Riley* decision that a statutory requirement of point-of-solicitation disclosure is indeed unconstitutional,[36] establishing one critical boundary for state solicitations regulation that would strongly influence the approaches of state charities officials in the following decades.

10.4 FUNDRAISING REGULATION SINCE THE 1980S: A FOCUS ON PROVISION OF INFORMATION

The Supreme Court's *Riley* decision rejected required point-of-solicitation disclosure of fundraisers' fees, but also included some advice to state charities regulators: "… of course, a donor is free to inquire how much of the contribution will be turned over to the charity … if the solicitor refuses to give the requested information, the potential donor may (and probably would) refuse to donate …"[37] Even before *Riley*, four states had enacted laws

---

[33] National Association of Attorneys General, *A Model Act Concerning the Solicitation of Funds for Charitable Purposes*, 1986, accessed January 7, 2016, www.muridae.com/nporegulation/documents/model_solicitations_act.html.

[34] Private Sector Advisory Group, "A Model Act Concerning the Solicitation of Funds for Charitable Purposes" [with the comments and resolution of the Private Sector Advisory Group], *Philanthropy Monthly*, 9(8) (1986): 10.

[35] Adam Yarmolinsky, "Talking Paper on Constitutional Aspects of Regulation of Charitable Solution," *Philanthropy Monthly*, 9(8) (1986): 11–12.

[36] *Riley*, n. 15.   [37] Ibid.

requiring solicitors to respond accurately if a prospective donor asked about the percentage that would be retained by the fundraiser or expended on the charitable purpose. In the years following *Riley,* nine more states added such a requirement.

With both statutory limits on fundraising costs and mandatory point-of-solicitation disclosure of fundraisers' fees declared unconstitutional in the 1980s, state regulators have since given increased attention to encouraging donors to look more closely at the financial performance of both parties involved in fundraising – charitable organizations themselves and commercial firms that assist with soliciting support from the public.[38]

A number of states have adopted broader rules that require charitable organizations, commercial fundraisers, or the office responsible for oversight to be prepared to respond to donor requests for information about the finances of most organizations that solicit contributions. At present, fundraising solicitors in eighteen states are required to provide information on how to obtain such information. Some, such as Georgia[39] and Wisconsin,[40] place the responsibility for providing such information on the commercial fundraising firm. Some, such as Maryland[41] and New York,[42] require the solicitor to provide contact information for the client who will receive the donated funds. The majority, including Washington[43] and Kansas,[44] direct the solicitor to provide information on how to receive financial reports from the state regulatory office.

Along with extension and refinement of the specific requirements for disclosures, registration, and periodic reporting by charitable organizations and commercial fundraisers, states increasingly rely on the Internet to offer information to the public about fundraising activities. As in all aspects of charitable solicitations regulation, there is considerable variation among the

---

[38] This approach was presaged by Harvard law professor Adam Yarmolinsky and Massachusetts lawyer Marion Fremont-Smith's report, *Judicial Remedies and Related Topics,* prepared for the Filer Commission on American philanthropy in 1975 recommending an informational approach to fundraising regulation. The report can be found in Rudney, n. 30, vol. 5, 2697–2704.

[39] Georgia Charitable Solicitations Act of 1988, §43-17-8(3)(B).

[40] 1991 Wisconsin Act 278, §440.455(b).   [41] Laws of Maryland 1987, chapter 117, §103E(D).

[42] Laws of New York, 1977, chapter 669, §174(b). (The information is to be available from the charitable organization or the Secretary of State; the mailing addresses of both must be supplied.)

[43] Washington Laws, 1986, chapter 230, §11(d). (The Secretary of State's toll-free number must be provided.)

[44] Kansas Laws 1988, chapter 96, §8(d).

states in the online presentation of information.[45] In most cases, though, the accompanying explanations suggest that prospective donors may use this information to determine whether or not an organization meets their personal standards for support. Some states also encourage referring to nonstate groups such as the Wise Giving Alliance, Charity Navigator, or other sources of information about soliciting organizations. These charity evaluators, though, use data from the federal Form 990 to inform their ratings and do not draw on information from the state regulators.[46]

10.5 CHARITABLE SOLICITATION REGULATION AND NONSTATE INTERVENTIONS IN THE DIGITAL AGE

In *Riley*, the US Supreme Court observed that "as a general rule, the State may itself publish the detailed financial disclosure forms it requires professional fundraisers to file. This procedure would communicate the desired information to the public without burdening a speaker with unwanted speech during the course of a solicitation ..."[47] Building on the Court's suggestion and taking advantage of technology not available in 1988, state regulation has changed: state regulators have increasingly provided and used web-based data, significantly superseding statutory requirements to provide specific information. As of 2015, at least thirty-six states offer some information of these sorts through the Internet.[48] Figure 1 highlights the states with such requirements.

In the first decade of the twenty-first century, congressional concerns with reported abuses of tax-exempt status[49] led to a major commitment by nonprofit organizations and foundations, spearheaded by the Independent Sector (itself

[45] Putnam Barber, "The Official Word: What State Charities Webpages Tell the Public" (paper presented at the Charities Law Conference 2013: The Future of State Regulation of Nonprofits, New York, February 7–8, 2013).

[46] A short-lived experiment that drew on state-level information to create profiles of fundseeking organizations, called "Charity Checker," was developed by the *Tampa Bay Times* and the Center for Investigative Reporting after their work on "America's Worst Charities." In 2015, the Charity Checker website was shut down. Visitors are instead referred to the *Tampa Bay Times* and Center for Investigative Reporting websites.

[47] *Riley*, n. 15.

[48] The details of the reports found among the state charities officials' websites vary widely. Some call attention to summary statistics on program services; others focus on costs of fundraising or provide a more extensive range of financial information. In some cases, images are available of the documents filed with the state, and some link to an online copy of the organization's Form 990.

[49] Senate Finance Committee, *Staff Discussion Draft*, accessed December 28, 2015, www.finance.senate.gov/imo/media/doc/062204stfdis.pdf.

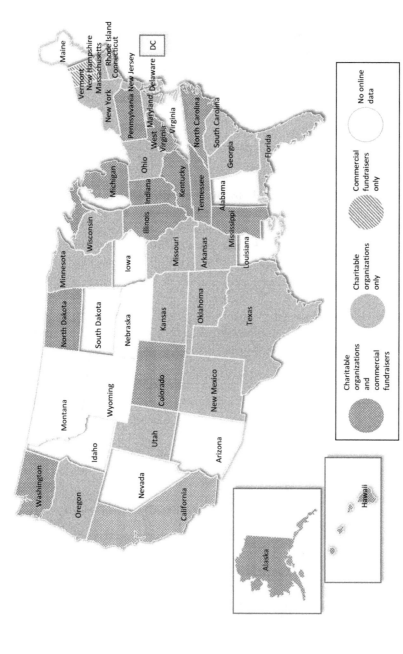

FIGURE 1: States with online access to data related to fundraising organizations. Kentucky: Information is in files (not a searchable database). New York: information on commercial fundraisers is for telemarketers only. Texas: Information is available only for law-enforcement organizations (not necessarily charitable). Vermont: Information on commercial fundraisers is for telemarketers only.

a nonprofit with many nonprofits in its membership), to publish a list of strong principles of governance with accompanying explanatory discussion and rec-ommendations. These recommendations included suggestions for congres-sional action and refinement of IRS financial reporting standards that, in many ways, parallel the recommendations of the earlier Rockefeller-supported Hamlin study of 1961 discussed above.[50] Many of the more recent recommen-dations have since been implemented, for example, mandatory termination of exempt status for federally recognized organizations that fail to file required reports for more than three years, filing of an annual "e-postcard" by public charities with less than US$50,000 in annual revenues (which previously could operate indefinitely without any contact with the IRS), and public access to federal tax information (Form 990) directly from the filing organiza-tions instead of by request to the IRS.[51]

The rapid increase in solicitations relying on the Internet to reach potential donors, in addition to the increasingly large proportion of contributions made through the Internet, has certainly attracted regulators' attention. In particular, there has been an increase in cooperation among the regulators with respect to online solicitations.

In 2001, the National Association of State Charities Officials (NASCO), a component of the NAAG, published *The Charleston Principles*, the most recent effort at collective policymaking on fundraising by state charities offi-cials.[52] In the *Principles*, NASCO offers recommendations "as a guide" for overseeing Internet solicitations, and not as proposed regulatory language. Although the members of NASCO are state charities officials from across the United States, NASCO does not have any authority over the actions of its members nor to publish regulations itself. Left unsettled by the recommenda-tions is any resolution of the question of whether a general appeal for funds on a website – obviously visible to anyone with access to the Internet – constitutes solicitation as defined by the charitable solicitations statute of any state where it may be seen.

In recent years, several states have implemented online facilities for use by commercial fundraisers and charitable organizations. As of 2016, a group of state charities officials is pursuing development of a "single portal" with

---

[50] Hamlin, n. 27.

[51] Independent Sector, *Report to Congress and the Nonprofit Sector on Governance, Transparency, and Accountability* (Washington, DC: Panel on the Nonprofit Sector, 2005), accessed April 2, 2015, www.neh.gov/files/divisions/fedstate/panel_final_report.pdf.

[52] National Association of State Charities Officials, *The Charleston Principles: Guidelines on Charitable Solicitations Using the Internet* (2001), accessed June 3, 2014, www.nasconet.org/wp-content/uploads/2011/05/Charleston-Principles-Final.pdf.

the goal of collecting all necessary information on fundraisers through one online facility and then distributing it electronically to all participating states.[53] Streamlining filings in this way should produce immediate efficiencies for both the regulators and the organizations supplying the required information. Costs will almost certainly be lower for regulators and filing organizations alike, and the information available is likely to be both more timely and more accurate. (Electronic filing programs typically flag faulty arithmetic and missing responses before accepting a submission.) Sharing of information (especially for enforcement) among regulators will be more feasible. Some of these advantages are already being realized. Increased attention to the utility of the Internet as a tool in regulation of charitable solicitations will bring further advantages and few, if any, new costs (except perhaps to those for whom remaining obscure is part of a business plan).

Much has changed since the development of *The Charleston Principles* in 2001. The Internet has significantly altered the way information about fundraising activities is available to the public. A concerned donor (or a curious researcher) can rapidly obtain vastly more information than was, in any practical sense, available in the 1980s when the Supreme Court considered the issues raised by point-of-solicitation disclosures. It is difficult to know whether these additional channels for accessing information about soliciting organizations have any effect on the choices made by donors.[54] There is a sense in which they resemble "regulatory disclosure" (such as the requirement in some jurisdictions that restaurants post easily viewed signs reporting the results of recent hygiene inspections). The processes by which donors make decisions about responding to appeals are so different from the question of whether to dine at a certain restaurant, though, that it is difficult to believe that the online publication of financial information about solicitors and their clients can make a significant difference.[55]

---

[53] National Association of State Charities Officials, "Urban Institute Selected to Build Single Portal Website," accessed June 3, 2014, www.nasconet.org/urban-institute-selected-to-build-single-portal-website/.

[54] Renee A. Irvin, "State Regulation of Nonprofit Organizations: Accountability Regardless of Outcome," *Nonprofit and Voluntary Sector Quarterly* 34(2) (2005): 161–178.

[55] The theory of regulatory disclosure is presented in Archon Fung, Mary Graham, and David Weil, *Full Disclosure: The Perils and Promise of Transparency* (Cambridge: Cambridge University Press, 2007). For a strongly argued statement of the limits of this approach, see Omri Ben-Shahar and Carl E. Schneider, "The Failure of Mandated Disclosures," *University of Pennsylvania Law Review* 159 (2011), 647–749. We have also discussed this issue in greater detail elsewhere; see Putnam Barber and Megan M. Farwell, "Charitable Solicitations Regulation and the Principles of Targeted Disclosure," *Nonprofit Policy Forum* (forthcoming).

10.6 THE INTERACTIONS BETWEEN STATE AND NONSTATE
ACTIVITY TO REGULATE CHARITABLE SOLICITATION

This review of the history of both state regulation and nonstate interventions raises important questions about America's efforts to limit abuse of popular generosity, of both the state regulatory and the nonstate variety. What is the relationship between them? How does state regulation affect nonstate intervention, and vice versa?

Although the federal government has no explicit role in the regulation of fundraising, its engagement with the finances of charitable organizations has a deep influence on the approaches of both state regulators and nongovernmental groups. In particular, the IRS Form 990 (the annual information form) has become the de facto source of charitable organizations' financial information. Not only does this form require organizations with more than US$200,000 in annual revenue to detail costs related to fundraising, but many states accept this form as a supplement or replacement to their own specific financial reports. The IRS has long offered a procedure by which anyone could request a copy of a nonprofit's Form 990; the information became even more accessible when, in the 1990s, Guidestar (under an agreement with the IRS) began scanning submitted Form 990s for online posting. In 2001, Charity Navigator began rating the larger charitable nonprofits (using zero to four stars) based on analysis of their finances as reported to the IRS. In short, these nonstate actors, nonprofit watchdogs, rely on IRS data to prepare reports that are available on varying terms to Internet users. Further, as noted above, since 2006 the public has been able to request a copy of this form directly from the filing organization; many post their Form 990 on the organization's own website.

Beyond just IRS data, there have been several occasions over the years when private-sector actors had a strong influence on the regulatory climate for charitable solicitations. The influence of the NIB extended through more than half of the twentieth century. The advisors from the fundraising industry shaped much of the model act created by the NAAG Committee in the 1980s. More recently, though, there have been few opportunities for fundraising professionals or nonprofit leaders to influence the patterns of regulation of fundraising by state governments. In most states, there is no regular forum in which discussion of the details of solicitations regulation takes place and little active attention to the regulations beyond advice about compliance. At the national level, the NASCO hosts a one-day meeting each year to which "the public" is invited (for a registration fee). The agenda at this meeting is highly structured and thus not particularly conducive to exploration of common interests or, for that matter, debates on policy issues.

Of course, a good deal of less formal discussion takes place throughout the year among such groups as the Association of Fundraising Professionals, the Better Business Bureau, the nonprofit section of the Direct Marketing Association, the American Association of Fundraising Counsel (now The Giving Institute), and the Association of Direct Response Fundraising Counsel, along with some active members of the bar primarily based in Washington, DC. Informal and anecdotal reports suggest that representatives of these and other associations discuss issues with state regulators on behalf of their members and other stakeholders, which often leads to clarifications of regulations or of their applicability in particular circumstances. In one notable instance, a coalition of commercial fundraisers operating as Americans for Reasonable Fundraising Regulation sued a local regulator (Pinellas County, Florida) and prevailed in the US District Court with the result that the rules in that county were significantly amended to be less burdensome.[56]

This dispersed and disconnected policy environment has been discussed from time to time as a source of problems for nonprofits in general and an opening for opportunistic solicitations that skirt – or cross – the line into unethical behavior. There have been intermittent proposals since the 1970s for some sort of central regulation of nonprofit activities by the federal government (for example, Joel Fleischman's work on regulatory reform[57]). But that seems unlikely to emerge in the present political environment. What is more likely is continued regulation at the state level, along with further developments in nonstate interventions.

The cooperation of the nonprofit Center for Investigative Reporting,[58] the *Tampa Bay Times*,[59] and the Cable News Network in the publication of "America's 50 Worst Charities" provides an example of the way nonstate actors use the expanding stock of data and the increasingly accessible tools for online research. Such developments may change the dynamic of charities regulation. The emphasis in these reports on identifying the bottom feeders in the field is

---

[56] American Charities for Reasonable Fundraising Regulation, "Combating Excessive Regulation of Nonprofits and Fundraising by Means of Litigation," accessed April 6, 2015, www.charityreg.org/.

[57] Joel Fleischman, "Public Trust in Not-for-Profit Organizations and the Need for Regulatory Reform," in *Philanthropy and the Nonprofit Sector in a Changing America*, ed. Charles T. Clotfelter and Thomas Ehrlich (Bloomington: Indiana University Press, 1999), 172–197.

[58] Center for Investigative Reporting, "Disciplinary Actions," accessed June 9, 2014, http://charitysearch.apps.cironline.org/.

[59] "America's Worst Charities," *Tampa Bay Times*, accessed April 20, 2015, www.tampabay .com/americas-worst-charities/.

promising. If the example stimulates more attention to identifying ways to prevent such abuses, it will be much to the credit of the investigating team.[60]

On the state regulatory side, since the 1960s there has been growth in the number of states operating "standard" solicitations regulation programs and increasing isomorphism among those programs as well. There have been three distinct approaches to the challenge of regulating solicitations (especially those that experience high costs): (1) limits on fees to solicitors (and variants), (2) point-of-solicitation disclosures, and (3) publication of data based on reports of fundraising activities.

The first two were found unconstitutional by the US Supreme Court, with the result that most states quickly removed related provisions from their statutes. Publishing information based on registration data has become a de facto standard across the country, though not every state has completely embraced the possibility of displaying solicitations details on a website in a format that can be used by prospective donors, inquiring scholars, and policy-makers. Today a donor, a regulator, a reporter, or any curious person can collect a great deal of data about almost any active secular charitable organization in the United States with a few minutes' time spent on a device connected to the Internet. The successes to date strongly suggest that the number and sophistication of investigations by nonstate actors relying on web services will grow. By emphasizing provision of information to the public, both the state regulations and the nonstate interventions are mutually reinforcing of each other and benefiting public understanding of the fundraising enterprise. Though there are continuing discussions among the members of NASCO and within the small group of engaged participants who address similar issues outside government, there are no signs of new major efforts (along the lines of the drafting of model acts in the 1970s and 1980s) to address continuing challenges in this arena.

10.7 CONCLUSION

Because of the Supreme Court's interventions in *Schaumburg*, *Munson*, and *Riley*,[61] point-of-solicitation disclosure never received a practical test of its efficacy in reducing unsavory fundraising. Gradually, over the quarter century

---

[60] The research team was spearheaded by Kris Hundley, a member of the *Tampa Bay Times* investigative team, and Kendall Taggart, a data reporter from the Center for Investigative Reporting.
[61] *Schaumburg*, n. 12; *Munson*, n. 13; *Riley*, n. 15.

since *Riley*, the emphasis in regulators' actions has shifted instead to the path suggested by the Court when it wrote in that opinion:

> In contrast to the prophylactic, imprecise, and unduly burdensome rule the State [of North Carolina] has adopted to reduce its alleged donor misperception, more benign and narrowly tailored options are available. For example, as a general rule, the State may itself publish the detailed financial disclosure forms it requires professional fundraisers to file.[62]

As with every aspect of Internet use at the present time, the connections between donors, charitable organizations, fundraising, and charities officials are changing rapidly and in myriad ways. With approximately US$250 billion in individual contributions in 2014 in the United States,[63] there is ample reason to explore the expansion and refinement of consumer protection–type information to support increasingly discerning giving by donors. In this important way, nonstate interventions geared toward greater provision of fundraising information are gradually playing a greater and greater role, and significantly complementing formal state regulation.

Legislatures, regulators, and nongovernmental oversight and ratings agencies have tried to prevent solicitations fraud for more than a century. Charitable solicitations statutes and related governmental agencies of some sort exist today in forty-seven states plus the District of Columbia (only Montana, Wyoming, and Nebraska have none). Yet reports of fundraising abuses are published frequently, and prosecutions resulting in arrests and convictions of violators of these laws, though infrequent, still regularly occur.

It is frustrating that calculated abuse of donors' generosity continues to occur with disturbing frequency. In addition to the *Tampa Bay Times* report mentioned earlier, Seattle area reporter William P. Barrett has an ongoing series of blog posts on his investigations of the would-be beneficiaries of the telemarketing calls he receives. The running series, "America's Stupidest Charities," questions the high valuations assigned to medical supplies shipped overseas (and hence low fundraising-to-program-service ratios) claimed by organizations that repeatedly call him asking for support.[64] The long-running (and scandalous) success of the bogus "U.S. Navy Veterans Association"

---

[62] *Riley*, n. 15.

[63] National Center for Charitable Statistics, "Charitable Giving in America: Some Facts and Figures," accessed December 29, 2015, http://nccs.urban.org/nccs/statistics/Charitable-Giving-in-America-Some-Facts-and-Figures.cfm.

[64] "Repeat Nomination in Seattle for 'America's Stupidest Charities,'" *New to Seattle*, accessed May 2, 2015, http://newtoseattle.wordpress.com/2014/05/27/repeat-nomination-in-seattle-for-americas-stupidest-charities/.

suggests that a determined thief can abuse people's trust not just to separate them from cash but to put their reputations at risk through provision of public endorsements.[65] And on a smaller but still dispiriting scale, it is good to know that after US$9.4 million had been stolen from donors, New York's "Coalition Against Breast Cancer" has been closed down and its operators successfully prosecuted by the Attorney General.[66]

The persistence of this sort of predatory behavior suggests that the tools available to regulators are not well matched to the challenges of preventing abuse of charitable impulses. Observers often cite the disproportion between the scale of fundraising activity in the United States and the resources available to the regulators – even the largest and most active state charities offices employ few professional staff members; funds for investigation and prosecution are, in many cases, unavailable. Observers also note that the number of existing, and presumably soliciting, charitable organizations appears to be significantly larger than the number of currently registered organizations. A recent estimate suggests, for example, that 130,000 charitable organizations are operating in California without joining the 230,000 already in the regulator's database.[67] This difference poses, of course, a complex question for already overburdened regulators. The twelve-member staff of this section of the California Attorney General's office already processes an estimated 1.2 million pages submitted annually by registered fundraisers and charitable organizations.[68]

There does not appear to be any broadly conceived initiative to further develop regulation of charitable solicitations. While working on his 1980 book, *Charity under Siege: Government Regulation of Fund-Raising*, Bruce Hopkins counted thirty-three states with charitable solicitations laws.[69] Since then, fifteen others have adopted such laws. Many include a central feature of the

---

[65] T.J. Sheeran, "Man Convicted in $100 Million Navy Veterans Fraud Case," *CantonRep.com*, November 14, 2013, accessed January 7, 2016, www.cantonrep.com/article/20131114/NEWS/131119717/0/SEARCH; Ken Stern, "The Charity Swindle," *New York Times*, November 25, 2013, accessed April 20, 2015, www.nytimes.com/2013/11/26/opinion/the-charity-swindle.html.

[66] Robert Kahn, "New York Sues 'Sham' Breast Cancer Charity," *Courthouse News Service*, July 1, 2011, accessed June 12, 2014, www.courthousenews.com/2011/07/01/37845.htm; *People of the State of New York* v. *Coalition against Breast Cancer*, Sup. Ct. NY (Suffolk), No. 20432-2011, May 2, 2013; jmt. aff'd, App. Div. NY, No. 2013-080222, Dec. 30, 2015.

[67] California Assembly Committee on Appropriations, "Bill Analysis. AB 2077," accessed June 9, 2014, http://leginfo.legislature.ca.gov/faces/billNavClient.xhtml?bill_id=201320140AB2077.

[68] Kendall Taggart, "Bill Targeting 'Scam Charities' in California Law Moves Forward," *Center for Investigative Reporting*, accessed January 7, 2016, http://cironline.org/blog/post/bill-targeting-%E2%80%98scam-charities%E2%80%99-california-law-moves-forward-6386.

[69] Hopkins, n. 28.

standard model of American fundraising regulation – registration and annual financial reporting by charitable organizations and commercial fundraisers. In other words, while state regulation is now widespread, it does not appear to be spreading in new directions.

Gradual expansion and refinement of various uses of the Internet in the mechanics of the states' programs is inevitable and expands the role of non-state actors. The trend toward using the Internet to interact with commercial fundraisers, charitable organizations, and the interested public offers many opportunities for refinements that could strengthen the protections provided by state charities officials while permitting savings of both expense and time. In particular, the plan to develop the "single portal" is an exciting development. On the other hand, a centralized effort to design and build tools for donors and other observers has never, as far as we know, been discussed seriously by the members of NASCO or others involved in efforts to prevent fundraising abuses.

These then are the challenges of the present day. How can the power of the Internet be used even more actively to strengthen the hand of regulators and nonstate actors and support the goals of donors in the midst of the countless thousands of appeals made on behalf of charity each year in the United States? And how can regulators and nonstate actors work together so as to more effectively protect both donors and American communities from selfish misappropriation of charitable resources? Our hundred years of history on these questions in the United States shows a complex relationship between the role of regulators and the role of nonstate actors, and in a digital era those roles and relationships must continue to evolve and strengthen. The generosity displayed by the millions of donors in America for whom it is a routine part of their lives to support charitable purposes deserves no less.

11

Regulatory Waves

A Conclusion

ALISON DUNN, OONAGH B. BREEN, AND MARK SIDEL

The aim of this book has been to explore whether there is an underlying relationship between statutory and nonstatutory regulation in the context of nonprofit regulatory frameworks. In so doing, we set out to investigate the extent to which the regulatory conversations occurring in sixteen jurisdictions inform the resulting regulatory models and regulatory relationships. By delving into the regulatory narrative and analyzing the factors that inform the interaction between statutory and nonstatutory regimes, this book has sought to glean a better understanding of the catalysts for regulatory change. In this final chapter we draw together the country narratives in order to highlight the common trends emerging in these case studies. We also set out some policy principles that may assist decision makers to choose the best options for effective facilitation and management of the nonprofit sector from among the array of regulatory tools on offer. These policy principles may also inform decision makers working in other fields of regulation on the relationships between regulatory tools.

11.1 THE UNDERLYING RELATIONSHIP BETWEEN STATUTORY REGULATION AND SELF-REGULATION

At the outset this book posited that there is an ongoing causal relationship between statutory and nonstatutory regulation. The country case studies provide a rich seam of evidence of the ways in which statutory regulation interacts with, and has impacted, the development of other regulatory tools – sometimes encouraging the emergence of self-regulation and at other times hindering it. Some of these impacts are part of a planned development by the state in concert with the sector (though this is rare in the case studies). Others arise independently as a reaction by the nonprofit sector to the existence and efficacy of statutory regulation, or lack thereof. Direct or indirect causal links between statutory and self-regulation aside, there is also evidence of self-regulatory initiatives arising as a response to public distrust so as to shore up the nonprofit sector's public profile, or as an instrument of professionalism to build the sector's reputation.

In this section we examine the impacts and relationships between self-regulation and statutory regulation as revealed by the country case studies. In so doing, it is worth emphasizing at the outset that statutory regulation is the dominant regulatory tool in nearly all of the country case studies examined in this book. Where this is the case, the focus of the nonprofit sector's attention has been on lobbying to make the statutory regulation comprehensive and fit for purpose. While it cannot be said that this focus has been entirely at the expense of exploring self-regulation for its own sake, the demand for and utilization of self-regulation as a regulatory tool by nonprofit organizations has been secondary to (and in some cases consequent on) its broader quest for appropriate regulation at state level.

The relationship between statutory regulation and self-regulatory initiatives is thus at the core of this book and the country case studies. In addressing the relationship between statutory regulation and self-regulation, this book is thus somewhat different from other excellent scholarly work on nonprofit self-regulation. Other recent efforts have focused more on the shape and dynamics of self-regulatory initiatives in the field. Sometimes they have treated these initiatives as forms of accountability collectives and collective action.[1] Some-times they have remained largely focused on the regulatory side, but with forays into and an understanding of the importance of voluntary self-regulation.[2]

In these and other cases, the stage has been set for a clear appreciation of the growing power and spread of nonprofit self-regulation and an increasing – and in our view entirely accurate – assessment that the goals of self-regulation are to strengthen accountability, transparency, and quality of activities and service in nonprofit organizations.[3] In particular, we recognize the role of collective action (sometimes called "club-like" activity) through self-regulation in attempting to enhance organizational and sectoral accountability, transparency, and quality. We are taking the next step: agreeing on the importance of collective action self-regulatory frameworks as analyzed in earlier work, while extending the analysis to ask how self-regulatory initiatives

---

[1]   Notably, Mary Kay Gugerty and Aseem Prakash, eds., *Nonprofit Accountability Clubs: Voluntary Regulation of Nonprofit and Governmental Organizations* (New York: Cambridge University Press, 2010).

[2]   Such as in Susan Phillips and Steven Rathgeb Smith, eds., *Governance and Regulation in the Third Sector: International Perspectives* (London: Routledge, 2011), and other work.

[3]   As in Gugerty and Prakash, n. 1.

and statutory regulation impact each other. That is a contextualized task (as it was in earlier works on self-regulation), and so we have explored these themes at country levels, to get a more detailed and nuanced sense of the relationship between regulation and self-regulatory collective action activities.

11.1.1 *The Impact of Statutory Regulation on Self-Regulation*

Direct impact of statutory regulation on self-regulatory initiatives and the rise of self-regulation as a response are apparent in all of the case studies considered in this book. The country narratives reveal that strictness of state regulation can sometimes be a motivating factor toward beginning work on self-regulation and on coordinating mechanisms that seek to strengthen professionalism and quality in the nonprofit sector. This is evident, for example, in both China and Vietnam. At the same time, the very strength of the state and its regulation in these two countries also hinders the emergence of those same self-regulatory frameworks, revealing the constant tension and contradictions that can exist between regulatory tools. This trend is not geographically limited and can also be seen in the Latin American, Asian, and African case studies.

Similarly, the country narratives reveal that the threat of statutory regulation that restrict the legal environment for nonprofits can, in fact, lead to discussion within the nonprofit sector about use of self-regulation as an alternative regulatory tool. This was the case in Ecuador, a country that already had restrictive statutory regulation to curb tax fraud and ensure transparency. Dialogue within the nonprofit sector in this country was also inspired by the Ecuadorian government's abandonment of its consultation for a more comprehensive nonprofit legal framework, leaving a regulatory void into which the nonprofit sector has stepped, at least on occasion, with self-regulatory initiatives. The threat of regulatory change from the state is also evidenced as a factor toward initiating self-regulation in several of the countries set out in the chapter on Africa, particularly Kenya and Uganda, though the strength of the regulatory threat, the state's initial response toward nonprofit initiatives, the participation of external donors, and the difficulties of collective action play very important roles too.

The Mexican state is another that has introduced stricter tax laws and made a show of making nonprofit organizations more accountable, but, unlike China and Vietnam though similar to Ecuador, effective follow-through or implementation of the statutory regulation was not always evident. This was the case with the poorly implemented legislation meant to allay the Mexican public's mistrust of philanthropy. The nonprofit Funds in Plain Sight initiative, for example, began as a response to government ineptitude, with self-regulation emerging to rule out both the corrupt use of nonprofit funds and state manipulation of the sector. The failure to sufficiently implement statutory laws served to create an empty space that the Mexican nonprofit sector could use to its advantage in an attempt to crowd out the state with self-regulation. Given the relative nascence of these schemes, the extent to which the Mexican nonprofit sector has been successful in doing so remains to be seen. Along somewhat analogous lines, though in a different context, the nonprofit sector used self-regulation in Scotland as an attempt to provisionally fill a regulatory void created by inadequate state regulation and years of policy neglect (while at the same time lobbying for a statutory regulatory framework fit for purpose). Similar patterns also emerge in Ireland in the context of the development of its fundraising regulation.

In a country where the waves of regulation are dominated by the state, the failure of statutory regulation to deliver on its promises also played a part in the limited growth of self-regulation in Brazil, primarily through the nonprofit Abong scheme. In other countries the vacuum left by a failure of the state to regulate (or an express decision not to) has had a direct impact on the creation of self-regulation codes of practice. This is evident, for example, in Ireland with the sector's creation of the *Code of Practice for Good Governance* and in England and Wales with the similar *Good Governance: A Code for the Voluntary and Community Sector*.[4] These two examples exist in countries with long histories of statutory regulation that have traditionally been concerned with putting in place the structural mechanisms of a nonprofit legal framework for the protection of funds and the needs of accountability (with varying degrees of success). But, in so doing, they have not addressed day-to-day nonprofit governance to which the self-regulation codes are aimed.

Mexico, Brazil, Ireland, and Britain stand in contrast to experience elsewhere. In Israel the dominance of the statutory regulatory system, coupled with the state's refusal to recognize existing self-regulatory schemes, has served to crowd out any attempt at regulatory activities by the nonprofit sector. Taken as a whole, the African country narratives exhibit similar echoes of the impact that a state's negative response to self-regulation has on the development and success of such initiatives; state repression of nonprofit sector self-regulatory initiatives is a significant problem in the Africa case studies and beyond. A different picture emerges in other countries, however, demonstrating that statutory regulation does not inevitably prompt self-regulation. State law is

---

[4] *Code of Practice for Good Governance of Community, Voluntary and Charitable Organisations in Ireland,* accessed January 6, 2016, www.governancecode.ie/about.php; *Good Governance: A Code for the Voluntary and Community Sector,* 2nd ed. (2010), accessed July 1, 2015, www.governancecode.org/about-the-code/.

dominant in the regulation of solicitations in the United States, for example, but here the strictness of the law has been tempered less by nonprofit initiatives at self-regulation (although they have played a role in developing the legal regime overall) than by use of the more traditional route in common law jurisdictions of challenge to state laws by defending constitutional rights within the court system.

A further way in which state regulation impacts self-regulation is the cooption of self-regulation by the state to serve its own regulatory objectives. There is evidence in some of the country case studies of nonprofit sector self-regulation being utilized to free up state regulators' time and resources to focus on other regulatory issues of priority. In Australia, for example, compliance with the Australian Council for International Development's (ACFID) self-regulatory *Code of Conduct*[5] is a prerequisite for Australian Agency for International Development (AusAID) accreditation for some government funding schemes. Being able to rely on self-regulation as a gateway provision relieves the state body from having to scrutinize organizations. This is important in the Australian state body context since the Australian command and control regulatory tools are not sufficiently resourced.

England and Wales has also coopted the nonprofit sector's self-regulation as a means of allowing the sector regulator, the Charity Commission for England and Wales, to conserve resources and focus on matters of regulatory enforcement rather than, say, advice giving. In China too, government support for nonstate actors coordinating data gathering is in part recognition that these organizations are doing the state's job for it. Although such cooption is not yet widespread, the benefits of utilizing nonprofit self-regulation for state purposes were recognized in a recent government policy paper in Israel and their use recommended.[6] In the US context, cooption would offer benefits to the overburdened fundraising regulators with low human resources and high numbers of filed reports to oversee.

11.1.2 *The Impact of Self-Regulation on Statutory Regulation*

The impact of self-regulatory initiatives on regulation at the state level and the rise of statutory regulation as a response to weak self-regulation are less

---

[5] Australian Council for International Development, *Code of Conduct* (2015), accessed January 5, 2016, www.acfid.asn.au/code-of-conduct/code-of-conduct.

[6] *Framework for Regulatory Impact Analysis – Draft for Comments* (Jerusalem: Prime Minister Office, 2013), accessed January 11, 2016, www.pmo.gov.il/policyplanning/mimshal/Documents/hashpaotregulatzya.pdf, 5.

prevalent in the country case studies, but by no means absent. While there is unsurprisingly little evidence of nascent schemes influencing government or government regulation – such as the self-regulatory scheme in Vietnam, which is only just starting – there are signs of impact elsewhere. In China, for example, where episodic attention to self-regulation goes back to about the year 2000, the state gives some support to nonstate coordinating groups that are not self-regulators but serve both sector and state by data gathering, strengthening professionalism and skills, and enhancing quality (such as the China Foundation Centre). This has been more successful than self-regulation per se in China, largely because of the real value of these activities and because they do not represent a threat to the state. At times there are state institutions and nonprofit coordinating institutions engaged in soft competition on reporting data in China, another partial state response to the rise of these institutions. The important role that data gathering and disclosure plays in conditioning behavior and setting quasi-regulatory expectations is a common theme in other country case studies too, particularly Ireland and Israel, both of which demonstrate how government backing to the nonstate data collector can be crucial to its success.

Two principal examples from the country narratives of self-regulation impacting statutory regulation are the fundraising self-regulatory initiatives in Britain and the use of a self-regulatory code of governance for international development in Australia. Both examples stand out for the way in which the respective nonprofit self-regulatory schemes received state backing – in what may be an indicator of the importance of state support for self-regulation to successfully exist within a broader regulatory framework. In England, Wales, and Scotland the responsibility for fundraising regulation was formally handed over to the nonprofit sectors, giving them responsibility for designing and implementing their own self-regulation scheme. In return, the respective governments provided initial funding and agreed to withhold statutory regulation on fundraising unless the self-regulation schemes proved to be ineffective (a threat that remains a very real one in the face of current fundraising scandals, and which has led to significant changes in the fundraising scheme and its regulatory body in recent times). A set of agreed principles were put in place alongside parliamentary reporting to measure the success or failure of the sector's initial self-regulation scheme.

If the impact on statutory regulation was by design in the countries of Britain, it occurred by default in Australia and as a result of the government failing to deliver statutory regulation. As the Australian case study explains, the ACFID self-regulatory code of practice was initiated as a temporary regulatory (and political) fix until broader legislative reform could be put in place. When the statutory regulation failed to materialize due to changing political administrations and altered political priorities, the self-regulation temporary fix became the permanent regulatory solution. The crucial difference between this example of self-regulation filling a regulatory void and the Mexican and Scottish case examples noted above of self-regulation doing the same is in the express impetus given to the Australian nonprofit scheme by a Minister-appointed advisory committee and the fact that the recommendation and the resulting self-regulatory code were accepted by the existing government and later incoming ones.

A salutary contrast to the Australian ACFID code and the British fundraising self-regulation schemes is the fate of nonstatutory regulation of public collections fundraising in Ireland. Although the Irish government supported extending nonstatutory regulation of fundraising (and using it to replace the need for state intervention if it was effective), successful implementation of the scheme has not yet been achieved. Although the scheme was supported by the Irish government, a lack of funding to promote public awareness and enable the development of detailed codes of conduct, a failure to appoint a monitoring group in a timely manner, and a lack of buy-in from the nonprofit sector have all hindered the scheme's success. The lesson here is that if government backing is a key to the success of nonstatutory regulatory schemes, it needs to be more than just in name, and the government needs to deliver on its funding promises.

The two examples above serve to show deferral of state regulation (by design or otherwise) as a result of self-regulation: the state holding back either because there is another regulatory tool in place or because the state simply does not get its act together. What the country case studies do not reveal is any evidence of state regulation arising as a direct response to a nonprofit self-regulation scheme, such as in the same way that we have seen self-regulation arise in reaction to statutory regulation. This is not to say that state regulation is proactive rather than reactive, but it is perhaps symptomatic of the way in which self-regulation is currently used in many of the countries as a means of filling in the gaps left by state regulation rather than vice versa. Indeed, as the case of Ethiopia exemplifies, at times self-regulation fails or is significantly weakened because the state has stepped up regulatory intervention.

11.1.3 *Contextual Factors*

While these causal points can be identified regarding the impact that self-regulation and state regulation have on each other, the country case studies do not support the view that it is the existence of a particular regulatory instrument alone that causes the development of others. Repressive statutory regulation will not always result in the creation of self-regulation, and self-regulation does not automatically arise when there is a regulatory vacuum that the state is unwilling to fill. Rather, the country narratives suggest that it is the relationship that exists between the nonprofit sector and the state that is more relevant, along with the respective strength or weakness and capacity of both. These relationships are born out of historical and political contexts specific to each country and are characterized by a range of factors, from adversarial and instrumental ones to those that are more supportive. Along with any prevailing political agenda, the country case studies reveal that the state/nonprofit sector relationship has a significant role to play in determining the type of nonprofit regulatory framework as well as the balance between regulatory tools within that framework. Because they are not linear, the contextual nature of these relationships and the impact they may have on resulting regulatory frameworks make them difficult to identify and so to compare. With the caveat that the relationships are rarely fixed, some common themes can be identified.

At one end of the scale stand those countries where the nonprofit sector is viewed by the state with a degree of wariness, hostility, or administrative ambivalence. The relationship between the state and the sector in these circumstances often belies a means of control, particularly of types of activities that nonprofit organizations pursue and their ability to challenge government or raise voices in dissent. This is the spirit and set of policies (at times expressly hostile) we see explored in the Ethiopia, Malawi, Tanzania, and Uganda case studies. In China and Vietnam, where the state retains tight control of legitimizing organizations, over the past several decades, and still today, the focus has been on the development of statutory regulation, that is to say, making sure that regulation effectively controls the nonprofit sector and prevents it (or parts of it) from developing into a political force, while encouraging the nonprofit and charitable activity (mostly focused on social service delivery) that the state knows that it must support and encourage in a new era.

Mexico and Ecuador are two further examples of these types of relationships. They also demonstrate the difficulty state/sector relationships have in moving beyond the past. There is a long, intertwined history between state and nonstate actors in Mexico, first in the guise of the Church, then later in the guise of secular nonprofit organizations. Hostility of the Mexican state toward nonprofit organizations flows from past conflicts with the Church. More recently it stems from jealousy of international support for Mexican nonprofits through international aid (echoes of which are also evident in Kenya and Uganda), which is flowing into such organizations rather than being channeled through the (corrupt) organs of the Mexican government. The Mexican nonprofit sector was traditionally weak and underdeveloped up to the point of the Mexican democratic transition to a market economy and electoral democracy in 2000. This democratic development caused a positive shift in the way that the state interacts with the nonprofit sector. But, notwithstanding an emerging regulatory transition from suppression of the Mexican nonprofit sector to minimize its voice to statutory regulation that seeks to create a better enabling legal environment (even with a repressive tax regime), the state/nonprofit sector relationship has yet to shrug off the mantle of its past. In turn this affects regulation. It has led to a Janus-faced government regulatory agenda: distrustful of the nonprofit sector yet also wanting to support it in the new democratic framework.

The Ecuador case is similar to that of Mexico. While Ecuadorian nonprofit organizations could not be described as politically weak, having assisted in the ousting of three presidents, the sector was both fragmented and unorganized prior to the country's democratic transition. With little access to power and in the absence of a working relationship, the sector was at best ignored and at worst excluded by the state. Post-democratic transition, and as the political mood toward the sector turned more adversarial in the aftermath of the 2007 presidential election, the sector was galvanized into action to work together for joint goals. The development of the nonprofit Collective of Civil Society was a key factor in developing the Ecuadorian nonprofit sector, both in improving perception of the sector's legitimacy and in providing a body with which the state could consult. There are now attempts to bring the nonprofit sector into regulatory consultation. But the continuing ability of the Ecuadorian president to proclaim decrees without sector involvement undermines the emerging process of consultation that had been developing in the discussion of drafts of statutory laws concerning a more comprehensive nonprofit sector legal framework. A similar coordinating process, whereby fragmented nonprofit organizations put aside their differences in order to work together in the face of a hostile regulatory and political environment, is also evident in Uganda.

Other countries might not have the same adversarial, hostile, or indifferent relationship between the state and the sector, but nonetheless remain dominated by the state, which in turn has determined the nonprofit regulatory regime. This is the case in the field of solicitations regulation in the United States, for example. This country narrative revealed extensive and pervasive statutory legislation in individual US states, with zealous regulators sometimes overstepping constitutional boundaries in their attempt to exclude and eliminate tax-exempt fraud and fraud at the expense of donors. In this relationship there is some use of the nonprofit sector in the context of publishing disclosure information, promulgating fundraising standards and standards for financial administration and governance, and making recommendations to improve the regulatory environment (such as the significant Independent Sector–led principles of governance and recommendations for reform[7] or the earlier use of the National Investigation Bureau of War Charities to review and comment on fundraising appeals). But this role for nonprofits is secondary to the dominance of statutory regulation, generally in fifty state jurisdictions. In Israel, too, the dominance of the state and the state regulator and a reluctance to share regulation has left little room for the nonprofit sector to successfully develop self-regulation – a characterization also evident in the regulatory experiences of Ethiopia and Tanzania. A similar picture emerges in Brazil too, where the multiplicity of state regulation has effectively crowded out self-regulation.

At the other end of the scale are those countries where the state and the sector have formed working alliances. These vary in their nature, scope, and purpose. Some are explicitly worked into the regulatory and political framework (such as the *Third Sector Scheme* established between the sector and the government in Wales and which has statutory force[8]), while others remain tacit. Either way, there is a realization on both sides that the sector and the state need to work together in order for their respective agendas to be achieved.

One common example of this relationship occurring in the country narratives is the alliance of the state and nonprofit sector in order to support a regime or build a nation. This was evident in Israel, which has a history of involvement of the nonprofit sector in building the independent state of Israel in its early years (although there has been a crowding-out of the nonprofit sector over time). In Brazil too, there were close linkages between the nonprofit sector and the formation of the Workers' Party, which later acceded to power. The alliance of the state and the sector to nation-build is currently evident in the post-devolution legal and policy environment in Scotland and in the development of Scotland-centric policies with specific forums in which the nonprofit sector can contribute.

In Ireland it was less the building of a regime or a nation and more the inexperience of the Irish state in providing social welfare that led to the need for a state/sector alliance, and an instrumental attempt by the Irish state to

---

[7] Independent Sector, *Report to Congress and the Nonprofit Sector on Governance, Transparency, and Accountability* (Washington, DC: Panel on the Nonprofit Sector, 2005).

[8] Welsh Government, *Third Sector Scheme* (Cardiff: Welsh Government, 2014).

stimulate the growth of social welfare nonprofit organizations to assist it in its task. This alliance, however, faltered in the face of a lack of a clear policy to underpin the Irish state and nonprofit sector relationship. Later attempts to bring the two sides together through the formal mechanism of a joint Implementation and Advisory Group eventually resulted in a deepening of distrust.

The Irish case illustrates that few of these alliances are equal ones. Most are characterized by some form of dependency, particularly financial dependency, of the sector on the state. Brazil is a typical example. The relationship between the Brazilian state and its nonprofit sector can be described as inclusive to the extent that nonprofit organizations are included in debates on policymaking. But it could not be described as an equal alliance since the extent to which the sector is listened to in these debates is limited. While the nonprofit sector is needed to help deliver a government program of state/sector partnerships (a program that has driven the agenda of Brazil's statutory regulation), at the same time Brazilian nonprofit organizations are dependent on the state for funding under this partnership scheme. It is telling that as a body taking part in the discussion on framing a new law for the sector, almost half of the members of the nonprofit Platform for a New Regulatory Framework for Civil Society Organizations were also in partnership with the government to deliver services.

Of course, such alliances and partnership programs also reveal a level of interdependency in the relationships between the nonprofit sector and the state, with the state most obviously reliant on nonstate actors to deliver state services. Even so, the relationship is rarely stacked in the nonprofit sector's favor. As with Australia, Brazil, Ireland, and later Israel, the British experience illustrates how this "new public management" agenda has shaped the relationships between the state and the nonprofit sector, as well as triggered recent regulatory reform agendas in England and Wales and Scotland.

At the heart of the new public management agenda is a drive for efficiencies in service delivery provided for by reliable and credible nonstate actors. For this to be achieved, a robust regulatory framework strong on accountability, governance, and supervision is required. In these new public management relationships, nonprofit organizations may get their desired and often long-lobbied-for statutory reforms and may be offered the opportunity to contribute to policy and service development as a result. But this is at the cost of dependency, competition over funding, and a real or perceived impact on their ability or confidence to raise their voices against the state in dissent or to undertake other acts of advocacy. The dependency in the relationship between the state and the sector allows the state to exert pressure on organizations via regulation, by using the threat of powers to revoke status or remove funding.

There can also be an internal impact of the new public management agenda on the sector. As suggested in both the Israeli and Brazilian case studies, being dependent on government funding may make it more likely that regulation will be primarily directed through statutory mechanisms. This is because organizations that are competing over state resources may not be in the mood to collaborate with one another or may be unable or disinclined to put their funding in jeopardy by antagonizing the state. Even in China, where state regulation trumps self-organization and self-regulation in virtually all respects, respectful alliances can happen as well. One example is the emergence of the China Foundation Center, which gathers data and promotes quality practice in the foundation sector, furthering policies supported by the state and often in more active ways than the state itself can.

The evidence from the country case studies is that the relationships between the nonprofit sector and the state are also rarely static. In Mexico, for example, both the government and the nonprofit sector are in transition, so the relationship between the two is unlikely to be stable. In fact, most of the country case studies examined in this book expose shifts over time (and not always progressive ones) as new political regimes, democracies, or agendas emerge. This is the case in most of the African country case studies, and particularly Ethiopia, where shifting policy toward, and relations with, the nonprofit sector has often undermined the potential for sectoral self-regulation and collective action.

Australia is also a case in point. There is evidence of government working together with the nonprofit sector, as seen in the use of the ACFID self-regulatory code of practice as a prerequisite compliance mechanism for government funding. However, at base Australia reveals a state/nonprofit sector relationship that has been in constant flux. With overlapping, inconsistent, outdated, and inadequately policed statutory regulation at state and federal levels, the time for reform has long been overdue. There have been two long decades of discussion about statutory reform of the nonprofit regulatory regime in Australia that have been significantly affected by the regularity with which the political agenda changes with the stripe of government. Even at the point at which legislation for a comprehensive nonprofit regulatory framework and a sector-specific regulator is in place, its implementation is threatened by another change of political administration with a different regulatory ideology. Although some flexibility and policy change is to be expected, such deep uncertainty as to the legal environment and the changing political agenda cannot help but negatively impact the relationship of trust between the two sectors. It also fails to provide conditions of stability and certainty into which self-regulatory schemes can confidently grow.

11.1.4 *Impacts on Self-Regulation*

The impact that these relationships have had on the development of self-regulation in the respective countries is equally varied and contextual. Of all the country case studies, the relationship between the state and the nonprofit sector in England and Wales could be described as the most supportive, at least in the last twenty years. Here self-regulation has been encouraged by the state, particularly in the fields of governance and fundraising. This, along with a concerted push from the main nonprofit peak/umbrella bodies, led to a boom in self-regulation schemes. By contrast in China and Vietnam, where the state/sector relationships are dominated by the state and regulation is used as a means to control nonprofit organizations, self-regulation emerges in only limited ways and in limited spheres. Any formal role for self-regulation now or in the future – for example, in certifying quality or even in some forms of tax determinations – would take place only with the acquiescence of the respective state and, most likely, state participation in or alliance with self-regulatory initiatives. In both of these countries the state is determinative of the regulatory regime and there is little space for the respective nonprofit sectors independently to develop their own regulatory tools.

State dominance in the state/sector relationship in Israel has had a clear negative impact on the development of its nonprofit self-regulation. The emergence of the Israeli Naot self-regulation scheme led by the Committee for Standards and Accreditation came as a sector response to the threat of further state regulation. The Naot scheme had a positive impact on driving up governance standards by enabling participating organizations to positively reflect on their accountability mechanisms and make changes to their procedures and processes as a result, but it suffered from lack of resources to enable external review and accreditation. The statutory regulator's failure to recognize this self-regulatory effort effectively thwarted its development and the impetus to initiate any subsequent self-regulatory schemes. The Naot scheme also suffered from being in quasi-competition with existing state regulation.

While there are recent signs that there may be a change of approach, the lack of division of labor on regulating the nonprofit sector in Israel demonstrates the chilling impact that a dominant centralized system of statutory regulation can have on the emergence of self-regulation. This is made all the more challenging for self-regulation in Israel where the sector lacks capacity and resources. It also shows the ease with which state regulation can override self-regulation. This latter point is one that may well be echoed in English and Welsh fundraising regulation – albeit in a very different context – where the threat of exercise of the state's reserve powers to introduce statutory regulation could come to fruition if, in light of recent fundraising scandals, the new co-regulation scheme is deemed to have failed.

State regulation is a strong factor too in the weak emergence of nonstate initiatives in the American fundraising sphere. With fifty state systems of charitable solicitation law, a confusing and difficult regulatory framework that takes up much organizational time and effort, nonstate initiatives in the American fundraising sphere have emerged only to deal with lacunae that multiple regulatory systems have let fall between the cracks – such as the problem of multistate fundraising registration – or to deal with the need for more public information in the wake of fundraising scandals.

In those countries where the nonprofit relationship with the state is marked by hostility or effective indifference, the emergence of self-regulation has been more prevalent, as a response to the strictness or absence of state law or as a mechanism by which the sector has attempted to address the high levels of mistrust that often also exist. Mexico is a case in point. Here self-regulation was initiated to combat negative perceptions of the sector created by a deep-seated public mistrust of institutions, as well as to address the failure of state regulation. Though active in voicing its concerns about state regulation and putting forward its own proposals, Mexican nonprofits' current self-regulatory initiatives are piecemeal, without coordination, and are not greatly supported by nonprofit organizations in terms of their buy-in to the different (and overlapping) self-regulatory accountability schemes (a state of affairs that also resonates in Malawi's nonprofit sector). This is unsurprising in light of the fact that the Mexican nonprofit sector was underdeveloped and fragmented as a whole and the self-regulatory initiatives are relatively recent. Indeed, it is a typical outcome in a country where the state historically suppressed the nonprofit sector and restricted the space in which organizations could flourish.

This was the case too in Ecuador, but a contrast lies in the sector's response. The Ecuadorian nonprofit sector initially lacked coherence but, in the face of restrictive state regulation, became more cohesive in an attempt to reclaim the sector's legitimacy in the eyes of a distrustful public. The catalytic effect of government threat on the development of collective nonprofit self-regulatory efforts is a theme that runs through the African case studies too. In those countries where the threat of repressive government regulation of the sector was imminent (for example, Uganda, Kenya, and Ethiopia), nonprofits were galvanized into collective action, whereas in those countries in which the threat of government repression was less hostile, as in Tanzania and Malawi, the impetus for the sector to work together was greatly lessened and negatively contributed to the success of the self-regulatory responses that flowed from the statutory reform.

Dominance by other organizations outside the state has also had an effect on the emergence of self-regulation, demonstrating that this is symptomatic not just of those countries with historically repressive regimes. The lack of development of self-regulation in Ireland pre-2000, for example, was a product of the dominance of the Church in delivering social welfare (a position that has similarities to the role of the Church in Mexico prior to the revolution and the subsequent effect that had on a weak and almost nonexistent Mexican nonprofit sector). Although the dominance of the Church in social welfare in Ireland eventually ended, its enduring legacy was a lack of peak/umbrella bodies and a more general lack of leadership capacity in secular nonprofit organizations. In turn, this emasculated nonprofits' ability to develop a coherent and cohesive sector, at least in the short to medium term.

The impact of the nonprofit sector's capacity and identity on its ability to develop self-regulatory initiatives should not be underestimated. Taken as a whole, the country case studies demonstrate that fragmented and weak nonprofit sectors, without strong leadership, have struggled to initiate, let alone develop or implement successful self-regulation. The Tanzanian experience of fragmentation among existing nonprofit umbrella bodies and their unwillingness to cooperate in the formation of new peak/umbrella bodies to the ultimate detriment of the sector is a case in point. In Mexico the lack of a coordinating peak/umbrella body also meant that there was no consensus around a single set of standards or agreement on appropriate and workable enforcement mechanisms. In both China and Vietnam, the relatively recent emergence of nonprofit sectors and their struggle to thrive in difficult circumstances have led to slow and fitful progress on autonomous or self-regulatory activities. Similarly, the Ugandan, Kenyan, and Ethiopian case studies reveal that the presence of preexisting collective action organizations is necessary for self-regulation to emerge.

Evidence of the positive difference these bodies can make is provided by England and Wales, where it was a peak/umbrella body that instituted an influential sector-led report on regulatory reform[9] (as it was too in Scotland) and that instigated a Quality Standards Task Group specifically to build the nonprofit sector's governance capacity through self-regulatory codes of conduct. In Ecuador, where self-regulation has not featured strongly, the lack of capacity and experience within its nonprofit sector has been a contributory factor, but the change to a more adversarial approach by the Ecuadorian government roused the sector to organize more effectively. The threat of

---

[9] Commission on the Future of the Voluntary Sector, *Meeting the Challenge of Change: Voluntary Action into the 21st Century* (London: NCVO, 1996).

repressive legislation became the vehicle around which organizations could unify and develop their identity as a sector – a situation also seen in Kenya and Uganda. By contrast, in Brazil, the nonprofit sector has traditionally been organized and has created coalitions to work for regulatory change at the state level, but it has not been an agent for change in its own right. As this country narrative revealed, actors within the Brazilian nonprofit sector suggest that there is little thirst to pursue self-regulation in a sector so diverse. Here, then, a clear sector identity is missing.

11.1.5 *Political Conditions and Timing*

A further point to address from the country case studies (and implicit in the foregoing discussion) is the impact that political conditions and timing have on the development and balance of regulatory frameworks. Political conditions can be moments of opportunity for the nonprofit sector but cannot always be extrapolated to a broader context. Some may be no more than one factor in a much wider picture that is constructed over time. As the Irish case study illustrates, they may involve a drive for regulation that is developed behind the scenes and difficult to unravel. While fundamental to the development of regulation in each country, these are more complex to piece together in terms of their range and influence, and so to compare. That said, the following broad political influences are evident from the country case studies.

New public management, identified above, is a political imperative that has cut across a number of countries (including Australia, Brazil, Britain, Ireland, and Israel) but not always with the same results. These case studies demonstrate the impact that contracting out delivery of state services to nonprofit organizations has had on a state's regulatory agenda. The creation of a market of service providers that are legitimate and accountable has driven forward reform of statutory regulation across the board, and strengthening legal frameworks is common in these countries. Where they differ is in the state's approach to the role of self-regulation in achieving the new public management agenda. In Israel, for example, the centrality of the state effectively crowded out self-regulatory initiatives, using only statutory regulatory tools to ensure appropriate accountability and supervision of nonprofit organizations. Thus far, this is also the situation in China and Vietnam.

England and Wales took a different approach. Here achievement of the new public management agenda was made in concert with the nonprofit sector. The government encouraged the sector to develop the legitimacy of its organizations through governance self-regulation, to be used in combination with a strengthened statutory regulatory regime. The circumstances of the government and the strategy of the nonprofit sector at the time go some way to explain the difference in outcomes with other countries. The incoming Labour government was keen to herald a new political approach and recognized that to do so it must harness nonprofit organizations. At the same time, the nonprofit sector was keen to put its interests on the political agenda and work toward achieving a better enabling legal and policy environment. That the timing of both coincided was propitious, and set the course for the use of a broader range of regulatory tools in England and Wales. That, in turn, served to pave the way for a more substantial use of self-regulation in fundraising a little more than a decade later. This political opportunity was fundamental to the subsequent self-regulatory wave.

An agenda toward participatory policymaking cuts across a number of the country case studies, including Brazil and Israel. In Ireland, a change in government perception on the problems the country faced opened the door for nonprofits to participatory policymaking. Nonprofits were invited into the Irish Social Partnership process, previously established by the state with the business, union and agricultural sectors. The extent to which this has had a direct or indirect impact on regulatory change in Ireland is not clear, but it was significant in raising the sector's profile, giving it access to greater political leverage and helping build capacity among nonprofit leaders who were able to learn negotiating skills from their partner peers in business and the unions. Devolution in Scotland and Wales was also a significant political moment in bringing the respective nonprofit sectors to the policy table, improving their political saliency and their leadership capacity, and triggering both policy and regulatory waves. In Wales (though not in Scotland) it resulted in the interests of the nonprofit sector being written into the government's strategic plan.

By contrast, the seismic democratic change that occurred in Mexico and Ecuador triggered waves of new statutory regulation in both countries but did not engender participatory policymaking. Neither was participatory policy-making even on the table – quite the reverse – in Uganda, Malawi, and Tanzania, where the introduction of stricter nonprofit statutory regulation coincided with upcoming government elections. These countries, with their less receptive political environment for nonprofits, illustrate the diverse impacts that electoral processes have on state/sector relationships, becoming part of a longer game of relationship transition in Mexico and Ecuador but serving to entrench existing relationships that constrain nonprofit action in Uganda, Malawi, and Tanzania.

Financial constraints are a further example of regulatory change triggered by wider circumstances requiring a political solution. In England and Wales the financial austerity measures put in place by the government as a response to the global financial crisis cut the sector regulator's budget by one third and directly led to a move toward retrenchment in its activities. This cleared a space into which peak/umbrella sector organizations could move, beginning an emergent wave on co-regulation. By contrast, financial constraints arising from the recession caused the Irish state to halt its regulatory wave, pulling back on implementation of its sector-specific regulator, the Charities Regulatory Authority (CRA), after deeming charity regulation not to be a priority in straitened financial times. The evaporation of state funding also affected the roll-out of self-regulatory efforts that were heavily state dependent (in terms of fundraising regulation) but had less effect on self-regulation of governance. With the return of Exchequer funding, the first to recover has been statutory regulation with the recent establishment of the Irish (CRA) in 2014.

External stakeholder influence, particularly when that stakeholder underwrites the funding, can also be an important trigger in the regulatory cycle. Donor influence, evident in Uganda and Kenya, has been particularly strong in the Kenyan case study, with the international donor community's threat to withdraw aid to the Kenyan government unless the government delegated some independent powers to the sector to govern itself, proving to be powerful enough to free up space for self-regulation to occur. Similarly, the impact of European funding of nonprofits on Ireland's accession to the European Economic Community in 1973 radically changed the composition of the sector in Ireland by providing funding for the emergence of secular organizations focused on community development and poverty relief, which in turn gave rise to a new generation of expressionist and advocacy organizations whose perspectives ultimately fed into the regulatory reform agenda.

External stakeholder influence has not always played to the advantage of nonprofits in initiating or developing regulatory cycles, however. In Tanzania, for example, donor support for the government's idea of a new apex nongovernmental organization (NGO) body, a plan not supported by most NGO associations, served to fragment the reform process. In Brazil, it was the reduction of foreign aid to Brazilian nonprofits in the 1990s that pushed them into partnerships with government. This had a domino effect, creating a higher focus on service provision by nonprofits and a shift away from advocacy activities.

The vagaries of political whim illustrate that just as political conditions can offer moments of opportunity, so too can the environment conspire to prevent regulatory reform. In addition to the effects of the recession, the lack of a clear vision for the state and nonprofit sector in Ireland – despite various commitments – has been identified as a major hurdle against effective regulatory reform. Similarly, in the field of American solicitations regulation, while the dispersed and disconnected policy environment at state level has not worked in favor of nonprofits, it has also not provided an appetite at federal level for reform. A comparable position existed in Australia where the federal government had no incentive to reform outdated or conflicting regulation simply because there were no charity scandals that demanded a regulatory or policy response. In all of these cases, neither the political environment nor the timing was favorable for reform.

In sum, an analysis of the foregoing country case studies in this book, and in particular the interactions between statutory and self-regulation in each, leads us to conclude that these studies do not support the argument that statutory and self-regulation follow a predictable pattern or arise necessarily in causally related cycles (although there is some evidence that the gaps created by repressive, ineffective, or nonexistent statutory regulation can have a direct impact on the emergence of nonprofit self-regulatory initiatives). What does emerge, however, is that the state of the relationship between the state and the nonprofit sector is a more likely indicator of future regulatory trends, and a study of these relationships provides greater insights into the consequent waves of regulation that arise in each jurisdiction. The caliber of the relationship and its effect on the regulatory wave cycle is determined by a complex array of factors, ranging from cultural to historical to environmental to political, the content of which will be different for each individual country. Timing, in the Kingdonian sense of open policy windows, is also critical to regulatory outcomes.[10] The interplay of these triggering events on regulatory reform is important, and studying them through the lens of the regulatory wave concept has value insofar as it allows us to better understand the relationship dynamic in place in a particular country and how this dynamic is likely to influence future regulatory waves in the context of the longer game rather than to view the outcome simply as a providence of circumstance.

11.2 WIDER LESSONS FOR REGULATION ON THE RELATIONSHIP BETWEEN STATUTORY AND NONSTATUTORY REGULATION: POLICY PRINCIPLES DERIVED FROM THE COUNTRY CASE STUDIES

The regulatory frameworks identified in the country case studies in this book demonstrate a predominance of statutory regulation. Self-regulation is limited and exists with varying degrees of success and support. It is, nonetheless, an

---

[10] John W. Kingdon, *Agendas, Alternatives and Public Policies*, 2nd ed. (New York: Longman Classics, 2003).

emerging regulatory tool steadily developing in scope and range. The country narratives indicate a growing appetite among a majority of nonprofit sectors and some regulators for nonstatutory forms of regulation, and not just as a tool of last resort. In this section we conclude by identifying policy principles drawn from the experience of the sixteen country case studies.

11.2.1 *Toward Encouraging Self-Regulation: The Ideal Conditions for Growth*

The country narratives have presented examples of a number of different attempts at self-regulation. Some of the schemes have flourished, while others have faltered. Even those that have not worked well have, at the very least, afforded learning experiences to nonprofit sectors and their organizations, experiences that may assist in developing the next self-regulation initiative. Along with the points identified in the discussion in the previous section, experience from the case studies suggests that the following nine factors go toward encouraging and sustaining self-regulation.

First and foremost is to have an organized sector, with interorganizational networks, linkages that bring the sector together, and sector-level bodies that have leadership capacity. That is not to say that self-regulation cannot succeed in the absence of an organized sector, only that collective action is a condition for success whether that be brought about through active participation on the part of all players or through passive acceptance by the majority. In various ways, all of the country case studies provide evidence of the ways in which fragmented or weak nonprofit sectors have failed to initiate or develop sustainable self-regulation schemes.

Second, it is useful to have a coordinating body either for self-regulation schemes or for the nonprofit sector as a whole, or for significant subsectors of nonprofit organizations. This can prevent the problem of development of overlapping schemes and reduce competition between schemes and organizations, encourage policy learning, and assist with public understanding and recognition. It can also provide an identifiable point of contact for government and regulators and become a conduit for consultation and representation. Every example of sustainable self-regulation in the country case studies has a driving body willing to take on the leadership role required for self-regulation to have the necessary direction and impetus not only to be viable, but also to evolve and grow over time.

Third, self-regulation must have clear and understandable purposes – be it to combat public mistrust, stave off state regulation, promote quality practice in the sector, or other aims – and it must be well publicized to its respective target groups, be they nonprofit organizations, donors, the government or current political elite, the public, and the media as relevant. Raising the profile of such regulation requires the investment of resources, which may take the form of substantive financial funding. The need for funding can be mitigated in cases where, as already set down in our first condition, a well-connected sector exists in which there is symmetry of information.

Fourth, nonprofit organizations must buy into the self-regulation scheme, that is to say they have to believe both that self-regulation is a worthwhile enterprise and that the particular scheme that is promulgated serves their internal and external interests. This means that the benefits of the self-regulation scheme to individual organizations and to the nonprofit sector as a whole must be certain and realistic, so that the costs of participation are offset by the benefits received.

Fifth, in creating a self-regulatory scheme it can be useful to start small with a defined or niche area or activity or with a specific group within the wider nonprofit sector. This enables the self-regulatory scheme to be tailored specifically for the needs of that area, activity, or group. This, in turn, helps to make the scheme relevant to the organizations for which it is designed and assists in achieving buy-in from those organizations.

Sixth, when determining the shape and format of the self-regulatory scheme, attention should be paid to the type of principles it will promulgate and the principles matched to the purpose of the scheme. Consider, for example, the different merits of broad macro-based principles that could apply to all organizations (for example, where the scheme is intended to be aspirational with the purpose of encouraging organizations to begin to think about good governance) versus detailed micro-based principles that may be tailored to specific situations (for example, where the scheme is intended to be enforceable with sanctions for noncompliance or intended to be for a discrete group for which broad-based principles would be too vague or would not serve the specific interests of the group).

Seventh, beyond the specific interests of nonprofit organizations, the self-regulation scheme should capture the vested interests of others by serving as many external interests as possible or by serving the needs or agendas of key interest groups – be they donors, the government, funding bodies, or the wider public – and avoid being in competition with the interests of others. This includes avoiding competition between self-regulatory initiatives. In serving external interests, however, care should be taken that the regulatory scheme does not become fragmented by losing sight of its key purpose(s).

Eighth, state support should be sought where possible. The most successful and enduring of the self-regulatory schemes identified in the country case studies have received some form of support at the state level. Support could be through direct resourcing, such as startup funding or infrastructure to assist the scheme, or it could be through an express or implicit agreement for the state to hold off regulating while the sector attempts to regulate itself. State support can bring costs, however, and nonprofit organizations need to be aware of the dangers of total dependency, the impact that might have on the sector's voice and advocacy activities, and the potential for the state to coopt the sector's regulatory regime for its own political agenda.

Ninth, the nonprofit sector must be cognizant and sophisticated political actors for self-regulatory schemes to work. Nonprofit self-regulation is an aspect of the relationship between states and their nonprofit sectors, and that is often even more of a political relationship than a legal one. So nonprofits not only must know the law, and the regulatory context, but must be knowledgeable and effective political actors to negotiate relationships with the state, including through self-regulatory initiatives.

11.2.2 *Toward Encouraging Self-Regulation: Additional Factors for Optimal Growth*

The following further four points may assist decision makers in creating the optimal conditions for a nonprofit regulatory framework.

Having a clear policy statement, preferably agreed between the state and the nonprofit sector. A policy statement provides structure and coherence to the state/nonprofit sector relationship. It can provide joint goals and a vision for the sector along with expectations and responsibilities to frame a working relationship. A policy statement can provide detail on matters such as policymaking, consultations, regulatory development, delivery of services and procurement, funding, support for the sector, respect for its voice, matters of funding, and so on. The country case studies in this book illustrate the value of written compacts (with the compact between the state and the sector being written into the Welsh Assembly strategic plan) and the damaging effect of the lack of an overall policy approach for the sector (particularly resonant in the Israeli and Irish case studies). At the same time, one must guard against the adoption of an inflexible "one size fits all approach," which may lead to distrust between the parties and a disconnected and dispersed policy environment (as evident in the United States case study).

Establishing opportunities for discussion: It is helpful to have a forum in which government, civil servants, and regulators along with the nonprofit sector and its actors have the opportunity to engage with each other. This can raise regulators' awareness and understanding of the nonprofit sector, its needs, experience, and priorities, and enable the sector's voice to be heard. It can also build capacity among the sector's leadership. Informal networks can work just as well as formal ones. Valuable lessons can be learned from both the positive and negative Irish experiences of these forums, as these relationships tend to succeed only when the players at the table are treated with parity of esteem and have authority to act. Nevertheless, some forum is better than none, as is illustrated by the negative effect of the lack of a forum on the development of nonprofit regulation in the United States.

Encouraging policy learning: This enables regulators and the nonprofit sector to draw inspiration, learn lessons, or gain an impetus to regulatory development from other sectors, communities, or countries. Positive examples of this abound throughout country narratives, from Ireland's experience of learning from the British fundraising codes and Uganda's experience of learning from and building on the self-regulation efforts in Kenya to Israel's consideration of the English Compact, the Canadian Accord, and the Irish Social Partnership process. Similarly, Australia's self-regulation dialogue in the development aid community at the international level gave momentum to the development of a sector-wide self-regulation code for Australian international development nonprofits.

Finally, *enabling self-regulation and state regulation to work hand in hand*, so that the utilization of one enables the other to focus more effectively on its matters of priority. The freeing-up of regulatory time and resources for the state regulators has the potential to offer efficiencies of action that will benefit both the public and the public purse. Just as important, it will enable the nonprofit sector to take ownership of its regulation and policing. This is an essential, but often overlooked, step in developing a viable and enabling legal environment for nonprofit organizations, and is something to which that the nonprofit sectors in all of the sixteen country cases can aspire.

Index